Brecht, Broadway and United States Theatre

Brecht, Broadway and United States Theatre

Edited by

J. Chris Westgate

CAMBRIDGE SCHOLARS PUBLISHING

Brecht, Broadway and United States Theatre, edited by J. Chris Westgate

This book first published 2007 by

Cambridge Scholars Publishing

15 Angerton Gardens, Newcastle, NE5 2JA, UK

British Library Cataloguing in Publication Data
A catalogue record for this book is available from the British Library

TABLE OF CONTENTS

Part III: The Future of Brecht on Broadway

LIST OF IMAGES

PREFACE

This book had two beginnings. The first was my growing concern with the ways that Bertolt Brecht's name was being bandied around in theatrical reviews, some of the more egregious examples I discuss during the following introduction. But the trend is much broader than the representative examples included there. Writing about the theater in the United States by the end of the twentieth century, in many cases, had become almost an implicit extension of the Broadway ethos of putting on a good show and not bothering with difficult details of what Brecht might have said—much less what he meant. It was enough to invoke the ghost of Brecht, when Broadway's validity in a world where terrorism could take place in New York City, to make us believe that U.S. theater mattered. The dumbing down of Brecht evident in more and more reviews isn't deliberate (I don't think) but rather demonstrates how little American reviewers and audiences care about what Brecht or any German or foreign (following Eric Bentley's argument) playwright might have to say about the relevance of theater. Eventually, I had read enough of such reviews.

The growing frustration I felt led to the second beginning: chairing a discussion panel at the Pacific and Ancient Modern Language Association (PAMLA) in 2005 at Woodland Hills, California. There, I discovered panelists (one of whom has contributed to this anthology) as well as members of the audience who were equally concerned with the clumsy ways that Brecht was being invoked. But further, there was growing anxiety about the fact that Broadway theater had—in an almost perfect illustration of hegemony—almost become theater in the United States. More and more people growing up in the United States and writing about theater did not have Brecht—or at least the Brecht whose writing about theater was always tinged with revolutionary fervor—as a touchstone for considering serious, political theater. This fact is particularly troubling today when the Bush administration has reinacted the worst dangers of *Mother Courage*, if not *The Resistible Rise of Arturo Ui*. This anthology, then, intends to challenge the indifference toward Brecht's writing about theater that has become more and more evident in reviews of theater in and around Broadway. My hope is that it will prompt discussion and debate about the past and the future of theater in the U.S. and elsewhere, an ambition that Brecht surely would have applauded.

ACKNOWLEDGEMENTS

We wish to thank the following people for their commitment and interest in this project, without which it would not have been possible. Thanks to Carl Weber, Sean Carney, and John Rouse, all of whom read and commented on this book in the manuscript stage. Thanks to Pacific & Ancient Modern Language Association that originally hosted the discussion panel on "Brecht and Broadway: A New Century of Political Theater" that gave rise to this anthology; to Amanda Millar at Cambridge Scholars Publishing, who nurtured this manuscript from the beginning. And thanks to Scott Shershow and W. B. Worthen who provided advice and encouragement very early in the process of editing this anthology.

INTRODUCTION

BRECHT ON BROADWAY: A DIALECTICAL HISTORY

J. CHRIS WESTGATE

When Bertolt Brecht left the United States in 1947, bound for what would become the German Democratic Republic (GDR), he had become thoroughly frustrated with Broadway. Broadway theater was mired in anachronism, more like German theater of the 1890s when naturalism and its assumptions about audience identification dominated German stages than the modern theater that had emerged in the 1920s and 1930s. "You have never heard of the new effects," Brecht told James Schevill the year before returning to Europe, meaning the experimentation with treadmills and film projections (among others) made famous by Erwin Piscator and Brecht himself, "or if you do use them, you use them briefly as tricks."[1]

Implied within this criticism are the problems that Brecht had with The Great White Way while living in the United States from 1941-1947. Relying on the idiom of fourth-wall realism, Broadway theaters—then and now—endorse passivity in audiences watching the story unfold along predictable, even formulaic lines. Never challenged to recognize or reflect on any dissonance within the play's staging or scenography, nor any dissonance between the representation of the world and the world represented, audiences are instead encouraged to *feel*: first curiosity, followed by anxiety with the mounting complications faced by characters, which gives way to renewed hope and further anxiety with sudden reversals of fate, which finally conclude with triumph if watching comedy or catharsis if watching tragedy. Although Brecht never mentions Broadway in "A Short Organum for the Theatre" (written in the years immediately after leaving the United States), it seems likely that Broadway exerted some influence on his complaints about audiences at

---

[1] Schevill, "Bertolt Brecht in New York," 101-102.

the mercy of "vague but profound emotions"—the fundamental problem that his epic theater intended to amend.[2] Broadway was (and still is) ideologically conservative, implicitly reassuring theatergoers about their commercialized society rather than aggravating them toward new—and Marxist—understanding.

Not surprisingly, Broadway demonstrated confusion about and hostility toward epic theater during the 1930s and 1940s, reactions Brecht experienced firsthand when Theatre Union (not a Broadway theater but nevertheless following Broadway's idiom of theater) staged *The Mother* in 1935. But Brecht's verdict on Broadway went beyond frustrations about the difficulty of getting his plays produced the way they were intended. His frustration, evident during the Schevill interview, in fact, probably owed as much to the 1946-1947 Broadway season he attended with Eric Bentley. Many of the plays debuting that year, like N. Richard Nash's *Second Best Bed*, Albert Mannheimer's and Frederick Kohner's *The Bees and the Flowers*, Ruth Gordon's *Years Ago*, have been forgotten to all save the theater historian. Revivals from this season, like *Hamlet, Lady Windemere's Fan, The Playboy of the Western World*, were more recognizable but were no doubt inhibited by the superstructure of commercialized escapism.

How many of these productions Brecht saw was regrettably not recorded in Bentley's *The Brecht Memoir*, but Brecht's general reaction was: "On the whole, he was not amused."[3] Brecht's most specific criticism dealt with Eugene O'Neill's *The Iceman Cometh*, though this production was famously flawed, and the play wasn't staged successfully until a decade later when revived at Circle on the Square—the year of Brecht's death. "'If you open a play with the image of a room full of sleeping men,' said BB, 'the audience will take the hint.'"[4] He was troubled by *The Iceman Cometh's* unwillingness to rouse audiences toward the socialist movement interwoven with much of the early dialogue among Larry Slade, Hugo Kalmar, and Don Parritt and that supplies historical backdrop of Harry Hope's Saloon. In fact, the ideological conflict between socialism and capitalism becomes secondary to the psychology of disillusionment that refuels the derelicts' need for their pipe dreams—more existential than political. This was probably another failure on the part of U.S. theater for Brecht, a failure to do more than wring emotions from audiences. If this play was the best that Broadway had to offer, Brecht may have concluded that there was no place for him as

---

[2] Brecht, *Brecht on Theatre: The Development of an Aesthetic*, 192.
[3] Bentley, *Bentley on Brecht*, 329.
[4] Ibid., 329.

a dramatist in the U.S., a conclusion confirmed when he was summoned before the HUAC (House UnAmerican Activities Commission) hearings the following year.

If Brecht had lived long enough to consider the history of his plays on Broadway, he would have known that he made the right decision in settling in the GDR. When *Galileo* debuted on December 7, 1947, after Brecht had left the U.S. behind, the play lasted a meager seven nights before closing. This, despite what Carl Weber describes as Brecht's determined efforts in rewriting the play with U.S. audiences in mind[5] and Charles Laughton giving a strong performance in the leading role. When *Galileo* was revived twenty years later, the more respectable but nonetheless discouraging run opened April 13, 1967 and closed June 17 of the same year. *The Resistible Rise of Arturo Ui*, which was influenced by U.S. gangster films of the 1930s starring Jimmy Cagney, George Raft, and Edward G. Robinson, and may have been written to introduce Brecht's plays to U.S. audiences,[6] flopped during its debut run: opening November 11, 1963 and closing November 16, 1963. Revived in 1968, it lasted two weeks before closing. *Mother Courage and Her Children*, considered Brecht's best play after the 1949 production at the *Deutsches Theater* in Berlin with Brecht's wife Helene Weigel in the leading role, opened March 28, 1963 and closed May 11, 1963—another failure by Broadway standards. When revived in 1967, it managed a month.

To appreciate just how poorly Brecht's plays have been received on Broadway, we need only put this stage history alongside the 1999 revival of *The Iceman Cometh*, with Kevin Spacey playing Hickey, which ran for 102 performances. Or John Patrick Shanley's *Doubt*, which opened March 31, 2005 and, after winning the Pulitzer Prize, ran through July 2, 2006. Why this discrepancy? Broadway follows a time-honored syllogism when it comes to mounting new or revived productions: what sells seats gets staged, and what sells the most seats are dramas that supply enjoyment through identification or musicals that deliver satisfaction through spectacle. *The Threepenny Opera*, of course, is the exception that proves the rule. Unlike other Brecht plays, *Threepenny* has enjoyed a six-year run on Broadway from the middle 1950s through the early 1960s and has been revived at least seven times to date, most recently by the Roundabout Theatre Company in 2006.

The fundamental tensions invoked by Brecht and Broadway when considered today, some seventy years after *The Mother* introduced epic

---

[5] Weber, "Is there a Use-value? Brecht on the American Stage at the Turn of the Century."
[6] Baxandall, "Brecht in America, 1935."

theater to U.S. theaters and audiences, no doubt seem irresolvable. When Broadway producers and owners discuss theater, as they do in Arvid F. Sponberg's *Broadway Talks*, they subsume everything under the discourse of business: they talk about marketing shows, recouping investments, and making profits; and make only uncomfortable mention of innovation or originality. The holy grail sought by producers becomes plainly evident: the extended run playing to sold-out houses like *The Mousetrap*, which, as of 2000, had been playing on London stages for some 20,000 performances. If you stand near the TKTS booth in Times Square, you can almost hear their whispered hopes of returns on investments, like the ghostly voice in *Field of Dreams*.

No wonder that Broadway theaters have historically privileged blockbuster shows: more songs, more dancing, more costumes, more glamour—anything to thumb their noses at Aristotle for relegating "spectacle" to an afterthought in *The Poetics* and to keep the paying public wowed. They intend to fulfill and simultaneously whet the most culinary of appetites of theatergoers with shows like *Wicked* and *The Lion King* and *Spamalot*: not merely to keep us paying increasingly exorbitant ticket prices but also to send us home satisfied with the production, ourselves, and our world. Brecht's dramas were completely foreign, as much conceptually as linguistically, to this kind of theater. Instead of having audiences identify emotionally with characters, Brecht intended them to judge historical or political implications of their actions. Instead of having worldviews confirmed for us while attending theater, he intended us to face epistemological challenge during the play and then undertake sociopolitical change following the play. Contributing to this chasm between Broadway and epic theater is the reality that Brecht intended many of his plays, like *The Threepenny Opera* and *Mahagonny*, to confront bourgeois audiences with the banality of their interests and others, like *The Mother* and *Saint Joan of the Stockyards*, to sow the seeds of revolutionary fervor in worker-audiences. With such divergent ambitions, it would seem there is little to say about Brecht and Broadway beyond the obvious.

But taking Brecht and Broadway as a rigid dichotomy means accepting a particularly unBrechtian (for want of a better word) view of history. Beginning from some endpoint, this kind of thinking reads the history of incidents proceeding that point teleologically: that is, as building steadily and inevitably toward that endpoint. Brooks McNamara's "Broadway: A Theatre Historian's View" demonstrates the implicit danger in this kind historiography in relation to the commercialism of Broadway. More opinion than history, McNamara's article nevertheless invokes the ethos of "history" or more accurately "historian" through its title and then suggests the "close attention" Broadway deserves should address the history of the theater district in New York City. Unfortunately, McNamara simultaneously insists upon a fixed definition of Broadway that constrains potential discovery when he contends, "it has always offered commercial theater and always has been devoted to making a profit."[7] The "always" here, repeated with the finality of an argument already won, forecloses at least some of the scrutiny called for in McNamara's essay. The "how" Broadway became wedded to making profits erases the question of "why" it did so, which McNamara rightly links to the geography of Times Square. The historical becomes the inevitable, implying that too common conclusion that Broadway's commercialism could not have been otherwise. Considered this way, history becomes a closed system, where all events are sedimented into patterns of fossilization that cannot questioned or challenged. Brecht's *The Resistible Rise of Arturo Ui* was intended to confront just this kind of thinking: the belief that the rise of Adolf Hitler (to change examples momentarily) could not have been avoided, that the history of post-World War I Germany could not have played out differently. In Brecht's parody, there is nothing inevitable about the buffoonish Hitler-figure Ui coming to power but rather was a product of the complicity and silence of others. While plainly admonitory in *Arturo Ui*, this view of history is empowering because it posits the possibility of change through action and intervention—if not then, then certainly when and if it were to happen again.[8]

Likewise, nothing was inevitable about Broadway becoming and remaining center of commercialism in the U.S. while Brecht has all but been forgotten on The Great White Way. Brecht himself did not initially surrender to this dichotomy, his frustrations with Broadway toward the end of the 1940s notwithstanding. Between the years 1935 and 1936, he described Berlin, Moscow, and New York as the "'theater capitals' that were 'modern, ie introduced artistic and technical innovations'" to the theater world according to Weber.[9] Notably, this was after Brecht's personal and professional frustrations that followed from *The Mother's* production by Theater Union described by Anne Fletcher in the opening section of this book. Weber additionally observes that *Galileo* and *The*

---

[7] McNamara, "Broadway: A Theatre Historian's Perspective," 126.

[8] *Arturo Ui* ends with a warning of just this repetition of history in the epilogue: "The womb he crawled from still is growing strong." The point for audiences is to recognize how they can intercede in history, which is still unfolding, and confront future tyranny.

[9] Weber, 227.

Caucasian Chalk Circle were "adapted by Brecht in America for America, with the viewing habits of the Broadway theater public in mind."[10] While living in the United States during World War II, Brecht made frequent efforts to get his plays produced on Broadway. Ronald Hayman, in fact, locates the exigency of *Chalk Circle* firmly in Broadway's commercialism: "Brecht started working on the play after Luise Rainer had told him how much the role in Klabund's version appealed to her. A Broadway backer, Jules Lowenthal, wanted to put on a show for her, and she persuaded him to commission a new adaptation from Brecht."[11]

Why did Brecht take this commission? Why did he make what Bentley calls "strenuous efforts" to get Broadway productions of his plays while living in the United States?[12] He may have been trying to make a name for himself at a time when few of his plays had been staged successfully outside of Germany. On the other hand, he may have intended his plays, even softened for Broadway audiences, to make the foundations of commercial theater—among Brecht's favorite targets—tremble. Whatever the explanation may be, the point for purposes of this anthology is clear: Brecht did not believe the opposition between epic theater and Broadway theater was irresolvable.

Brecht on Broadway

In 1965 Eric Bentley considered the following in a *New York Times* article: Why has Broadway rejected Bertolt Brecht? Intending to challenge the dismissal of Brecht's dramas by one of the central arbiters of theatrical success in the United States, Bentley maintained that Brecht's communism and irony (the dark irony of Frank Wedekind or Carl Sternheim rather than the whimsical irony of Oscar Wilde) became blockades to successful productions of *Mother Courage* or *Chalk Circle*. Joseph McCarthy's "Red Scare" certainly disinclined producers and audiences toward Brecht's plays, many of which involved overtly Marxist pedagogy, during the 1950s—when there were no New York productions of Brecht plays mounted except for *The Threepenny Opera*. Worth asking then as well as now, Bentley's question suggests a better methodology for considering the difficult encounters between Brecht and Broadway than the throwing up of hands that usually follows when Brecht and Broadway are included in the same sentence. By addressing cultural causes, Bentley

---

[10] Ibid., 233.
[11] Hayman, *Bertolt Brecht: The Plays*, 81.
[12] Bentley, 252.

foregrounds ways of considering not just why Broadway rejected Brecht but what that rejection demonstrates about the particular assumptions of dramaturgy, performance, and reception in U.S. theater during particular historical moments.

Like Bentley, the contributors to this anthology ground discussion of Brecht's difficult encounters with Broadway in history—a history remarkable for its messy details—rather than inevitability. But it's worth noting that that this anthology does not share Bentley's belief that Brecht needs to be exonerated from his Marxism.[13] In fact, nothing could be further from the ambitions and approach here. More importantly, this study intends to push Bentley's question further to consider the conceptual as well as the cultural differences between Brecht and Broadway. Of particular interest are conflicts about representation in and responsibility of theater. The first includes questions of performance and production (considered by David Kornhaber and Ilka Saal); the second includes the function of theater in relationship to society (considered by Dominic Symonds and William Burling). Brecht's encounters with Broadway during the seventy years leading up to and following Bentley's *New York Times* essay, then, has not yet been sufficiently considered.

More noteworthy are the questions never addressed by Bentley: When and why has Broadway embraced Brecht? While infrequent, Brecht's plays and politics (at least in name) do make it to Broadway stages, usually during some reactionary moment in U.S. history, when Brecht's plays, ironically, become ways of comforting ourselves. *The Threepenny Opera*, Brecht's most commonly performed work on Broadway, is the best evidence of this tendency. Although *Threepenny* initially debuted in a botched production in 1933, which suggested that it would fare no better than *Mother Courage* or *Galileo* on Broadway, it received new life when revived shortly after Senator McCarthy's Icarus-like fall from national prominence. In 1954, Marc Blitzstein's "tempered" version, reworked toward entertainment rather than excoriation of bourgeois audiences, won enormous popular success, running for six years and breaking "all records for the run of a musical theatre piece at the time."[14] Brecht's musical, though he would have perhaps disowned this production if he had seen it, served a necessary end: it supplied escapism from politics when the U.S. public had become weary of national debates about democracy and communism.

---

[13] Bentley is hardly subtle in this ambition. See *Bentley on Brecht*.
[14] Weber, 228.

This blunted version of *Threepenny* is well known in theater history, but what's hardly considered is how this trend of commodifying Brechtian plays during times of historical or cultural crisis continues half a century later. Not long after the World Trade Center attacks in September of 2001, Benjamin Barber wrote "*Oklahoma!—How* Political is Broadway?" Defending the relevance of Rodger's and Hammerstein's musical, which had been revived on Broadway in 2002, Barber invoked Brecht's *Chalk Circle* as the centerpiece of his argument for U.S. musicals following the terrorist attack. It hardly matters to Barber that *Oklahoma!'s* politics are unabashedly conservative, arguing for reconciliation between isolationists and interventionists during World War II, through the trope of property ownership no less! Or that *Chalk Circle*'s politics are rather radical: Brecht depicts Governor Abashwili and his wife as the epitome of a bloated aristocracy that deserve to be overthrown. What matters after 9/11 was finding a way of making musical theater comforting to audiences, who may have suddenly found themselves doubting the significance of such pastimes, and Brecht's name became a convenient touchstone.

Taking such questions as starting points, this book considers Brecht and Broadway in the tradition of dialecticism. This methodology involves seeking out and investigating the tensions between Brecht and Broadway in U.S. theater history, an approach that corresponds with dialecticism's positing "everything is itself and not itself at the same time, that is, everything is and is becoming, nothing is static or self-contained."[15] This dialectical methodology rejects history as a closed system and welcomes the contradictions of Brecht and Broadway as contributing to U.S. theater. How else to account for the fact that with the exception of Shakespeare and Beckett, Brecht is the most influential dramatist in university classrooms (and many university theaters); but the Broadway that has historically rejected Brecht functions as one of the final arbiters of the canon of dramatic literature published, taught, and studied in universities? How to make sense of the obvious importance of epic theater to playwrights and directors working successfully on Broadway during the 1990s—like Tony Kushner and George C. Wolfe—during a decade when hardly any Brecht plays were staged on The Great White Way? Or to account for the enormous influence of the Berliner Ensemble on generations of practitioners working in regional and nonprofit theater when more and more small theaters have begun to adopt the plays and production models of Broadway during the last few decades?

---

[15] Friedman, "Dialectical Method in the Work of Brecht," 45.

If we consider theater history as still unfolding through numerous contradictions, we can make sense of the fact that from the middle 1990s, we have witnessed the Disneyfication of Times Square at the same time that overtly political (if not Brechtian) plays like *God of Hell* by Sam Shepard and *Guantanamo: Honor Bound to Defend Freedom* by Victoria Brittain and Gillian Slovo as well as *Caroline or Change* by Tony Kushner were staged on Broadway. What this anthology intends, then, is to consider the many encounters between Brecht and Broadway during the seventy or so years since *The Mother* was produced by Theatre Union in terms of dramaturgy, performance, and reception.

Before going further, it's worth defining what this anthology means by "Brecht" and "Broadway." Beginning with the latter, Broadway means, first of all, the geography of Times Square, with its venerable theaters like the Helen Hayes and the Plymouth as well as recently refurbished theaters like the New Amsterdam. This New York City district was historically an "occupational district," as McNamara rightly observes, rather "like the Diamond District to the east and north or the Garment District to the west and south."[16] As such, Broadway theaters have been long influenced by pressures of place, culture, and history toward making profits rather than producing innovative or political theater. Although the Off-Broadway and Off-Off Broadway theater movements, which often took innovation as their mandate, demonstrate how these pressures can be resisted at historical moments and suggest the limits of Broadway hegemony.

But "Broadway" is also used in this anthology as synonym for commercial theater beyond New York City and even beyond the United States, like London's West End. Using this flexible definition of Broadway is justified by the fact that Broadway has become as much a way of producing theater (escapism, lots of spectacle, etc.) as it remains a locale for theater. Elizabeth Wollman, in fact, has demonstrated that Broadway has produced a trickle-down effect on the regional theaters that were originally defined against Broadway commercialism. Moving away from this traditionally "adversarial relationship," regional non-profit theaters have begun to embrace "a partnership in which the commercial realm looks to the non-profit for new works and smaller houses in which to test Broadway-bound material."[17] Many non-profit theaters, in effect, have become rather like a farm-system for Broadway, testing shows without having to pay the exorbitant costs of mounting a production in a Broadway theater, an arrangement that has benefited both theaters

---

[16] McNamara, 126.
[17] Wollman, "The Economic Development of the 'New' Times Square and Its Impact on the Broadway Musical," 461.

economically, if not artistically. For the regional theater, they draw fuller houses and for Broadway, regional theaters replace the process of touring a big-budget extravaganza, which has become too expensive to be feasible during the last few decades.

Defining "Brecht," curiously enough, proves more difficult than defining "Broadway." This is true not just for this anthology but for the books on Brecht since his death in 1956, most of which attempt to *find* a new Brecht through their approach. Eric Bentley first recognized the significance of Brecht's dramaturgy but has too often tried to define Brecht as "poet and dramatist" and not, notably, theorist, Marxist, or philosopher.[18] This approach is dubious in that trying to separate Brecht the dramatist from Brecht the Marxist may prove impossible since one continually nourished the other. Carl Weber defines Brecht as "genius," a definition that is potentially problematic in that it downplays the historicism of Brecht's thinking and writing in favor of the ahistoricism of humanism (although I doubt Brecht would have resisted the term himself). But Weber carefully locates this genius in Brecht's keen eye for paradox, a perceptiveness that grew out of his Marxism, and thereby avoids the pitfalls ignored by Bentley. Other books have "found" Brecht the poet,[19] Brecht the rhetorician,[20] and Brecht the thinker.[21]

Regardless of the methodology employed in reading Brecht, it's difficult to define him because Brecht's opinions or at least the articulation of those opinions about dramaturgy, production, and reception frequently changed during his lifetime. His attitude toward the thinking/feeling dichotomy wrongly attributed to Brecht by many, for instance, softened over the years as demonstrated by reading "A Short Organum" (1946-1947) alongside "The Modern Theatre is the Epic Theatre" (1930). The tempering of his opinion about enjoyment has historical roots: in the earlier essay, he was fighting against the conventions of identification in Germany; in the latter, he was allowing for the coexistence of criticism and enjoyment. (A change that emerged from his experience with Broadway perhaps?) This anthology acknowledges these tensions but makes little effort to resolve them. In fact, the contributors have written about differing aspects of Brecht and Broadway, from Brecht's plays produced on Broadway to Brecht's name invoked on Broadway, to the theory of epic theater alongside commercial theater.

---

[18] Bentley, 14.
[19] Morley, *Brecht: A Study.*
[20] Speirs, *Bertolt Brecht.*
[21] Oesmann, *Staging History: Brecht's Social Concepts of Ideology.*

Instead of resolving these tensions this anthology intends to "rediscover" the tensions *between* as well as *within* Brecht and Broadway. The word "rediscover" is borrowed from Manfred Wekwerth[22] of the Berliner Ensemble, who used it to describe the ways that any theater practitioner should come to Brecht, and indicates the ways that U.S. criticism has forgotten Brecht in its complacency of knowing Brecht. The tensions between Brecht and Broadway have not been resolved, however much the stage history of Brecht's plays suggests otherwise. Brecht's dramas occasionally make it to Broadway stages and, more recently, Brecht's name has been invoked by reviewers and writers of Broadway theater, something that proves troubling when we consider closely how loosely terms like "epic" and "Brechtian" are deployed in ways that further confuse dramaturgical and ideological difference. This interest in Brecht, however misguided, prompts the historicism demonstrated by Norman Roessler's contribution to this book: "when, where, what, how, and why does American Theater reach for Brecht?" Asking such questions without presuming answers allows us to reconsider the history of modern and postmodern theater in the United States as growing out of competing and, yes, even contradictory traditions. An anthology of essays, each considering different encounters of Brecht and Broadway during the last seventy years and making their own competing and complementary claims about those encounters allows scholarship to "rediscover" Brecht through those encounters. What does it reveal about Brecht? About Broadway? More importantly, what do Brecht and Broadway reveal about the way theater is written and produced, performed and received in the United States? Less of a history of Brecht and Broadway, this anthology functions more as an intervention in history, particularly in the calcified view of history as closed: the divisions between Brecht and Broadway inevitable and not worth considering; the divisions within unacknowledged.

Brecht On Broadway

The Threepenny Opera revival by the Roundabout Theatre in 2006 demonstrates how much these tensions need to be rediscovered. Following the trend of casting popular actors and musicians,[23] this production included movie star Alan Cummings (*X Men 2, Son of the Mask, Pride and Prejudice*) as Macheath and singers Cyndi Lauper (*She's*

---

[22] Wekwerth, "Questions Concerning Brecht."
[23] In 1989, John Dexter's *Threepenny Opera*, for instance, cast Sting as Macheath.

So Unusual 1983, *True Colors* 1986, *Wanna Have Fun* 1996) as Jenny and Nellie McKay (*Get Away from Me* 2004) as Polly. This casting strategy of loading the show with recognizable stars intended to attract audiences through name-recognition extends from Shakespeare to O'Neill to Brecht when revived on Broadway: a way of winning enthusiasm and thereby recouping investments. If Jim Schachter's op-ed piece published in *The New York Times* is any indication, this production was rather successful in the former ambition. The solitary complaint about *Threepenny* to emerge from this article was regarding the ending: "The finale ends with the performers filing off the stage in darkness. Nobody applauds, let alone stands and applauds."[24] Troubled by being denied the opportunity to show enthusiasm for the show—become necessary for closure for plays or musicals on Broadway these days—he offers this plaintiff query: "Why should the director get to take away my chance to register my judgment on his show?"[25] From the word "judgment" emerge the tensions between Brecht and Broadway being increasingly overlooked today. Determined to make some judgment, Schachter confuses judgment about the representation of the bloated and moribund society brought to the stage (which concludes with that worst of Broadway sins—having not fully satisfied audiences) with judgment about the bloated and moribund society beyond the stage (that deserves judgment in Brecht's estimation). So far has Brecht's concept of epic theater fallen in the U.S., a concept which intends to awaken and energize the critical faculty of audiences in relation to society, that his musical that indicted bourgeois tastes has become judged largely, if not entirely, on whether or not it satisfies those tastes thanks to the idiom of Broadway theater.

This confusion about Brecht and Broadway or Brecht *on* Broadway is subsidized by theater reviews like Ben Brantley's for *The New York Times*. Brantley found this production "shrill" and "numbing" rather than worthy of applause like Schachter.[26] But Brantley's criticism becomes thorny when he attempts to enumerate the revival's failings *as* epic theater. "This production has nothing like the sustained point of view that might hook and hypnotize audiences," he notes, and consequently "this *Threepenny* takes Brecht's notion of the theater of alienation to new self-defeating extremes."[27] I find nothing troubling about Brantley's conclusion that this production, which privileged sexual debauchery instead of capitalist exploitation, might fail as epic theater. But I am troubled by the reasoning

---

[24] Schachter, "All Over But the Clapping," par. 2.
[25] Ibid., par. 4.
[26] Brantley, par. 13.
[27] Ibid., par. 4.

of this argument. Linking this failure to "hypnotize" audiences to its failure as epic theater, implying that lulling audiences into a condition of suggestibility was a precondition for the critical engagement that Brecht intended, means misunderstanding or simply ignoring much of what Brecht wrote about epic theater.

In "A Short Organum," Brecht describes the kind of theatergoing (perhaps inspired by encounters with Broadway) that his epic theater was intended to replace in the following terms: "True, their eyes are open," he says of contemporary audiences, "but they stare rather than see, just as they listen rather than hear. They look at the stage as if in a trance."[28] More than simply anachronism, this kind of reception was a vestigial holdover from the era of witches and priests when superstitions clouded reasoning—*and certainly not part of epic theater.* In fact, Brecht describes epic theater as a way of amending the cultural problem that follows from theater producing what he elsewhere calls "a cowed, credulous *hypnotized* mass" [emphasis added].[29] Brantley fails to recognize and, more importantly, fails to acknowledge this abiding principle of epic theater while chastising the Roundabout Theatre Company, whether through clumsiness (perhaps implying what he didn't intend) or confusion (simply not knowing). I might allow for the former except for the fact that Brantley demonstrates more confusion in the review by lamenting the production's inability to integrate "stylistic" components toward coherent criticism.

Unfortunately, Brantley's confusion is part of a larger misunderstanding of Brecht on and off Broadway demonstrated by a survey of reviews on Brecht plays since 2000. Writing for *The Washington Times*, Jayne Blanchard has similar difficulty with locating *A Man's a Man* in epic theater. "Galy [Gay] is meant to be an Every-Schlub," she says, supplying a summary of the play, "being exploited by a bunch of British soldiers, the widow Begbick and others until he is so estranged from his true self that he begins to adopt the persona of others."[30] While she captures the basics of the plot, she confuses the fundamental argument of *A Man's a Man*, which demonstrates the Marxist belief that there is no "true self"—a humanist concept that privileges individuality and psychology—beyond social identity. Blanchard apparently fails to grasp this tenet of Brechtian theater, even though Brecht makes this argument frequently, perhaps because she cannot escape emotional identification as means of audience reception when she talks

---

[28] Brecht, 187.

[29] Ibid., 188.

[30] Blanchard, " '*A Man's a Man*' Numbing, Inane," par. 8.

about Galy Gay. "He is supposed to be a blank slate, but the audience must experience some sense of shared humanity to want to join him on his bizarre journey."[31] But surely anyone who has read Brecht's writing about theater can imagine other ways of engaging with Gay's journey.

Graydon Royce's review of *The Resistible Rise of Arturo Ui* for *The Star Tribune*, though, was more perplexing. He, too, demands psychology rather than sociology in staging Brecht's plays: "We seldom see the wheels of transformation working in Ui's mind, charting his course from small-time thug to supreme boss."[32] This, despite the fact that Brecht rejects psychology, again beyond the social, and despite the fact that the psychology of Arturo Ui is second to the criticism of audiences watching the play, who become implicated in the rise of the eponymous Ui. More noteworthy is Royce's difficulty with the distinction between topical references and politics,[33] which contributes to his bizarre admonishment of those staging Brecht's plays: "let Brecht's work speak for itself and spare us the tortured politics."[34] Although not entirely representative of writing about Brecht, these reviews are nonetheless typical.

The irony of how poorly Brecht has been reviewed in the United States becomes plain if we remember Brecht's beginnings in theater. When he had written only *Baal* and an early version of *Drums in the Night* titled *Spartakus* in 1920, he was already writing "regular drama criticism for the *Volkswille*, a left-wing newspaper" in Augsburg.[35] Demonstrating a determination to test the limits of German theater at the time, Brecht soon became known as an *enfant terrible*. "Already in these early articles can be found in his impatience with reactionary trends in the drama and with production techniques of the time" that followed conventions instead of daring innovation.[36] More significant was his loudly announced antipathy toward the abiding mode of audience engagement: "he was demanding that the production should have 'intellectual format' rather than merely satisfying the emotions of audiences."[37] To evaluate the seriousness of plays, Brecht frequently made comparison to Upton Sinclair's *The Jungle* instead of considering how satisfied the play left audiences, a habit that reveals how seriously Brecht took his responsibility as a reviewer who was

---

[31] Ibid., par. 9.
[32] Royce, "'Ui' Resonates but is Bogged Down by Politics," par. 7.
[33] At the end of the review, Royce complains about the production making reference to the WTO riots in Seattle and becoming too bogged down in politics.
[34] Ibid., par. 8.
[35] Morley, 6.
[36] Ibid., 6.
[37] Speirs, 36.

influencing the assumptions of a theatergoing public. He intended to educate that public by making them confront not just the banality of what they were watching but further the consequences of watching such banality.

This kind of reviewing stands in stark contrast to reviews today which tend to dumb-down audiences by misrepresenting what they describe—in particular in regards to Brecht's epic theater—or by describing superficiality as significance. There are notable exceptions, of course. Mark Blankenship of *Daily Variety* and Robert Hurwitt of *The San Francisco Chronicle* have, more often than not, written engaging and insightful reviews about Brecht's plays—without the aforementioned confusion about epic theater. Nonetheless, it's hard to quibble with Charles Lyons's conclusion about reviewers of theater: "this pervasive unwillingness to address either the past, the new, or the difficult ... insures the undistinguished writing about the theater in the American press."[38]

It's easy to say, as Eric Bentley did in 1986 during a conference entitled "Brecht Thirty Years After," that Brecht cannot be held responsible for much of what is termed "Brechtian" today and wash our hands of the aforementioned confusion about Brecht and Broadway. After all, the legacy of Brecht never depended upon productions in the United States, much less on The Great White Way. But this confusion poses noteworthy problems for continued influence of Brecht on U.S. dramatists and directors as well as for theatergoing since without Brecht as what Tony Kushner describes as a possibility of alternatives,[39] theatergoing will become further conditioned by Broadway. Having survived the doldrums of the 1980s, Broadway theaters are now enjoying a boom in attendance, ticket-pricing, and overall profits the likes of which were almost unimaginable a decade earlier. Complaints about the costs of tickets then, which topped out around $100 for orchestra seating, have turned into nostalgia today considering the new trend in premium tickets, which run from $300 to $500 per seat, described by Campbell Robertson. "Who buys these tickets? Those in the industry rattle off a list: people who want great seats at the last minute, people who have expense accounts, people who are not regular theatergoers and consider a show a special occasion and, that loveliest of all breeds, people who paying a high price is a pleasure in itself."[40] Attending a Broadway show, musical or play, has

---

[38] Lyons, "Addressing the American Theater" 166.
[39] See Carl Weber's interview with Kushner, "I Always Go Back to Brecht" in *Tony Kushner in Conversation.*
[40] Robertson, "Broadway's New Math: Top Dollar Tickets Equal Bigger Sales," par. 14.

always been a form of conspicuous consumption. But this commercialization of theatergoing has expanded exponentially with the investment of Disney in Times Square, in particular the refurbishment of The New Amsterdam for *The Lion King* and other shows like *Beauty and the Beast*, intended simply as escapism. Susan Bennett's "Theatre/Tourism" looks closely at how theatergoing within New York City and Las Vegas has been subsumed within the tourist industry. Citing the 2003 "Who Goes to Broadway?" report produced by the League of American Theatres and Producers, she stresses that "domestic tourists made up 49.3 percent of the audience for the year ending 1 June 2003" up from 46 percent the previous year, something that Disney has carefully marketed.[41]

Bennett warns against dismissing this cultural tourism, and she's right. This kind of theatergoing is what Kushner lampoons in *Angels in America,* the most successful U.S. play on Broadway that was influenced by Brecht. "*Cats!* It's about cats. Singing cats, you'll love it. Eight o'clock, the theatre's always at eight," Roy Cohn barks into the telephone, adding to Joe with his hand over the receiver, "Fucking tourists."[42] Beyond expressing Kushner's frustration with the schlock mounted on Broadway in the name of returned-investments, this brief scene highlights what Kushner understands to be at issue in U.S. theatergoing today. Broadway is producing not just escapism on the stage but a particular kind of theatergoing that demands escapism and finds any socially or politically-conscious theater too heavy, too didactic, too unsatisfying to even be considered. When they come to New York City, tourist-theatergoers want the most culinary of theatrical fare rather than anything that might interrupt their holiday. It hardly matters what kind of tickets Cohn offers his clients since much of what is consumed during this cultural tourism depends on wowing audiences with spectacle and then lulling them into inert but fully satisfied trances with only thoughts of buying more tickets for their next trip. Audiences laugh, cry, clap—and then go home, after buying merchandise marketed alongside shows, without thought of any serious problem in their world.

The phrase "Broadway theater" is increasingly becoming redundant in the U.S.: Broadway *is* theater, is a kind of theater that promises and delivers escapism from the world's problems. Political theater, whether from Brecht or from those writing in the tradition of epic theater, is desperately needed today when journalism has abandoned much of its

---

[41] Bennett, "Theatre/Tourism," 415.
[42] Kushner, *Angels in America*, 13.

responsibility for informing the public beyond the latest pop-culture trend or in confronting abuses of power in our government. Saying Brecht isn't responsible for the confusions about Brechtian theater is tantamount to surrender to this kind of theatergoing. It means accepting the indissoluble opposition between Brecht and Broadway, with Broadway having won the future of theater. Or, it means accepting the co-opting and commodifying of Brecht's plays by Broadway.

The following essays, which consider the historical and dramaturgical encounters of Brecht and Broadway, work against this complacency. The ambition of this anthology is to rediscover the tensions *between* and *within* these traditions of theater that have influenced U.S. theater history since the 1930s. The anthology considers these encounters in three sections, the first of which traces the early clashes of Brechtian and Broadway theater. Anne Fletcher's study of *The Mother* when staged by Theatre Union in 1935 demonstrates the fundamental tensions from the beginning. Arminda Apgar's study of the mystifications of Brechtian theater during the years following *The Mother* up until recent productions in the U.S. transitions toward contemporary concerns. Then Ilka Saal's essay on Erwin Piscator's directing while working in New York City extends the problems outlined by Fletcher and Apgar toward a case-study of the diverging ambitions of epic and commercial theater during the 1940s and 1950s.

The next section looks at productions of Brecht's plays or Brecht-influenced performances on Broadway during the 1980s, 1990s, and 2000s. Norm Roessler's study of *The Resistible Rise of Arturo Ui* at the National Theatre considers ways in which Brecht has been produced against the backdrop of Broadway after September 11, 2001. Kathryn Edney's essay turns toward the reviewing and marketing of *Urinetown: The Musical* through Brechtian reference and the confusions that followed. Then David Kornhaber's reading of Sarah Jones's one-woman show about ethnic politics on Broadway considers how Brechtian techniques might function without investment in Brechtian politics.

The final section looks toward the future of Brecht on Broadway, toward the (im)possibility of bridging the gap between epic and commercial theater. Dominic Symonds's reading of *Jerry Springer: The Musical* considers how Brecht finds surprising resonance in London's West End theaters, England's Broadway. William Burling's consideration of the U-effect, though, argues for the necessity of transforming theatergoing culture in the U.S. before Brecht can find resonance here. Ultimately, this book considers the following question from competing and even contradictory perspectives: What was the past, what is the present, and what will be the future of Brecht on Broadway?

Works Cited

Barber, Benjamin. *"Oklahoma!—How Political is Broadway?" Salmagundi* 137-138 (2003): 3-11.

Baxandall, Lee. "Brecht in American, 1935." *TDR (1967-1968)* 12, no.1 (1967): 69-87.

Bennett, Susan. "Theatre/Tourism." *Theatre Journal* 57, no.3 (2005): 407-428.

Bentley, Eric. *Bentley on Brecht*. Revised 2nd ed. New York and London: Applause, 1999.

Blanchard, Jayne. "'A Man's a Man' Numbing, Inane." Review of *A Man's a Man*, by Bertolt Brecht. *The Washington Times,* 9 February 2004, B05.

Brantley, Ben. "'Threepenny Opera' Brings Renewed Decadence to Studio 54." *The New York Times,* April 21, 2006. <http://theater2.nytimes.com/2006/04/21/ theater/reviews/21thre.html> October 7, 2006.

Brecht, Bertolt. *Brecht On Theatre: The Development of an Aesthetic.* Trans. John Willett. New York: Hill and Wang, 1964.

Friedman, Dan. "Dialectical Method in the Work of Brecht." *Communications from the International Brecht Society* 31 (2002): 44-50.

Gardner, Elysa. "Do Not Resist 'Rise of Arturo Ui.'" Review of *Resistible Rise of Arturo Ui*, by Bertolt Brecht. *USA Today,* 22 October 2002, 4D.

Geary, Dick. "Brecht's Germany." *Brecht in Perspective.* Ed. Graham Bartram and Anthony Waine. London and New York: Longman, 1982. 2-10.

Gray, Ronald. *Brecht: The Dramatist.* Cambridge: Cambridge UP, 1976.

Hayman, Ronald. *Bertolt Brecht: The Plays.* London: Heinemann, 1984.

Hurwitt, Robert. "Baby, You Don't Know the Half of It—This is Bigger than You." Review of *The Caucasian Chalk Circle*, by Bertolt Brecht. *The San Francisco Chronicle*, 26 July 2004, C2.

---. "Filet Mignon and Fatty T-bone from Brechtian Meat Market." Review of *Saint Joan of the Stockyards*, by Bertolt Brecht. *The San Francisco Chronicle,* 12 April 2004, E3.

---. "It's Perfect Timing for Brecht's Popular Tale of Justice Prevailing." Review of *The Caucasian Chalk Circle*, by Bertolt Brecht. *The San Francisco Chronicle,* 5 October 2005, E6.

---. "War Ravages Human Virtue in Brecht's Sharp 'Mother.'" Review of *Mother Courage and Her Children*. *The San Francisco Chronicle,* 12 August 2003, D2.

Lob, Ladislaus. "Germany Drama Before Brecht: From Neo-Classicism to Expressionism." *Brecht in Perspective*. Ed. Graham Bartram and Anthony Waine. London and New York: Longman, 1982. 11-29.

Kushner, Tony. *Angels in America: Part One: Millennium Approaches*. New York: Theatre Communications Group, 1992.

Lyons, Charles R. "Addressing the American Theater." *American Literary History* 5, no.1 (1993): 159-171.

McNamara, Brooks. "Broadway: A Theatre Historian's Perspective." *The Drama Review* 45, no.4 (2001): 125-128.

Morley, Michael. *Brecht: A Study*. London: Heinemann, 1977.

Reinelt, Janelle. *After Brecht: British Epic Theater*. Ann Arbor: U of Michigan P, 1994.

Robertson, Campbell. "Broadway's New Math: Top Dollar Tickets Equal Bigger Sales." *The New York Times,* May 8, 2006, E1.

Royce, Graydon. "'Good Person' Opens Minds and Hearts." Review of *The Good Person of Szechwan,* by Bertolt Brecht. *Star Tribune,* 15 November 2003, 4B.

---. "'Ui' Resonates but is Bogged Down by Politics." Review of *Resistible Rise of Arturo Ui*, by Bertolt Brecht. *Star Tribune,* 22 September 2001, 4B.

Schachter, Jim. "All Over But the Clapping." *The New York Times,* April 30, 2006. sect. 2.

Schevill, James. "Bertolt Brecht in New York." *The Tulane Drama Review* 6, no.1 (1961): 98-107.

Speirs, Ronald. *Bertolt Brecht*. Modern Dramatists Series. New York: St. Martin's, 1987.

Sponberg, Arvid F. *Broadway Talks: What Professionals Think About Commercial Theater in America*. New York: Greenwood P, 1991.

Tenschert, Joachim. "The Origins, Aims, and Objectives of the Berliner Ensemble." *Re-Interpreting Brecht: His Influence on Contemporary Drama and Film*. Ed. Pia Kleber and Colin Visser. Cambridge: Cambridge UP, 1990. 38-49.

Weber, Carl. "Is there a Use-value? Brecht on the American Stage at the Turn of the Century." *German Monitor: Bertolt Brecht: Centenary Essays*. Ed. Steve Giles and Rodney Livingstone. Amsterdam and Atlanta: Rodopi, 1998. 227-239.

Wekwerth, Manfred. "Questions Concerning Brecht." *Re-Interpreting Brecht: His Influence on Contemporary Drama and Film.* Ed. Pia Kleber and Colin Visser. Cambridge: Cambridge UP, 1990. 19-37.

Wollman, Elizabeth L. "The Economic Development of the 'New' Times Square and Its Impact on the Broadway Musical." *American Music* 20, no.4 (2002): 445-465.

PART I

INITIAL ENCOUNTERS:
BRECHTIAN & BROADWAY THEATER

THE THEATRE UNION'S 1935 PRODUCTION OF BRECHT'S *THE MOTHER*: RENEGADE ON BROADWAY

ANNE FLETCHER

The year 1935 is often considered the apex of American political drama in production. This appellation does not derive from the sheer convenience of this season's situation as mid-decade, nor solely because of the premier of *Waiting for Lefty*, but from a number of circumstances. By 1935, theatre practitioners and audiences alike suffered the impact of the long Depression. Partially in response to economic deprivation, workers theatre companies burgeoned in the United States, reaching an all-time high of some 400 mid-decade. An increasing number of artists and intellectuals turned to Marxism and even to the Communist Party as potential panaceas for their economic woes and the poor socioeconomic state of the country.

As Harold Clurman suggests in speaking of the Group Theatre's production of *1931-* in *The Fervent Years*, however, not all audience members wanted to watch the deprivation of their lives traverse the stage.[1] Broadway still, therefore, offered a variety of styles ranging from such staples as the works of Gilbert and Sullivan and William Shakespeare to classic pieces by Henrik Ibsen, mysteries, comedies, historical and poetical plays. The mid-1930s, however, saw considerably more black theatre, social drama (most pointedly with the emergence of playwright Clifford Odets), political plays, and the living newspapers and other productions of the Federal Theatre Project. In fact, Brecht's *The Mother* found itself situated, with its opening 19 November 1935, a little shy of midway between "Lefty" and the Robert Sherwood's anti-war play *Idiot's Delight*.[2]

---

[1] Clurman, *The Fervent Years: The Group Theatre & the 30's*, 70-73.

[2] Selected plays considered for this study include: *Awake and Sing!* (9 Sept 1935); *Waiting for Lefty* (9 Sept. 1935); *Winterset* (25 Sept 1935); *Paths of Glory* (26 Sept 1935); *Porgy and Bess* (10 Oct 1935); *Mulatto* (24 Oct 1935); *Dead End* (28 Oct 1935); *Let Freedom Ring* (6 Nov 1935); *The Mother* (19 Nov 1935); *Paradise Lost*

Although earlier in the decade the Group Theatre staged *1931-* , a sort of Depression "Everyman" that can be examined retrospectively in Brechtian terms with its alternating scenes and chorus and epic-like devices, American theatre practitioners and audiences were not yet familiar with the work of Bertolt Brecht. In 1935, apart from a couple school productions of *He Who Says Yes* and the Philadelphia Symphony's performance of the music from *The Flight of the Lindberghs*, Bertolt Brecht was known in the United States only by a short-lived English version of *Three Penny Opera* staged in New York in 1933.[3] He received scant mention in even the most leftist American publications.

In fact, Brecht has endured a less than auspicious Broadway career overall; the Internet Broadway Database, for example, lists only eighteen New York productions of plays by Brecht, eight of them *The Threepenny Opera.* Brecht's work found little acceptance with American audiences until theatre scholars like Eric Bentley, whose translations made Brecht's work more accessible or Bernard Beckerman, whose fascination with Brecht's theories and practices infected his studies of the Elizabethan stage, brought Brecht studies into the academy. Brecht's association with actor Charles Laughton who played the title role in *Galileo* in 1947 at the Los Angeles Coronet Theatre under the direction of Joseph Losey[4] increased Brecht's profile in America. Brecht's infamous HUAC testimony and his hasty departure from the United States in October of the same year, however, aborted his interaction with the American audience and forever marked him as suspect, an "Other." Thus, the American public's tangential exposure to Brecht through reading or hearing of these events had little to no effect on his reception by Broadway audiences. It remains Brecht's fate, despite recognition as one of the foremost theatre theorists (and practitioners) of the twentieth century, to meet with production outside The Great White Way rather than on Broadway. The average American theatergoer might identify Brecht as the lyricist of "Mack the Knife" but more likely would more recognize recording artist Louis Armstrong[5] or Bobby Darin[6] for their popularizing of the song.

Even in academia today, despite Brecht's obvious influence on practitioners like Augusto Boal and playwrights like Caryll Churchill,

---

(9 Dec 1935); *The Case of Clyde Griffiths* (13 Mar 1936); *Triple-A Plowed Under* (14 Mar 1936); *Idiot's Delight* (24 Mar 1936).
Dates of openings from www.ibdb.com 1 Oct 2006.
[3] Lyon, *Bertolt Brecht in America,* 6.
[4] Much later, in 1975, Losey adapted the play for a film version that starred Topol.
[5] Recorded in 1955.
[6] Recorded in 1958.

reception of his work consistently illustrates the same tensions between empathy and alienation that it elicited in 1935 with the Theatre Union's Broadway production of *The Mother*. From personal experience, I can note the distaste and even offense some undergraduates took at conventions utilized in a Brecht-influenced production of *The Crucible* at Southern Illinois University Carbondale in 2006. In classes several of us met with resistance similar to that exhibited by Broadway critics in 1935, with students declaring that they did not need to be "beaten over the head." I speculate that such violent reactions, then and now, indicate that by eschewing traditional audience involvement and thwarting the audience's expectation of a catharsis *per se*, a "Brechtian" production touches a nerve so to speak, creates discomfort, and indeed to some degree accomplishes Brecht's intents. Rather than encouraging complicity between audience and production, the disengagement of Brechtian convention elicits in its unwitting viewers, then, unexpected and unwelcomed responses; nonetheless, in doing so, it ironically provokes the thought Brecht insisted was so vital to his *Lehrstücken*. Brecht's lack of Broadway appeal leads us, as Americans, to the unflattering conclusion that perhaps the American audience is generally unaccustomed to or reticent about tackling *thinking* as its charge!

The Theatre Union

In 1933 America's first self-proclaimed professional leftist theatre joined the ranks of the New York production companies. The Theatre Union attempted to redefine Broadway practices and sought to effect social change. Its founding members were comprised of a potpourri of intellectuals who shared a leftist ideology and identified with America's working class, but most of whom had little practical theatre experience apart from playwriting. The Theatre Union's *modus operandi* might be viewed as an amalgamation of the collective nature of the Group Theatre, the immediacy of the workers theatres and the business practices of the Theatre Guild.

Producing over the course of just four years (1933-1937), the company's productions included Albert Maltz's and George Sklar's, *Peace on Earth* (1933); Paul Peters's and George Sklar's *Stevedore* (1934); Friedrich Wolf's *Sailors of Cattaro* (1934/35), Albert Maltz's *Black Pit* (1935), Bertolt Brecht's *The Mother* (1935), Albert Bein's *Let*

Freedom Ring (1935)[7], and John Howard Lawson's *Marching Song* (1937*)*.

The company emanated from a number of meetings that included Edmund Wilson, editor of *The New Republic*; John Henry Hammond, entrepreneur and social activist/writer; John Dos Passos; Charles Walker (leftist writer on the steel industry in particular, who later turned to academia); Michael Gold (formerly Irwin Granich at the Provincetown) editor of the *New Masses*; song-writer Margaret Larkin (later Mrs. Albert Maltz); Mary Heaton Vorse, insurgent and Provincetown alumnus; Paul Peters (a pen name for *New Masses* writer Harbor Allen); prominent American Socialist writer Liston Oak; and other writers,[8] then extended to George Sklar and Albert Matz because of their piece *Merry-Go-Round*.[9] The Executive Board included Michael Blankfort (screenwriter of record later for *Broken Arrow*, as a front for blacklisted Albert Maltz and *Born Yesterday*), Sylvia Fensington (who had assisted Joseph Losey with *Little Ol' Boy*), Albert Maltz, Paul Peters, George Sklar, Charles and Adelaide Walker. Its Advisory Board included such notable figures as Sherwood Anderson, Sidney Howard, Elmer Rice, Paul Muni, Lynn Riggs, and Rose McClendon. Prominent members-at-large included John Dos Passos (no longer playwriting), Stephen Vincent Benet, H. W. L. Dana, and Ida Rauh. Lending regular assistance, also, were John Howard Lawson, Molly Day Thatcher (Kazan) and scene designer/theorist Mordecai Gorelik. A tacit understanding existed among the active Executive Board that new members were recruited primarily because of contacts they had that would increase production attendance and widen the scope of theatregoers beyond the "already converted." Members of the Theatre Union "practiced what they preached," becoming actively engaged in the sociopolitical issues of the time. In fact, the *Stevedore* cast, although they arrived too late to participate, attempted to join the Macaulay publishers employee strike,[10] and the cast for *Sailors of Cattaro* were jailed and a performance was canceled when the actors picketed on behalf of departmental store workers.[11] The Theatre Union's Executive Board was a

---

[7] Albert Bein refused to comply with the cutting of his text, recommended by the Theatre Union. As a result, the play was first produced by Bein himself, along with Jack Goldsmith, on Broadway, at the Broadhurst Theatre. It was then moved downtown and remounted by the Theatre Union for a longer run.

[8] Press Release, Maltz Collection.

[9] Maltz in Jay Williams Collection.

[10] Newspaper Clippings, Theatre Union Scrapbook.

[11] Scrapbook, NYPL.

working board, and they had their work cut out for them as they mounted their production of Bertolt Brecht's *The Mother*.

Nonetheless, not only was the Theatre Union the only New York theatre company interested in producing *The Mother*, but it was also the best equipped to do so. At its inception, the company took great care in outlining its mission and remained true to its guiding principles throughout its existence. Each production program set forth the Theatre Union's goals in the form of a mini-Manifesto that was repeated in most of the company's press material. The Theatre Union's ideology was clearly defined and cogently articulated on playbills as well as in its plethora of press releases.

> One of the company's foremost goals was to "dramatize significant aspects of this period in which we live."[12]
> The Theatre Union is not guided by reigning social standards... Its point of view is the only one which offers a constructive guide—the interests of the great masses of the people, the working people, the workers as a class... Our attitude has nothing in common with the 'social service' approach....[13]
> The company identified a niche on the theatrical scene—one to which its founders were committed—and defined its place:
>> The Theatre Union is the first professional social theatre in America...
>> First—we present plays that deal boldly with the deep-going social conflicts, the economical, emotional, and cultural problems that confront the majority of people....
>> Second—we have established the lowest price scale in New York....
>> Third—we organize our own audience.[14]

In short, the Theatre Union targeted the working class audience for whom Broadway prices precluded theatre attendance and sought scripts that dramatized the workers' economic and social struggles. In 1935, the average Broadway ticket price was approximately $5.75—a rather hefty sum considering the average yearly income for a family of 3.7 in New York City was $ 1,745.[15] To contextualize ticket prices, we need only note that 1) Most families were operating on a yearly deficit across 1934-1936; 2) A five-pound bag of flour cost $.25, and pork was $.26 a pound; 3) A government employee averaged $.78/hour in wages, and a construction worker just under half-a-dollar, a miner just over a $.50 but,

---

[12] Press Release, Albertz Maltz Papers.
[13] Ibid., Maltz Papers.
[14] Playbill, *Bitter Stream*.
[15] Moore, "The Demand for Broadway Theatre Tickets," 82.

of course, many were unemployed.[16]   For the first three years of its existence, the Theatre Union's highest priced tickets were $1.50,[17] and the company offered free tickets to all sorts of workers on a very regular basis. The Theatre Union, it is important to note, however, (although it was accused of political assignations) was not officially affiliated with any party.   In fact, the company consciously diversified its Board to include liberal, Socialist and Communist alike.

Apart from reduced ticket prices, the Theatre Union employed numerous strategies in its effort to bring workers into the theatre, at the same time maintaining cordial relationships with other producing companies, especially the Group Theatre with whom it conducted a policy of reciprocity regarding complimentary tickets.   A fundamental tenet of the company was its emphasis of theatre as an educative force, and to this end the company maintained a library of plays for workers, offered symposia connected to each of its productions (The speakers at the symposium on *The Mother* were Archibald MacLeish, Aaron Copeland, theatre scholar/critic John Gassner, and Mother Bloor.[18]), conducted a reduced price and even free ticket campaign targeting trade unions and a variety of associations, aired radio broadcasts of mass recitations and plays, and taught classes.

One list for free ticket distribution to the unemployed from the Theatre Union archives includes over fifty organizations, including both the Henry Street and Grand Street settlement houses, International Ladies Garment Workers #22, the Textile Trimming Workers Union, the American Federation of Labor (AFL), the International Workers of the World (IWW), and more. Another—for group sales, and perhaps more reliable in terms of documented regular attendees—exhibits the variety of walks of life the company targeted: the Dentists' Wives Association, the Godmothers' League, the University Teacher's Association, the Dairy and Fruit Clerk's Union, the Bryn Mawr School Alumni Association, the National Student League, the United Millinery Salesmen, the Friends of the Chinese People, the Nature Lovers, the Protestant Young People's League, and more.[19]

The Theatre Union's free weekly radio coverage on WEVD included programs entitled, "Social Plays from All Over the World" and "Glimpses into a Workers Theatre."   The latter featured a mass chant, written by Paul Peters and George Sklar.   The announcer's copy includes an explanation

---

[16] Maltz Papers.
[17] Theatre Union Scrapbook.
[18] Maltz Papers.
[19] Maltz Papers.

of mass recitation and pointers for the listening audience.[20] In its overall approach to audience development, the Theatre Union was unparalleled in its efforts.

The Executive Board for the Theatre Union was what we call today a working board. Its members literally took to the streets, procuring speaking engagements before a wide range of liberal and working class organizations. Albert Maltz remembers giving speeches three times a week in addition to reading potential scripts, and, as part of the Production Committee, attending nightly rehearsals.[21] "Working in the TU was an all-consuming thing... [There was] no aspect of the life of that theatre in which I wasn't involved, George too, Paul Peters too, and so on..."[22]

Given the Theatre Union's sincere interest and the socioeconomic circumstances of 1935 and it would seem that the stage was set for a successful run of *The Mother*, Brecht's depiction of working class struggles; but such was not the case.

While some of the company's founders and early participants worked with the New Playwrights in the 1920s and with the Workers Theatre, the Theatre Union was hardly *avant garde* in either its script selection or its style of production. In dramatic form it gravitated toward a distinctive brand of socialist realism (according to Maltz, then called "social" realism), produced with realistic scenery. A sub-committee comprised of Executive Board members supervised the evolution of performance texts, and although their desire was simply to assure the scripts' suitability to their mission, the appearance was that the Theatre Union was exclusive in its selection of material and unwelcoming to new playwrights. Well-intentioned as they were, the Theatre Union board members were not as daring in their season selections as they might have been. In fact, their misjudgments concerning the box office potential of what turned out to be significant productions for other companies (Peters's and Sklar's *Parade*, a presentational labor piece the Theatre Guild accepted and *Bury the Dead* by Irwin Shaw are examples.)[23] contributed to the company's financial demise. Producing *The Mother*, then, was problematic for the company from the outset. Theatre Union members found the play intriguing, but they misinterpreted its intended style of production and sought to mold the script to their notion of social realism rather than celebrating its unique form. This misjudgment not only ruined chances of a seamless rehearsal process with Bertolt Brecht but precluded opportunities for promoting the

---

[20] Ibid.
[21] Maltz, Transcript.
[22] Maltz, Transcript.
[23] Williams, *Stage Left*, 184-186; 190-191.

play's United States premiere on grounds of its epic form and style. The Theatre Union's experience with *The Mother*, once again, foreshadowed receptivity of Brecht across the decades—and points to the irony that often even today Brecht audiences respond best to his theories when they are couched in more familiar *mis en scene* and his characters elicit empathy rather than alienation.

Nonetheless, the company never wavered from its mission and worked tirelessly to reach its desired audience. Their efforts to promote *The Mother* were no exception. The Theatre Union's assault on the New York media was impressive. Margaret Larkin (Secretary) and her assistants, primarily Martha Dreiblatt for *The Mother*, worked tirelessly to devise human interest stories in addition to typical production press releases. A draft of one sensationalizes Brecht's notoriety in his native Germany:

> Bert Brecht, author of the adaptation of the novel was complacently enjoying the beginning of his smash hit in Berlin, when the Hitler regime assumed power and the play was forced to close. Brecht fled Germany to a neighboring country. Helen Weigel who played the leading role was arrested on the stage in full view of the audience.[24]

The release goes on to explain that composer Hanns Eisler escaped arrest and to link the New York production of *The Mother* to Eisler's introduction of the text and score to Executive Board members.

Another release features actor Lester Lonegan's lineage and explains his theatrical heritage, making special note that his son by the same name was appearing on Broadway as well. A third focuses on designer Mordecai Gorelik and harkens back to his constructivist set for *Loud Speaker* almost a decade earlier, capitalizing on stories of stage hands sliding down the scenic chutes as a way into discussing the designer's ingenuity and his settings for *The Mother*.

A release marked "Labor press 'Mother'" quotes Mother Bloor, "If only because it shows the work in getting workers and farmers to unite, a problem that is facing us here in America right now, all workers should see 'Mother' this week before it closes."[25] The author continues to draw a comparison between activist Bloor and the play's enlightened protagonist, calling the former "an American Pelagea Vlasova."[26] In the two-page document Mother Bloor goes on to emphasize the educative aspects of the production, pointing out how leaflets, as they appear onstage, are

---

[24] Dreiblatt, Press Release for *The Mother*, Maltz Papers.
[25] Ibid.
[26] Ibid.

efficacious in the contemporary American workers movement and urging workers to arise from their complacency, attend the production, and take its message to their compatriots.

An extant flyer for the company's symposium concurrent with the production bears the title, "Music and Poetry in the Working-Class Theatre," subtitled "A Symposium on 'Mother'—the Theatre Union's Current Provocative Production." A modest admission fee of twenty-five cents was charged for the event. MacLeish's discussion focused on "Poetry and Realism in the Theatre," Copeland addressed Eisler's music, and Gassner lectured on dramatic style."[27]

Both Gerald Rabkin (*Drama and Commitment*) and Ira A. Levine (*Left-Wing Dramatic Theory in the American Theatre*) very deliberately introduce their discussions of the Theatre Union with the same pithy quotation from Erwin Piscator that emphasizes the revolutionary theatre's dependence on a continued revolutionary audience. Ultimately, the Theatre Union did not find a "revolutionary audience"; the American theatre-going public found drama of social concerns infinitely more palatable than outright political theatre. And, the investment the company made in *The Mother* signaled the beginning of its financial demise, for despite pre-sold showings to workers groups and others, the production did not appeal to a wider audience, and it met with decidedly unsatisfactory reviews, from left, right and centrist critics. It is no small irony that the Theatre Union's undoing was due, in part, to its bravery in bringing to the New York stage the first significant production of a Brecht piece.

The Mother Pre-Production

Brecht's association with the Theatre Union was an unlikely and unpleasant one. The Theatre Union found *The Mother* compatible with its ideals, but its members scarcely knew who Bertolt Brecht was. Theatre Union Board member and playwright Albert Maltz recalled: "To my best recollection none of us had any knowledge of Brecht's concept of the epic theatre…"[28] The Theatre Union entered its alliance with the German laden with all the naiveté characteristic of "bleeding heart" liberals in Depression-era America. Nonetheless, and despite themselves, the German playwright and the company produced what can be viewed as the first epic production in America.

---

[27] Flyer "Music and Poetry in the Working-Class Theatre," Maltz Papers.
[28] Baxandall, "Brecht in America 1935," 71.

Problems with the Theatre Union's production of *The Mother* began with issues of translation, and once Brecht arrived in America, became issues of production. Company members thought they had, *via* their association with composer Hanns Eisler, obtained permission from Brecht to utilize Paul Peter's adaptation of the Stark-Weisborn translation. Dispatching one of their company, Manuel Gomez, to meet with Brecht in Denmark brought back no assurance. Brecht was apparently determined to take advantage of a potentially free trip to America and insisted upon supervising the production himself. Theatre Union members were taken aback by the playwright's resounding refusal and further astounded by his rage when he arrived in New York, his passage at their expense. The Theatre Union awaited his arrival, mere days away from opening, and according to Maltz they were well into the production process, having already "started the machinery of production, not only hire[d] the set designer, having scenery built, but [the] whole mechanism of booking theatre parties..."[29] In fact, Maltz's vote before Gomez even departed to negotiate with Brecht, was to cancel the production regardless of financial loss. Maltz's premonitions about the production experience upon Brecht's arrival proved telling.

With no knowledge of Brecht's epic theories, Theatre Union members could not understand why the playwright/theorist was outraged at the reconfiguration of the order of scenes, the addition of melodramatic scenes and the omission of others, especially given their customary process or revision work with playwrights. Ironically, Peters struggled to overcome what he and the company believed to be weaknesses in Brecht's text: "its fragmentary quality, its abrupt changes of mood and style and its insufficient dramatizations of personal scenes..."[30] Like its audiences, ultimately the Theatre Union Board was accustomed to traditional character "arcs," a building of suspense to crisis proportion reaching a climax followed by adequate denouement. Although familiar with expressionism (especially Maltz and Sklar as exhibited in their early piece *Pinwheel*), the notion of eschewing identification with the protagonist's plight was shocking to them. The only sociopolitical drama to which they had been exposed centered around the emotional impact of given circumstance on character.

Theatre Union Board members, then, although champions of the working class, had no idea how Brecht's political views and dramatic theories informed his productions. Maltz recalled, "Brecht's theory of

---

[29] Maltz, Transcript.
[30] Baxandall, 71.

epic theory—he gave us a written document to try to make us understand what he wanted. I thought the document was nonsense and I still think so."[31] Mike Gordon was even bolder in his assessment, "I thought Brecht's technique was bullshit and I still do."[32]

Inspired by Gorki's novel of the same title, *The Mother* is set in czarist Russia in the decade prior to the Revolution. All versions of the story utilize a series of short scenes, unified by the appearance of Pelagea Vlassova, "the Mother," to illustrate conversion to Communism. At first, the Mother does not understand the workers' plight or their potential rights. She thinks of economics only in personal terms (i.e. how she can stretch the quantity and quality of soup she has to feed her son, with wages decreased again). Motivated by allegiance to her son, rather than to a cause, she takes part in revolutionary activities. Gradually she becomes both literate and independent, evolves into a revolutionary in her own right and works for the Communist Party, trying to educate others, even after her son is killed. The Theatre Union sought to emphasize the play's relevance to socioeconomic issues in America.

Although obviously sympathetic to the workers' cause, The Theatre Union wanted its audience to enjoy the show, to follow the play's action, and to be swayed toward political action by *empathizing* with the workers' plight. Therefore they adapted Brecht's text to meet their socialist realism expectations. Attempting to build dramatic tension to a climax, Peters rearranged the order of the scenes— the antithesis of what Brecht extolled. "The result was a hybrid production which satisfied no one."[33] It lacked the epic structure and hard-line political punch Brecht sought; at the same time, it failed to satisfy the traditional audience, accustomed to the linearity and causality of the dramaturgy of the Freytag triangle.

Brecht was furious, and he sought to reinstate scenes that Peters cut and to emphasize the visibility of lighting apparatus and the two pianos onstage. He was appalled at the Theatre Union's efforts to incorporate the staging elements indicated in his text with traditional fourth wall style. The company tried valiantly to seamlessly fuse music and book as well— the antithesis of Brecht's desired glaring juxtaposition. Peters and director Victor Wolfson made changes that affected the rhythm and tempo of the script in production. For example, they moved the moment in which the Mother learns of her son's death. Brecht's intention was for her to remain a clear-headed revolutionary; Peters and Wolfson sought universality and

---

[31] Maltz, Transcript.
[32] Gordon, Transcript of Interview with Jay Williams.
[33] Lyon, 9.

a humanity; they wanted to project the experience of a mother's loss. Naturally, Brecht's response to this change was indignation.

The Mother In Rehearsal

Rehearsals with Brecht in the room were chaos. Brecht did not speak English, but no translator was needed for the resounding expletives, "*Das is Scheisse! Das is Dreck!*" that shook the Civic Repertory Theatre. George Sklar recalled:

> Brecht would sit in the audience, mutter to himself, then take off like a beechcraft [sic] plane, hop up on the stage and start screaming… Day after day he'd come in with 'rewrites'—one scene at a time. It was soon clear that the 'rewrites' were simply reversions to the original script.[34]

Maltz told of the endless "Sitzungs" called by Brecht, meetings that could last an hour or two, *via* translator.[35] Then there were seemingly endless written notes from the playwright, some directly addressed to actors. It was years before Albert Maltz confessed his innermost thoughts:

> …I came to be so furious at him, becos [sic] I thought what he [was] doing would destroy us, that I once talked seriously with some Board members about getting rid of him for the last week of rehearsals, make the thing what we wanted and get it back on the boards. I even talked with a doctor friend and asked how to get rid of Brecht without hurting him; doc suggested we inject croton oil in an orange so he'd be knocked out—it was a laxative they give to elephants. But I never had the courage to go through with it.[36]

Brecht's perspective, of course, was that the company was bowdlerizing his script and desecrating his theories. At the very least, in his view, the Theatre Union would present a bourgeois interpretation of *The Mother*. So, he took his complaints to V. J. Jerome, chief cultural officer of the Communist Party in the United States. "Comrade" Jerome moderated the argument between the playwright and the producers, but Brecht broke the tentative agreement almost immediately, stating that he was not a Party member. The Theatre Union people were not, either, so Jerome had no jurisdiction over either side, arbitration failed, and the rehearsal process returned to mayhem.

---

[34] Sklar, Transcript of Interview with Jay Williams.
[35] Maltz, Transcript.
[36] Maltz, Transcript.

Brecht continually bullied twenty-three-year-old director Victor Wolfson[37] to whom he had apparently taken an immediate dislike.[38] Finally, when Wolfson could see no other alternative, he seized Brecht by the collar, literally dragged him up an aisle, and threw him out the theatre door, locking it behind him.[39]   Set designer Mordecai Gorelik found Brecht and Eisler on the street, near the stage door. Apparently afraid to attempt to go back inside, they asked Gorelik to fetch them their caps![40]

Brecht was not the only problem with the Theatre Union's rehearsals. The promptbook for *The Mother*, kept by Stage Manager Peter Xantho alludes to drunken actors, dissatisfactions—an overall malaise.   The technical strain the production presented is reflected in Xantho's notes as he repeatedly mentions the incredible difficulty the technical crew experienced integrating and implementing the more than thirty-five projections required. This particular promptbook is far more detailed than Xantho's others for Theatre Union productions and includes a rudimentary light plot and a detailed list of slides. The notebook ends with Xantho's exclamation, "Thank God!" The slides indicate the notion of *gestus* as applied to *mis en scene*, that is, the selection of a particular visual image to convey the overall message of the scene. For example, one slide was of a shopping list in kopeks; another photograph of four women bore the text, "In every country of the world there are…" pointing to the universality of protagonist Pelagea Vlasova's plight; another emphasizes the economics at play with a photograph of a factory; yet another bore the image of a membership card in the Russian Social Democratic Labor Party, and so on.

Both scene designer Gorelik and Brecht retrospectively describe a revolving stage, visible lighting apparatus, onstage pianos, and other elements of Brechtian staging techniques recognizable to us as such today.

The Production

According to James Lyon, in *Brecht in America*, subsequent to their eviction from the theatre—which Lyon states as having resulted from Brecht's physical assault on a pianist—neither Brecht nor Hanns Eisler attended *The Mother's* opening.[41] Brecht apparently continued his barrage

---

[37] Wolfson, "Brecht Harrangued in German But the Elegant Man Said Nothing," 30.
[38] Baxandall, 73.
[39] Wolfson, 30.
[40] Gorelik, Letter to Lee Baxandall.
[41] Lyon, 9.

of letters after his expulsion, right up until opening night, but he and Eisler opted to go to a movie rather than brave the production's opening.[42] Bertolt Brecht did not see the American staging of *The Mother*; he was informed of its closing in a letter written to him by the Theatre Union's secretary. It is somewhat surprising that the production managed to eek out a respectable thirty-six-day run.

Reviews of *The Mother* exhibit critics' difficulty with the production's style. Many reflected the irony that has come to be identified with the work of Brecht—the notion that productions of his plays are more effective when they encourage the very empathy he so eschewed. Helen Henry, playing the title role, was said to display "a quiet dignity about her that gives the piece a quality of genuineness despite its tendency to spell everything out on a black-board or throw it on a screen."[43] Ironically, Brecht was rather taken with Henry's work. James Lyon attributes Brecht's preference of her acting over that of other members of the company to her prior experience in vaudeville, a genre Brecht enjoyed.[44] Wilella Waldorf of the *New York Evening Post*, Arthur Pollock of the *Brooklyn Daily Eagle*, Richard Lockridge of the *New York Sun* and an anonymous reviewer for *Women's Wear Daily* all comment on the

---

[42] Fuegi, *Brecht and Company: Sex, Politics, and the Making of the Modern Drama*, 337.
[43] Waldorf, *New York Evening Post*.
[44] Lyon, 10.

redundancy of the projections: "The proscenium arch bears quotations from Thomas Jefferson and Karl Marx."[45] "The scenery is only intimated, and after a thing has been said four or five times, and sung twice, it is spelled out on a motion picture screen. There is certainly no excuse for anyone's missing the point"[46] and "...one wondered why the audience should learn from screen titles what the dialogue can and does describe."[47]

Brooks Atkinson stood alone in his qualified defense of the production. While he found the dramaturgy lacking, he was intrigued by the style of production:

> The style of production is considerably more interesting than the drama... The scenery is hardly more than a skeletonized background lighted by batteries of lamps that are quite visible. Above the background is a screen where movie titles are shown to clarify the story, to announce the title of the chant or to show photographs that symbolize the significance of the scene. In the shadows of the wings are two pianos.
>
> ...Although the style of production may sound eccentric in this description, it seems thoroughly logical in the theatre, and in its free confession of stage mechanics it has a refreshing frankness. All the bars are down between the actors and the audience.[48]

In his review, Atkinson even acknowledged Brecht's indebtedness to Piscator.

Post-Production

While Manuel Gomez served as Brecht's official translator, the other German-speaking member of the Theatre Union, designer Mordecai Gorelik, became intrigued by Brecht's theories, if not by his behavior. While Brecht criticized Gorelik's work as overly "picturesque" at first, apparently Gorelik to some degree wed his style of production to Brecht's dramatic form.[49] While he knew nothing of *Verfremdung*, Gorelik knew a great deal about the German theatre. He was even better acquainted with the workers theatre in America. Breaking the fourth wall was a goal Gorelik passionately pursued, and Brecht's use of signage and projections as social commentary was a technique Gorelik utilized instinctively in the past. With this production he learned how to systematically select

---

[45] A. Pollock, *Brooklyn Daily Eagle*.
[46] R. Lockridge, *New York Sun*.
[47] *Women's Wear Daily*.
[48] Atkinson, *New York Times*.
[49] Gorelik, "Brecht: I Am the Einstein of the New Stage Form," 72.

appropriate elements upon which to focus, a skill he utilized throughout the duration of his career, in his designs and in his playwriting as well.

Gorelik internalized the epic design process. His depiction of the factory scene illustrates the epic design process as parallel to Brecht's idea of *gestus* in acting. According to Brecht,

> …the factory was represented not so much by a photograph of the building as by the picture of the owner; the point of the scene was not that the workers were in a factory, but that the factory belonged to Mr. Sukhlinov and not to them…[50]

The selection of the precise object or property to epitomize an idea is the root of epic design. Gorelik was quite proud when Brecht complimented him on his knack for identifying the "right" objects,

> As a designer, the highest praise I ever received from Brecht came during a visit to the staging of his Round Heads and Peaked Heads in Copenhagen… Brecht was especially troubled by the major setting—that of a town square. For this the designer had furnished a view of houses in an open area, center stage. I suggested that the property man bring in all the shopkeepers' signs he could round up: a sugar cone from a confectioner's; a wooden umbrella; a big, gloved hand from the mercer's; an enormous pretzel from the baker's, and so on. Hung in one assortment in the middle of the stage, these conveyed some of the activity of small business in the center of a modern town. 'The Gorelik effect,' according to Brecht.[51]

Almost twenty years later, in an article entitled "Brecht: I am the Einstein of the New Stage Form," Gorelik acknowledged that the set for *The Mother* was primarily Brecht's creation. Apparently when the designer challenged Brecht with the question, "Why don't you simply say you don't want settings — only properties?" the playwright answered in the affirmative, and the two of them took it from there.[52] Gorelik's description of the set corroborates Brecht's:

> A small revolving stage partitioned through the center stood just under a projection screen. At stage right were two grand pianos. The stage was illuminated by rows of visible spotlights… The projection screen was in constant use as an editorial commentary… For many people the screen

---

[50] Gorelik, *New Theatres for Old*, 423.

[51] Gorelik, "Brecht: I am the Einstein of the New Stage Form", 87.

[52] Ibid., 72-73.

was especially disturbing; it was resented as making obvious statements and detracting from the action[53]

Production photographs[54] and photographs of Mordecai Gorelik's model reveal his application of the screen and projections.[55] In a letter written more than thirty years after the fact, Gorelik recalled how he used the screen:

> One example bore the caption 'Class Struggle,' Another showed a grocery list written down by Mother, imitating her untutored writing — written for projection with my left hand. On occasion the screen complemented the setting below it. For instance, the factory scene was represented only by an acetylene tank with workers grouped around it. Projected on the screen was a photo of the outside of the factory, combined with a photo of Mr. Suekhlinov [sic], the owner.[56]

At the time, predating even the Federal Theatre Projects' *Triple-A Plowed Under*, the screen effect was considered unusual: "the screen... on

---

[53] Gorelik, *New Theatres for Old*, 396.
[54] Berlau, et. al. *Theaterarbeit Progress-Verlag Johann Fladung Düsseldorf,* 334 .
[55] Gorelik Collection.
[56] Gorelik, Letter to Baxandall.

which titles and photographs are flashed while the action transpires below, is not a success."[57]

Why Did *The Mother* Fail?

It would seem that *The Mother* fit perfectly with the Theatre Union's mission and practices, so why did the production fail—in terms of process, product and financial profit? Surely, a great deal of the blame sits with the Executive Board for its misunderstanding of Brecht's theories, intentions, and perhaps even his comments and actions when he arrived in the United States. On the other hand, Brecht himself seems not to have fully understood the ramifications of "adaptation" or the subtlety of "translation," nor may he have fully grasped the machinations involved when a playwright puts a piece in the hands of a producing agency other than his own, something Brecht was not wont to do. Undoubtedly the backstage turmoil surrounding the final rehearsals for *The Mother* contributed to the production's failure. Chaotic processes contribute to the demise of many a production, on Broadway or off. What is more fascinating, I think, is to view *The Mother* within the context of the 1935 Broadway season and to ponder its failure in that light.

Many comparisons can be drawn among the plays produced in the 1935-1936 Broadway season—in terms of form, content, emphasis on the concerns of previously marginalized groups *vis a vis* subject matter. The most important conclusions with regard to *The Mother's* position in this season are that the work of Clifford Odets was constantly in the public eye; realism still dominated the American stage; and the popularizing of the techniques of Piscator and Brecht would remain the task of the government-funded Federal Theatre Project whose *Triple-A Plowed Under* opened four months after *The Mother* closed.

The ruckus caused by *Waiting for Lefty's* premiere in January 1935 (ten months before *The Mother's*) as a New Theatre performance added to its cachet which has diminished only slightly over three quarters of a century. "Lefty" shares much with *The Mother* in form and production style, but the differences between the two pieces point to those that most affected the poor critical response with which *The Mother* met. Despite its mosaic structure of vignettes, its limited set pieces, its obvious sociopolitical message, and its encouragement of audience participation, "Lefty" relies on audience identification and empathy for its impact.

---

[57] Barnes, *New York Herald Tribune.*

Throughout its history, the American audience has responded more favorably to emotion over reason.

In May-June 1935—just six months before *The Mother*'s opening—the political musical revue *Parade* ran for forty performances, only four more than *The Mother*. With part of its book by the Theatre Union's team of Paul Peters and George Sklar, some speculated that *Parade* would have fared better with them than with the politically hesitate, more conservative Theatre Guild. The two pieces can be compared in message, but the revue format *Parade* takes was far more familiar to the 1935 audience than *The Mother*'s production style. It seems odd that *Parade*'s authors did not take heed of its limited success as they approved *The Mother* for production by their company.

Robert Sherwood's political drama, *Idiot's Delight*, opening four months after *The Mother*, couched Sherwood's political message in a familiar, realistic dramatic form, garnering a Pulitzer Prize and a run of 300 performances. Others cast in realism from the season include *Awake and Sing!* (185 performances, with a return engagement of 24); *Dead End* (687 performances); *Let Freedom Ring* (Theatre Union, 108 performances) and *Paradise Lost* (73 performances).[58]

We can glean, then, from response to just these productions where audience receptivity in 1935 lay. Regardless of the internal havoc *The Mother* raised with the Theatre Union, the production may have been doomed to failure from its outset. The American audience, unfamiliar with the work of Bertolt Brecht—in fact, by and large unsophisticated with regard to European production styles—and unaccustomed to burlap curtains, pianos onstage in a non-musical production, visible lighting equipment, and slides—simply could not adjust to the play no matter what its message was. As Mordecai Gorelik wrote in 1940 in *New Theatres for Old*, "[*The*] *Mother* may have alienated some with its subject matter, but its chief offense was undoubtedly its strange approach in script and stage form."[59] How ironic, indeed, that *The Mother* failed for its attempt to "make the familiar strange"— one of Bertolt Brecht's lifelong goals.

Works Cited

Atkinson, Brooks. *New York Times*. 20 November 1935. n.p., Mordecai Gorelik Collection, Special Collections Research Center, Southern Illinois University Carbondale, Carbondale, IL.

---

[58] www.ibdb.com 1 Oct 2006.
[59] Gorelik, *New Theatres for Old*, 396.

Barnes, Howard. *New York Herald Tribune.* 20 November 1935.n.p., Gorelik Collection.

Baxandall, Lee. "Brecht in America 1935." *The Drama Review,* 12 (1967): 71.

Brecht, Bertolt, Ruth Berlau, Klaus Hubalek, Peter Palitzsch & Käthe Rülicke. *Theaterarbeit: 6 Aufführungen des Berliner Ensembles.* Düsseldorf: Progress Fladung, 1952.

Clurman, Harold. *The Fervent Years: The Group Theatre & the 30's.* New York: Da Capo Press, Inc., rpt. 1983.

Fuegi, John. *Brecht and Company: Sex, Politics, and the Making of Modern Drama.* New York: Grove Press, 1994.

Gordon, Michael. Transcript of Interview with Jay Williams. Jay Williams Collection, Mugar Library, Boston University, Boston, MA.

Gorelik, Mordecai. "Brecht: I Am the Einstein of the New Stage Form." *Theatre Arts* (March 1957): 72.

—. Letter to Lee Baxandall. Gorelik Collection, Special Collections Research Center, Southern Illinois University Carbondale, Carbondale, IL.

—. *New Theatres for Old.* New York: Samuel French, 1940, rpt. 1957.

International Broadway Database. http://www.ibdb.com/.

Lockridge, R. *New York Sun.* 20 November 1935. n.p., Gorelik Collection.

Lyon, James K. *Bertolt Brecht in America.* Princeton, NJ: Princetown UP, 1980.

Maltz, Albert. Interview by Jay Williams, transcript, Jay Williams Collection, Special Collections, Mugar Library, Boston University, Boston, MA

—. Albert Maltz Papers, Wisconsin Center for Film and Theater Research, Wisconsin Historical Society, Madison Wisconsin.

Moore, Thomas Gale. "The Demand for Broadway Theatre Tickets." *The Review of Economics and Statistics* 48, no. 1 (1966): 82.

Pollack, A. *Brooklyn Daily Eagle.* 20 November 1935. n.p. Gorelik Collection.

Sklar, George. Interview by Jay Williams, transcript, Jay Williams Collection, Special Collections, Mugar Library, Boston University, Boston, M.A.

"Theatre Union Scrapbook," Billy Rose Collection, New York Public Library, Lincoln Center, New York, New York.

Waldorf, Wilella. *New York Evening Post.* 20 November 1935, n.p., Gorelik Collection.

Williams, Jay. *Stage Left.* New York: Charles Scribner's Sons, 1974.

Wolfson, Victor. "Brecht Harrangued in German But the Elegant Man Said Nothing." *The Dramatist Guild Quarterly* 30 (Winter 1990): 30.

Women's Wear Daily. n.a., n.d., n.p., Gorelik Collection.

MISCONCEPTION & MISUNDERSTANDING: BRECHT & AMERICAN THEATRE

ARMINDA APGAR

Bertolt Brecht remains a controversial playwright in contemporary American theatre, highly susceptible to mixed audience and critical reactions. His notions of audience alienation and the *Verfremdungseffekt*, the A-effect, though almost entirely assimilated into modern drama, continue to be a source of confusion and, often, animosity, especially for American audiences. His plays have been tailored therefore to fit the expectations of the liberal humanist American audience, thus minimizing or even negating the critical potential of his drama. American directors and actors tend to view Brecht as merely a historical figure, the mastermind of an historical era that faded away long ago. As a result, Brecht's work is misunderstood and misrepresented by both American audiences and the American theatre community—to such an extent that productions of Brecht's work have lost everything that ever made them Brechtian. This neutralizing of Brecht's revolutionary, critical theatre is necessary, of course, in order to transform it into sheer entertainment that generates box-office revenue.

In this project, I argue that Brecht's work has been consistently misunderstood by a mystified American culture and will continue to be aestheticized and commodified by that culture in order to dampen its revolutionary potential. The first section outlines theatrical reviews of *The Threepenny Opera* (1928), *The Mother* (1932) and *Mother Courage and Her Children* (1939) from Brecht's initial run in the United States during the 1920s and 1930s, 1950s and 1960s, and more recent theatrical productions, focusing on the manner in which Brecht's work is misunderstood and routinely misrepresented. I pay special attention to the critics' focus on the acting, the music, and the emotion of each respective production, and how that focus represents the exact theatrical attributes Brecht wished to minimize. I then contend that American audiences and critics have reinterpreted Brecht's plays to such an extent that they have become either liberal humanist "classics" or simply song and dance routines, stripped off any critical potential. The second section focuses on American acting, exploring the way in which Brecht's work is substantively eviscerated even before it reaches the audience due to the irreconcilable differences in Brecht's form of acting and that taught to American actors (e.g., Method acting). The third section explores ideological mystification in American culture—the central argument being that American ideology continues to mystify critical art by automatically transforming it into liberal humanist, aesthetic terms. In conclusion, I argue that though America claims to love and respect Brecht, it neither recognizes nor understands the intent of his work, and is ideologically incapable of doing so due to the requirements of capitalist cultural logic. I also argue that for Brecht's work to serve any revolutionary function in American society, a radical transformation of the current ideological system must occur that will open a space in which genuinely revolutionary, critical art might be both presented and received.

The Initial Introduction of Brecht to the United States (1954-1963)

Joseph Wood Krutch places Brecht in a group of "radical and eccentric dramatists in post-war Germany … [who] demonstrates the fact that the left-wing writers of Europe have rather more of something besides their conviction to go on than most of the less-experienced American 'proletarian' dramatists have."[1]   This is an accurate portrayal of the American response to Brecht at the time, a sort of questioning of the artist's ability to transcend cultural boundaries. Krutch does appear to admire the style and form of Brecht, but he goes on to question whether Brecht has had "time to develop these qualities within the framework of a new culture," or if he is "merely … trailing some still clouds of glory from a previous existence as a 'bourgeois' artist."[2] It is this type of uncertainty that ultimately shows America's main concern with Brecht: of what use is Brecht to *us*?

In 1933, shortly after Brecht fled Germany and the rise of Nazism, an English language version of *The Threepenny Opera* opened at New York's Empire Theatre. Of the production, Ben Brantley writes, "an immediate, scandalous hit in Europe, 'Threepenny' failed to generate the same frissons when it first arrived in New York" and quotes *New York Times* writer Lewis Nichols as saying "[it was] a gently mad evening in the

---

[1] Krutch in Lyon, *Bertolt Brecht: The Despair and the Polemic*, 659.
[2] Ibid., 659-660.

theater for those who liked their spades in the usual nomenclature of the earnest."[3]   The production was an utter failure, and closed after only twelve weeks. James K. Lyon wrote that this failure "galled [Brecht], for he recognized that theatrical success in America meant New York City."[4] Later, in mid-1935, Brecht was called upon to spearhead a production of *The Mother* being performed by the Theatre Union. *The Mother*, though not the main emphasis of this paper, is still a noteworthy example of American audience reaction to Brecht and his work. He agreed, and later received a copy of the translation used to produce the play. Lyon writes that in Brecht's view, the translation had "transformed his play into the kind of hypnotic theater he abhorred."[5]   Brecht was later thrown out of the theatre and, coincidentally, off the project after continued controversial behavior, as Anne Fletcher describes in the preceeding essay.   The production was, again, an utter failure. Critics called it "an unhappy marriage of revolutionary exhortation and stage experimentation."[6] Krutch called the production "an interesting experiment … not addressed at the average theatergoer."[7]

It was twenty years later, in 1954 and just two years before his death, when *The Threepenny Opera* arrived at the Theatre de Lys in New York, that Brecht gained any semblance of popularity in the United States. Reviews of the productions indicate that, while Brecht's popularity was finally a fact, his work was judged only by the amount of entertainment it provided its audience. The opera has, since then, been aesthetized to such an extent that the content of the play is lost entirely to both the critics and the viewers, and stands stripped of possible revolutionary potential. Little emphasis was placed on the content of the plays or any potential political lesson. Rather, critics emphasized specifically the acting, the music, and the overall aesthetic quality of the productions. For example, one review in the *New York Times* remarks that, "Vocally, [the production] is entirely satisfactory. Dramatically, its performance is somewhat rough around the edges and there is evidence of inexperience. From time to time it is difficult to avoid being conscious of a lack of bite and style."[8]   Brooks Atkinson, known for his critical focus on purely aesthetic production values, remarks, "Although the production is about as poverty-stricken as Mr. Peachum's corps of knavish beggars, the songs are full of gusto and

---

[3] Brantley, "'*Threepenny Opera*' Brings Renewed Decadence to Studio 54," par. 8.
[4] Lyon, 6.
[5] Ibid., 7.
[6] Lyon, 10.
[7] Krutch "Black Bread and a Circus," 659.
[8] L.F., "At the Theatre," 26.

humor, the orchestra is light and charming, and, despite inequalities in the acting, the performance captures the acid drollery of the story."[9]   These reviews show little evidence of understanding the meaning or form of *Threepenny*, and in fact fail to recognize the overall revolutionary potential of Brecht's work.   The production appears as merely another theatrical experience—a "strange and unexpectedly thrilling experience."[10] *The Nation* critic Harold Clurman recognizes some semblance of Brecht's purpose in his review of the production.   He writes that the play sums up an entire epoch and state of mind.[11]   He then goes on to say that this epoch is one in which a "lurid rascality combined with fierce contrasts of prosperity and poverty shapes the dominant tone of society" and that the state of mind is one of "social impotence so close to despair that it expresses itself through a kind of jaded mockery which mingles a snarl with tears."[12]   This review, in itself, is a fairly accurate portrayal of the play, but what Clurman emphasizes is the fact that Americans may be unable to fully comprehend the play because they cannot connect with its historical implications.   He does attempt to connect the play with the Great Depression, stating that the tone of *Threepenny* is quite similar.[13] Clurman remarks on the potential historicism of *The Threepenny Opera,* something he feels Americans could eventually understand:

> [*The Threepenny Opera*] makes the mood so irresistibly present and, strangely enough, induces us to take it to our hearts with a kind of pained affection … it fosters a bitter sense of regret that we live so scabbily in relation to our dreams and also a kind of masochistic attachment to our wounds, as if they were all we have to show as evidence of our dreams.[14]

Here we see that Clurman has, for the most part, grasped a deeper sense of Brecht's work.   Where many other critics of the time are unable to see past the entertainment value or historicity of Brecht's work, Clurman has found a use for Brecht in his own time.   Clurman, however, does not dwell on this concept for long—he quickly switches focus back to the music and the "ambiguous, corrupt seduction of a half-world akin to that which Francois Villon sang of long ago."[15]   Clurman's overall focus on the aesthetic value

---

[9] Atkinson, "Made With Music," X1.
[10] "'*Threepenny Opera*' Wins Praise, Scorn," 83.
[11] Clurman, "Theater," 265.
[12] Ibid., 265.
[13] Ibid., 265.
[14] Ibid., 265-266.
[15] Ibid., 266.

of the production is no surprise, however, given his background as a member of the Group Theatre and The Actor's Studio of the 1940s and 50s—liberal humanist groups that ultimately popularized the familiar notion of "Method Acting."[16]

Mother Courage and Her Children, though of a drastically different sort in both style and content, received similar reviews during its initial run in the United States. Peter Thomson focuses on a 1956 production of *Mother Courage* performed at The Actors Workshop in San Francisco. This event was the play's maiden voyage into America, and sparked immense controversy.   Thomson writes that joint-founder of the workshop, Herbert Blau, "laid bare his passionate commitment to a theatre that participates in the politics of its own place and time," indicating that Blau attempted to produce the work in its proper form.[17] Despite Blau's attempts, the effort failed on several accounts. Thomson argues that the initial problem with the production was that the American actors struggled with Brechtian acting. He cites Blau as saying:

> What American acting has little sense of is the thing that astonishes you in the acting of, say, Ekkehard Schall, the young, crew-cut, intensely Communist Marlon Brando of the [Berliner] Ensemble, who played Arturo Ui. He is a political actor. And it is really eye-opening to see somebody get so much out of himself by force of *external* conviction.[18]

Thomson writes that it was this problem, the difficulty in training actors to act by way of *external* force rather than *internal* force, which created a momentary barrier to progress in the play.[19] The Brechtian form of acting requires actors to consider the social and political connotations (the *external*) rather than the internal conflicts and emotions of the character. Actors trained to "become" the character were not, in other words, able to come to terms with the Brechtian form. As result, the play's success maintained its position behind that barrier, little known and little revered. Thomson writes that "even within the city there was insufficient interest to

---

[16] Method acting, derived from the "Stanislavski System" of the Russian director/producer Konstantin Stanislavski, in its very nature stands in stark contrast against Brecht's *Verfremdungseffekt*, discussed later in this project. The inability of the American actor to move away from Method acting explains, at least in part, the difficulty the American actor has with the Brechtian form.

[17] Thomson, *Brecht: Mother Courage and Her Children*, 106.

[18] Blau in Thomson, 107.

[19] Thomson, 107.

sustain a long run," and Blau was eventually forced to cancel to stave off financial disaster.[20]

The other problem cited by Thomson is in the audience's reception of the production. Prior to the production, Blau and his company performed a version of Samuel Beckett's play *Waiting for Godot*, which earned the workshop its national reputation. The play was revered as the "Beat's play," capitalizing on the then-popular Beatnik movement. When *Mother Courage* appeared on the stage, its form, style, and content could not compete, nor could the little-known, mildly eccentric Brecht against the increasingly popular, highly philosophical Beckett.

Rather than viewing the play as having a potential use during their own time period, critics often focus on the play's "universal" anti-war message. In a review of a 1963 production of *Mother Courage*, Howard Taubman writes that "'Mother Courage' is a play about war and what it does to people. Its tone is bitter and sardonic. As a turncoat chaplain murmurs sanctimoniously, 'Blessed are the peacemakers.' That's a good slogan in wartime."[21] Taubman focuses on the fact that Brecht, though he wrote the play on "the eve of a holocaust," intended it to solely reflect the 30 Years War of the 17th century. There is no mention of how *Mother Courage* might reflect American lives at the time. The review focuses solely on facts and details of the play as though it were, perhaps, merely a historical event in a textbook. Taubman does, however, acknowledge that the play is "unconventional in form, style and purpose. Brecht reveals his plot in advance—scene by scene."[22] He also writes that "what Brecht has to say—and he has a lot to say—is communicated in amusing, striking and moving stage terms."[23] The recognizable problem with this statement, and with the entire review, is that though Taubman realizes *Mother Courage* carries a more significant meaning, he does not acknowledge that meaning, perhaps because he does not understand it.

What is interesting to note about these reviews is the fact that Brecht was not only considered a shocking and even eccentric playwright, but that his work was considered by some critics, including Clurman, to be devoid of a use value (that is, something worthwhile to the audience) because it carried with it historical connotations that the audience could not comprehend. Were critics, and likewise audiences, unable to look past the shadow of historical emphasis to notice a far more perilous present meaning? Even Brecht himself claimed *Mother Courage and Her*

[20] Ibid., 108.

[21] Taubman, "Theater: *'Mother Courage'* by Brecht," 51.

[22] Ibid., 51.

[23] Ibid., 51.

Children was not merely a historical tale of terror. Hugh Rorrison quotes Brecht as saying that *Mother Courage* is meant to show that "in wartime, the big profits are not made by little people. That war, which is a continuation of business by other means, makes human virtues fatal even to their possessors. That no sacrifice is too great for the struggle of war."[24] In other words, though the play is set in wartime, and though Brecht published the play during wartime, it remains just as apt (or perhaps more so) during peacetime in a capitalist society. Charles R. Lyons furthers this sentiment when he writes, "War ... becomes a metaphor for business. In Brecht's terms, the war itself is the business of big men who manipulate politics for their own advantage, exploiting mankind, and this ethic of exploitation pervades the social structure."[25] *Mother Courage* as a critique of the capitalist regime does not appear in the aforementioned reviews, however, nor is the play considered a critique of much at all. The focus, rather, is on the aesthetic qualities of the production and its abilities to illicit its anti-war sentiments.

The Threepenny Opera, on the other hand, may offer a different explanation for its misinterpretations. Ralph Manheim and John Willett write that:

> *The Threepenny Opera* undoubtedly appealed to the fashionable Berlin public and subsequently the middle classes throughout Germany, and if it gave them an increasingly cynical view of their own institutions it does not seem to have prompted either them or any other section of society to try to change these for the better. The fact was simply that 'one has to have seen it,' as the elegant and cosmopolitan Count Kessler noted in his diary after doing so with a party that included an ambassador and a director of the Dresdner Bank.[26]

Though this explanation regards the European, or more specifically, the German reaction to Brecht, the American reaction was likely quite similar. What is remembered and discussed about *The Threepenny Opera* is not its message, but rather its aesthetic appeal. The work is most well-known for its music and its eccentric flair, not its commentary on social inequality.

---

[24] Brecht, *The Good Person of Szechwan*, XXX.

[25] Lyon, 99.

[26] Willet and Manheim in Brecht, *The Threepenny Opera*, XV.

Brecht's Continuing Influence on American Theatre (1998-2006)

When considering Brecht in more recent permutations, it is important to note that, while the plays may be performed with more frequency, and the reviews may be more in-depth, the overall critic-audience response remains similar to the initial reviews. Brecht is still firmly placed within an aesthetic framework, and his plays are still seen as unconventional representations of the past rather than commentaries on the social and political state of our world—commentaries that could be viewed as more relevant than ever. Stephen Henderson writes of a particularly Brechtian homeless couple panhandling on the streets:

> One wonders what Bertolt Brecht, were he alive today, would make of such street theatre. No doubt he would richly enjoy the layering of contradictions, the fortunate being confused by the panhandlers' refusal to play by the rules of how pans are supposed to be handled. And, since this scene of class struggle might have flowed from his own pen, Brecht would no doubt be reassured that his plays were more relevant today than ever.[27]

But is this truly the case? Are we more likely to understand Brecht now that the American capitalism Brecht so abhorred has proved near-indestructible? As a culture, it is unlikely. In fact, we are, perhaps, more inept at understanding Brecht than ever before. In a time when our entertainment has reached the point of pure, mindless leisure, there may be no room left for Brecht's crucial life lessons, unless of course they are co-opted into an allowable form by the commodity process of modern capitalism. Henderson writes that "not surprisingly, for a playwright so enamored of life's paradoxes, whose work and personality embraced such extremes as good/evil, poverty/wealth and power/powerlessness, reactions to Brecht a century after his birth are highly polarized."[28] In the section to follow, I will outline theatrical reviews from contemporary Brecht productions, in order to contend that, indeed, an overall critical understanding of Brecht (as Brecht intended) still appears out of reach.

Henderson quotes Bartlett Sher, director of a 1998 production of *The Threepenny Opera*, who views it as a play about "how everyone learns to look out for number one" and goes on to say that "each individual becomes his or her own organization, only looking to satisfy their own needs. Issues of justice and the economic conditions of wealth are the

---

[27] Henderson, "The Persistence of Brecht," par. 4.
[28] Ibid., par. 8.

very fundamentals of Brecht."[29]   Here we see Brecht's intentions used to explain modern America.   Despite what other critics may claim, Henderson shows that Brecht may be more relevant today than we think. The problem, writes Henderson, is that most people are not prepared to acknowledge what he sees as the present use for Brecht. He quotes Blanka Zizka, who says of her *Threepenny* Production at the Wilma:

> It was our best-selling play ever. But I realize now that many of those who came didn't really know the play—they knew its reputation and the Kurt Weill songs. In actuality, Threepenny is very grim. The point of view is cynical, nihilistic. It was shocking to our audience and caused a strong reaction. Even I was surprised.[30]

The Threepenny Opera continues to be the most popular Brecht production in the United States—roughly every fourth Brechtian play produced has been *Threepenny*.[31] Klaus Schmidt writes that this "may in part be due to Weill's music, but much more so to the fact that the genre itself is generally experienced as less alien by American audiences."[32]   Whatever the case, more than thirty years later, it is evident that *The Threepenny Opera* is still revered not for its content but for its musical aesthetic.

Despite Henderson's emphasis upon the play's importance in today's society, his views are not shared by the typical theatre critic. David Littlejohn, for example, writes in a review of a 1999 performance that the plays popularity hails from, first, Kurt Weill's "brilliant, raunchy music" and, second, from its "star tunes, modeled after the 69 ballad tunes John Gay inserted into its source, 'The Beggars' Opera' of 1728."[33] In addition, Littlejohn notes that many of the highpoints of the play come from "deliciously sexual and amoral" songs.   This indicates that the true message of *The Threepenny Opera* has been entirely lost, at least for Littlejohn. MacHeath's character is seen as the "evil antihero" of the play, rather than Brecht's original ideal of what we might call "the man struck down by capitalism."   Furthermore, there is no mention in Littlejohn's review of any further meaning within the play. It is merely viewed as a form of crude entertainment.

In a similar fashion, Ben Brantley writes that a 2006 production of *Threepenny* at Studio 54 in New York focuses merely on the spectacle of

---

[29] Sher in Henderson, par. 12.
[30] Henderson, par. 28.
[31] Schmidt, "B.B. 1986: Still a Resistible Force in the American Theatre?" 148.
[32] Ibid., 148.
[33] Littlejohn, "Theater: Brecht Returns to Bay Area," A46.

the opera, rather than on any original Brechtian meaning. This production attempts to modernize Brecht by adding homosexual relationships and pushing the play's obscenity boundaries even further. Brantley writes:

> MacHeath again finds himself torn between two brides: the demi-virginal Polly Peachum and Lucy Brown. But in this case Lucy is a man, who makes a point of showing the audience exactly what lies beneath his skirt. MacHeath's friendship with Tiger Brown, Lucy's father and the chief of police, is of the crotch-grabbing, kissing kind. And for a copulatory free-for-all brothel sequence, the participants' underwear glows luridly beneath a black light.[34]

Though Brecht's original intent was indeed to estrange his audience, this production appears to have entirely lost the point of exactly *what* is supposed to be estranged. Brantley writes that the production pushes the audience further away than what Brecht would have ever intended in "presenting Brecht's lowlifes as exotic, feckless party animals instead of as pseudo-bourgeois materialists ... their censoriousness registers as just a random dip on a pharmaceutically induced roller coaster of moods. Another line of cocaine or two, and these hedonists will forget all about the poor and hungry."[35]   What is evident, then, is that, though Brantley appears to understand Brecht's original intent in *Threepenny* and the epic theatre form, this production has missed the mark, so to speak.

Theatrical reviews of *Mother Courage and Her Children* during this time period also serve to illustrate the current misunderstanding in the United States. The play is still viewed as an anti-war play with little modern usage potential. What is also evident is that, in many cases, there is little emphasis at all on the play's message; instead, reviews focus on the production's portrayal and characterization of Mother Courage. Here again the misrepresentation of Brecht's work is clear—the emphasis on acting detracts from Brecht's original intent, rendering *Mother Courage* as little more than a historical play recast for modern entertainment. Though a handful of critics point out that *Mother Courage* carries with it a series of modern lessons, the minute number of major theatrical productions of this play indicates that both the theatrical community and its audience fail to acknowledge those lessons, if they are even aware of their existence.

Patrick O'Connor's review of a 1995 production of *Mother Courage* illustrates the typical misrepresentation of the play. In this review, O'Connor writes that Mother Courage is "a character who has an answer

---

[34] Brantley, par. 11.
[35] Ibid., par. 17.

for everything until the end, when, completely isolated and alone, 'everyone else sings and she is at last silent.'"[36]   This representation of *Mother Courage* fails to emphasize that Mother Courage, in the end, has learned nothing and that she continues on in the same selfish mental state she has maintained throughout the play. O'Connor also writes of Brecht's alienation effect, claiming what Brecht was really looking for was "more direct communication with the audience" rather than some form of audience alienation.[37]   This indicates that American critics still misunderstand Brecht, even if their interpretations are much closer to his original intentions. If critics and audiences are still hoping for some form of connection with the performers onstage, then Brecht's intentions are still being confused with traditional American theatrical techniques.

America's positioning of Brecht as a merely historically-concerned playwright returns in a review of a 2001 performance of *Mother Courage*. Author Joel Henning writes that the play is "about ordinary people living and dying through unceasing war that is driven by unrelenting greed and fueled by religious hatred."[38]   This confuses the play as merely a depiction of a country stricken by war-time grief. This mystification arises again when he writes that the play is "almost impossible to appreciate in a country that hasn't faced war's devastation on its own soil in almost a century and a half."[39]   In Henning's opinion, America cannot even begin to understand Brecht's message because we have not faced the horrors of war in recent times.   Perhaps Americans don't understand Brecht's message because, like Henning, they still haven't realized the message's existence.

Henning does, however, make a noteworthy comment regarding the performance of Mother Courage in the production.   He admires the director for succeeding "where most Americans previously failed" and writes that, "too often she is played as a charming and plucky survivor, a mother tiger who will do anything to save her children and herself. But Brecht's Mother Courage is not charming. She is cunning, self-serving and cowardly. She only occasionally tries to protect her three children.[40]" Henning praises the fact that Mother Courage is not created to be an admirable character, which is in keeping with Brecht's notions of audience alienation. Even his interpretation of the end of the play, where he writes "Back to business, she continues to peddle whatever she can at the edges

---

[36] O'Connor, "Haggle with Mother," 22.

[37] Ibid., 22.

[38] Henning, "Theater: One Tough Momma," A24.

[39] Ibid., A24.

[40] Ibid., A24.

of the endless war" is at least slightly on target.[41]   However, despite his notable representation of the meaning of the play, Henning still insists that the main idea behind the production is the selfishness during an unending war, rather than the battle of the little man to survive under capitalism.

Margaret Jefferson's review of a 2004 production of the play, on the other hand, illustrates an understanding much closer to Brecht's original intent.   One might say, even, that though the critical meaning is exemplified in the play, Jefferson merely fails to make the connection. She writes that "'Mother Courage' is a great antiwar play. Like war itself, it is brutal yet devious. We are alienated and implicated. We are repelled by much of what we see, but we can't pretend we are astonished."[42]   She also comments that she is aware that the audience understands that Mother Courage is a representation of what we are and could be under any given circumstance. She continues, "Brecht did not want those in the audience to sympathize or identify with what they saw. He wanted them to think and judge. His characters address one other and the audience clinically. The characters feel emotions, but they use them, too."[43]   Here we see that Jefferson understands Brecht to some extent. What she misses is the idea that we do not need to be under the influence of war to realize that such selfish and indomitable actions as Mother Courage's could and do occur every day under the capitalist regime.   This seems to be a common misconception of the American audience.   We may question the implications of a war, but we are far more hesitant to question the implications of the capitalist system.   Stephen Henderson quotes Dikran Tulaine, who argues that "America, it shouldn't be forgotten, is a country founded by Puritans. Even though a lot of this morality was outdated when first enforced, a curtain of morality still hangs over this country. It's a chain on the American Psyche. There's this idea here that all archetypes have to fulfill an absolutely ludicrous moral code."[44]

Despite many misconceptions of *Mother Courage and Her Children*, a review by Bruce Weber does manage to acknowledge the implications of the play today. Weber examines a 2004 production of the play in Harlem and writes that the play is "unashamedly confrontational … [and] is meant to illustrate just the kind of self-satisfying human behavior that will resonate in an era of Enron, Halliburton, terrorism and Iraq."[45]   Here we finally see a review that takes into consideration a use for Brecht in

---

[41] Ibid., A24.

[42] Jefferson, "War Shows its True Colors as Both Friend and Foe," E1.

[43] Ibid., E4.

[44] Tulaine in Henderson, par. 13.

[45] Weber, "Uptown Boys," AR6.

modern America. Though Weber does place it in a historical context, calling the play a "prickly tragicomedy about the demeaning effects of war on ordinary citizens," he acknowledges that, yes—Brecht's ultimate message does have a place in modern America. Weber also notes that the play takes into consideration the idea that Mother Courage is a character who is "determined to protect and support her family but whose integrity is compromised through petty profiteering and shifting of allegiances."[46] Again Weber, like many other critics, places his focus on Mother Courage; however, here we see that Weber's interpretation of her character is much more akin to Brecht's original intent.

Though both *The Threepenny Opera* and *Mother Courage and Her Children* are well-known to the American theatre community, it is apparent from the above analysis that, for the most part, there is a severe disconnect between Brecht's original intent and what is understood by both the American audience and the American actor. Klaus Schmidt writes, "a common belief within the theatre world would have it that [Brecht] has come back with a vengeance, as an irresistible force"[47]— however, the nature of these productions and Brecht's corresponding popularity indicate that it is not Brecht that is popular in the United States; it is the humanized, commodified interpretation of his work. Nearly all attempts to produce Brecht in his original form, as has been shown, have failed; most attempts to produce Brecht in non-Brechtian, purely-for-entertainment form have succeeded and gained headway in the American theatre community.

Misunderstandings and Misrepresentations: Brecht and the American Actor

The Brechtian form has failed in the United States on two accounts. First, Brecht's work typically fails before it reaches its intended audience. This is due to the structure of American theatre and the training of its actors. The Brechtian form stipulates focusing attention *away* from the character, while the American actor is trained in Method acting, that is cultivating empathy and emotion from his viewer, pulling attention *toward* the character—ultimately resulting in the disappearance of the alienation theoretically necessary to Brechtian theatre. Second, and perhaps more imperative, given the nature of American culture and its tendency toward mystification, Brecht's message fails to motivate the American audience in

---

[46] Ibid., A6.
[47] Schmidt, 147.

any way. American audiences do not and will not respond to a theatre designed to *teach*, only to a theatre designed to *entertain*. In the paragraphs to follow, I will explore both causes, beginning with an analysis of the structure of American theatre, the training of its actors, and the irresolvable contradictions between American acting and the Brechtian form.

In "A Short Organum for the Theatre," Brecht writes, "We need a type of theatre which not only releases feelings, insight and impulses possible within the particular historical field of human relations in which the action takes place, but employs and encourages those thoughts and feelings which help transform the field itself."[48] This transformation, Brecht argued, would come about via the restructuring of traditional dramatic theatre, in an effort to create a new, "epic" theatre. This theatre would turn the spectator into an observer, and motivate him toward action; it would cause the spectator to face a societal truth; it would show that the world is alterable and able to alter; and, finally, it would motivate action via reason more than emotion.[49] Though Brecht employed a variety of methods to achieve his theatrical model, arguably the most important was Brecht's reconsideration of acting.

Acting becomes central to Brecht's *Verfremdungseffekt*, or the A-effect, and he writes that, to create this alienation, the actor must "discard whatever means he has learnt of getting the audiences to identify itself with the characters" and that "at no moment must he go so far as to be wholly transformed into the character played."[50] In other words, the actor must cultivate a distance from the character he portrays, one which prohibits the audience from experiencing empathy or understanding for the character. He must not *become* the character, as in Method Acting; rather, he must *present* the character, allowing the audience to make their own judgments. The inability to empathize with the character thus allows the audience to recognize that the character is not doing what he or she *must* do, but rather what he or she *chooses* to do.

Brecht suggests this distance can be created in several ways. First, the actor must portray the character in such a way that the audience recognizes that they are witnessing a play rather than events of a real-life situation—there should be no attempt to "blur the distinction between art and reality."[51] Brecht writes, "It is of course necessary to drop the assumption that there is a fourth wall cutting the audience off from the stage and the

---

[48] Brecht, *Brecht On Theatre: The Development of an Aesthetic*, 190.
[49] Ibid., 37.
[50] Ibid., 193.
[51] Esslin, "Some Reflections on Brecht and Acting," 138.

consequent illusion that the stage action is taking place in reality and without an audience. That being so, it is possible for the actor in principle to address the audience direct."[52] In addition, the actor must participate in more "reading rehearsals" in an effort to continue the understanding that the actor is *reading* the part instead of *living* it.[53] Brecht also posits three ways in which the actor can train himself in the art of alienation: transposition into the third person, transposition into the past, and speaking the stage directions out loud.[54] These methods, argues Brecht, prohibit the actor from creating a relationship with the character he is portraying; rather, he maintains a necessary distance that will be evident to his audience. Brecht writes that "the object of the A-effect is to alienate the social gest underlying every incident"[55]—in other words, the audience must be able to ascertain the fundamental social relationships underlying all actions in the production.

The above methods, though explicated in great detail by Brecht in many of his writings, illustrate what could be called the American theatre community's "problem" with Brecht—in other words, it is the American actor's misunderstanding and misrepresentation of the Brechtian form that results, at least in part, in the general misunderstanding of Brecht's work. Martin Walsh writes that American actors often have a "very superficial view of Brecht's theatre as a *style* like 'Restoration.' 'Restoration' equals foppish gestures, and Brecht means a certain grittiness and stringency, probably picked up from second hand knowledge of *Mother Courage* or *Threepenny Opera*."[56]   What has happened is that Brecht has been aestheticized to such an extent that the *purpose* of his theatre has been lost—transformed into merely another artificial historical period in the theatre timeline. Modern actors are trained to live the character, not be critical of it; thus Brecht becomes "too cold ... he doesn't allow the actors to get at any emotional truths."[57] This resistance to the Brechtian method of acting, then, transitions into the misrepresentation of his work and often to the complete misunderstanding of what it means to act in the Brechtian form. When actors are trained to place emphasis on the character, that training will carry over to all productions, including productions of Brecht's work.

---

[52] Brecht, 136.
[53] Ibid., 137.
[54] Ibid., 138.
[55] Ibid., 139.
[56] Walsh, "Producing Brecht for the Contemporary American Theatre Audience," 209.
[57] Ibid., 209.

Klaus Schmidt postulates another problem concerning Brecht and the American actor—that the Brechtian form is viewed by many actors as merely a necessary step in their formal training. He quotes directors Guy Sprung and Steven Kent, who argue that Brecht, in the mind of many young actors, is "something you have to go through before you get out into the real world."[58] In other words, Brecht's form is once again stripped of its modern purpose and viewed only as a historic style. Schmidt also argues that it is a lack of any Brechtian tradition in the United States, as well as poor instruction regarding Brecht's style of acting that cause students to "quake in their boots" before they approach a Brecht production.[59] It becomes evident, then, that the American actor sees Brecht as a historical playwright with little to offer modern American theatre, thereby showing clearly how Brecht's messages could be so easily stripped out of the equation and lost entirely.

In the end, the issue of Brecht's form versus the American acting style comes down to two main issues: lack of interest and lack of knowledge. Directors agree it is difficult enough to find actors to *play* the roles demanded in Brechtian theatre—it becomes even more difficult to find actors who know *how* to play the roles, as few actors are trained in Brecht's form. Stephen Henderson quotes director Bartlett Sher, who claims, "With Brecht, an actor has to consider his character not only in relation to the other cast members, but in terms of politics and history … you can't assume your actors are going to know what the lumpenproletariet is."[60] Brecht clearly requires an amount of work that American actors simply are not willing to give—both because it contradicts their formal training and because, ultimately, their work is gauged on a standard that is entirely non-Brechtian. American actors are trained to seek a step-by-step technique, something Brecht and epic theatre can't offer the modern actor. Martin Walsh argues, "It's very hard to convince … actors that the attitude towards the work is as important, if not more so, than anything you can isolate as the technique of Epic actors, that in a sense the attitude becomes the technique. A critical attitude, of course, is actively discouraged in actor training in the United States."[61] With such training in the United States, it is simple to see how Brecht could so easily fail on stage. More important than the difficulties of bringing Brecht to the stage, however, is the ideological mystification that occurs once the work is presented to its audience. It is here that the true

---

[58] Sprung and Kent in Schmidt, 150.
[59] Schmidt, 151.
[60] Sher in Henderson, par. 34.
[61] Walsh, 209.

failure of Brecht's work becomes clear, a failure to be explored in the next section.

A Culture Mystified: America, Brecht, and the Culture Industry

When Brecht arrived in the United States in 1941, he entertained the notion that his theatre would not only be accepted, but would ultimately flourish in what he felt was one of the modern "theatre capitals" of the world.[62]   His stay turned out to be a radical disappointment, however—one that Brecht carried back to Europe six years later:

> Despite his profound contempt for Capitalism's mode of cultural production, it seems that Brecht still harboured some illusions about the American theatre when he arrived ... By the time Brecht decided to return to Central Europe, however, he had lost his trust in the American theatre's potential to explore an innovative, politically progressive aesthetics that might be responsive to his work.[63]

Brecht, as well as his work, was largely ignored by the American populace—the professional productions of his work, *The Private Life of the Master Race*, *The Duchess of Malfi*, and *Galileo*, failed both commercially and responsively, as did his efforts to situate himself in the Hollywood screenwriting community. Less than ten years after his return to Europe, however, Brecht's popularity exploded alongside the commercial success of *The Threepenny Opera*. Some critics attribute the fall of McCarthyism in the United States to Brecht's rise in fame, both occurring in approximately the same time period. What this claim fails to recognize, however, is that, by the time *Threepenny* reached the stage, it had undergone massive changes, most of which stripped its potential for "social attack."[64] The fall of McCarthyism, though it may have aided in the overall acceptance of Brecht as a playwright, did little to pave the way for social critique. The problem with Brecht is not to be blamed on American culture or its theatrical community, but rather on the capitalist system that created it. In other words, Brecht *cannot* be done properly, because to honor the spirit of his art would be to foster a savage critique of

---

[62] Weber, "Is There a Use Value? Brecht on the American Stage at the Turn of the Century," 227.

[63] Ibid., 227.

[64] Ibid., 228.

the American status quo (i.e., the "American way") and thus to encourage the overthrow of capitalism.

In his text *One-Dimensional Man: Studies in the Ideology of Advanced Industrial Society* (1964), Herbert Marcuse argues that the progression of advanced industrial society (in this case, the progression of American society) is such that it promotes a one-dimensional thought structure, and that in this thought structure, "ideas, aspirations, and objectives that, by their content, transcend the established universe of discourse and action are either repelled or reduced to terms of this universe."[65] The dominant ideology, in other words, has become so entrenched in society that it ultimately pushes away that to which it is opposed. This society "bars a whole type of oppositional operations and behaviors" that could potentially spark actions against the dominant ideology.[66] The result is a society that pushes away those thoughts, beliefs, and opinions that it has been taught to avoid, thereby creating a one-dimensional thought pattern incapable of accepting (or even recognizing and understanding) that which stands outside its ideological realm. In modern American society, this translates into the overall rejection of critical thought by the majority of society—especially that critical thought that might negate the validity of an overtly conservative capitalist system. American society chooses to accept only that which perpetuates its self-imposed ideology, and, in turn, degrades itself below the level of social critique.

In the theatre world, this has resulted in an art form whose sole purpose is to entertain its audience and generate mass capital. It is no wonder, then, that there is little use value for Brecht's work—in its original form—in the United States. Instead, producers have chosen to transform that work from its once revolutionary potential to that which promises viewers the aesthetic pleasure to which they are accustomed and which is ultimately required for any amount of commercial success. Furthermore, once the transformation (and, likewise, the humanization) of Brecht's work occurs, the aesthetic pleasure *must* ultimately outweigh any revolutionary thought for there to be any prospect for overall success, otherwise it will be rejected by theAmerican audience as "eccentric" or "radical." Stephen Henderson writes that the problem of "what to do with Brecht" remains at the forefront of theatre simply because it is, at its core, so controversial:

---

[65] Marcuse, *One Dimensional Man: Studies in the Ideology of Advanced Industrial Society*, 12.
[66] Ibid., 15.

After the bloat of too many Noel Cowards, Terrence McNallys or Rodgers and Hammersteins, a good stiff Caucasian Chalk Circle or Arturo Ui is seen as a purgative. Like exercise, vegetables and reading poetry—things Americans don't naturally have much enthusiasm for—Brecht is included in the well-balanced diet in the hopes that theatregoers will be provoked and thereby improved. What many producers and directors are finding, however, is that their audiences may only think they want to be challenged.[67]

It is due to American society's apathetic nature about what is "good for it" that the Brechtian nature has started to disappear from modern Brecht productions. American society refuses to respond to a theatrical form that could potentially require any amount of critical thought, both because of its growing apathy and because it finds itself ideologically conflicted. The productions must then be humanized and stripped of their conflicting qualities, should the theatre community hope to remain afloat. Modern media presents a continued challenge for the theatre community, and, as Klaus Schmidt writes, for Brecht: "Contemporary audiences in America literally have to be lured away from the tube with a mouth watering meal,"[68] a meal that, rest assured, Brecht could not provide the American audience. The end result is a watered-down, stripped version that only vaguely resembles the playwright's initial theatrical ambitions.

What remains in productions during both Brecht's initial American introduction and in contemporary theatre is, then, exactly what Brecht abhorred—emphasis placed upon the characters, the songs, and the various aesthetic elements within the production. Inherent, too, in Brecht productions is the museumification of his work, the presentation of it as an historical artifact with little or nothing to offer an American audience. It is interesting to note, however, that the continued advancement of the American capitalist regime has, unbeknownst to much of American society, given Brecht's work continued urgency and relevance in the United States. Henderson writes that, "at the end of a century transformed by media and technology, when the capitalism Brecht deplored has emerged virtually triumphant, when the ideologies he embraced have been outdistanced by history, the relevance of his work has become a thorny question."[69] The problem, to return to Marcuse, is that the dominant ideology has so effectively immersed itself in American culture that there is little chance for the recognition of Brecht's importance in modern times.

---

[67] Henderson, par. 27-28.
[68] Schmidt, 152.
[69] Henderson, par. 4.

American society, and its focus on "mass-produced, mind-numbing entertainment,"[70] has little understanding of, or need for, Brecht and his ideologically-conflicting lessons; however, the transformed Brecht, stripped of its critical meaning and political potential, has a small window of opportunity, given its focus on the aesthetic pleasures of the theatre. The disappearance of the political and critical potential in his work has pushed Brecht toward popularity—in other words, the misrepresentation of Brecht (the non-Brecht) that has allowed him to flourish in the spotlight of American theatre.

It is, then, both the misrepresentation and the misunderstanding of Brecht and his work that is at the heart of America's "trouble" with Brecht. When performed according to Brechtian standards—utilizing alienation, disjointed scenes, stark scene design, and characters with whom the audience cannot connect—productions cannot generate the audience numbers or the revenue they require to maintain any quantity of theatrical success. First, given the nature of American acting and its emphasis upon characterization and empathy, it becomes difficult for productions to achieve anything close to a Brechtian standard. Furthermore, even if a production were to achieve that standard, it would ultimately be rejected by its American audience on the basis that it would conflict with the ideologies of that culture. American society has demonstrated, thus far, neither the understanding nor the patience to gain the understanding of the lessons inherent in Brecht's work. Instead, his work must be tailored to meet the requirements of an American audience and theatre community that bases its value judgments on the aesthetic qualities of a production. Klaus Schmidt quotes Peter Farran, who rightly argues that "Brecht will never make headway in American theatre as long as our theatre remains, as Brecht identified it in his '*Arbeitsjournal*,' ... a whore selling worn-out pleasure to an impotent customer."[71] Brecht, then, must be transformed into a commercial "whore," to be at least partially successful in American theatre, even if that "whoring" entails the loss of anything that was ever Brechtian about a given production—the end result: a *Threepenny* that is little more than a homosexual orgy bent on the ultimate shock-value, and a *Mother Courage* whose hardy, just-keep-going attitude offers a model to businesspersons across the country.

What is most amazing in analyzing America's response to Brecht—both by the theatre community and its audiences—is that Brecht's work has indeed managed to find a niche in American culture. That niche,

---

[70] Ibid., par. 4.
[71] Farran in Schmidt, 151.

however, is not the one which Brecht wished to permanently achieve. Whether or not America will finally come to terms with Brecht's critical message is still yet to be seen, but what is certain is that, both fifty years ago and today, Brecht is still vastly misunderstood and misrepresented by American culture—a culture that, more than many others, is in need of the critical messages his work has to offer. Given the growth and expansion of capitalism, and the continued push of its accompanying ideology, there appears to be little chance for Brecht's pertinent life lessons to shine through to all of society; rather, Brecht's work will remain a sometimes thrilling, sometimes confusing, and often bizarre experience for American theatregoers. It will not be until the radical transformation of that capitalistic system and its ideology, both of which serve to keep the true Brecht spirit captive, that any critical or political use value will be visible to American culture. Until then, Brecht cannot and will not succeed in changing the world with which he fought; instead, his message will continue to be misrepresented by the American theatre community which presents it and misunderstood by the American audience that perceives it—something Brecht may have known too well.

Works Cited

Atkinson, Brooks. "Made With Music." *New York Times*, 21 March 1954, X1.

Brantley, Ben. "'Threepenny Opera' Brings Renewed Decadence to Studio 54." *New York Times on the Web*, 21 April 2006. <http://theater2.nytimes.com/2006/04/21/theater/reviews/21thre.html> (21 April 2001).

Brecht, Bertolt. *Brecht On Theatre: The Development of an Aesthetic*. Trans. John Willett. New York: Hill and Wang, 1964.

—. *The Good Person of Szechwan, Mother Courage and Her Children, Fear and Misery of the Third Reich*. Trans. John Willett. New York: Arcade, 1993.

—. *The Threepenny Opera*. Trans. John Willett and Ralph Manheim. New York: Arcade, 1994.

Clurman, Harold. "Theater." *The Nation*, 27 March 1954, 265+.

Esslin, Martin. "Some Reflections on Brecht and Acting." *Re-interpreting Brecht: His Influence on Contemporary Drama and Film*. Ed. Pia Kleber and Colin Visser. New York: Cambridge UP, 1990. 135-146.

Henderson, Stephen. "The Persistence of Brecht." *American Theatre* 15, no. 5 (1998): 12-18.

Henning, Joel. "Theater: One Tough Momma." *Wall Street Journal,* 23 October 2001, A24.

Jefferson, Margo. "War Shows its True Colors as Both Friend and Foe." *New York Times,* 13 Februrary 2004, E1+.

Krutch, Joseph Wood. "Black Bread and a Circus." *The Nation,* 4 December 1935, 659+.

L.F. "At the Theatre." *New York Times,* 11 March 1954, 26.

Lyon, James K. *Bertolt Brecht in America.* Princeton: Princeton, 1980.

Lyons, Charles R. *Bertolt Brecht: The Despair and the Polemic.* Carbondale: Southern Illinois UP, 1968.

Littlejohn, David. "Theater: Brecht Returns to Bay Area." *Wall Street Journal,* 18 October 1999, A46.

Marcuse, Herbert. *One Dimensional Man: Studies in the Ideology of Advanced Industrial Society.* Boston: Beacon, 1964.

O'Connor, Patrick. "Haggle with Mother." *TLS,* 25 November 1995, 21-22.

Schmidt, Klaus M. "B.B. 1986: Still a Resistible Force in the American Theatre?" *Gestus: The Electronic Journal of Brechtian Studies* 2, no.3 (1986): 147-156.

Taubman, Howard. "Theater: 'Mother Courage' by Brecht." *New York Times,* 1 April 1963, 51.

Thomson, Peter. *Brecht: Mother Courage and Her Children.* Cambridge: Cambridge UP, 1997.

"'Threepenny Opera' Wins Praise, Scorn." *New York Times,* 12 February 1956, 83.

Walsh, Martin. "Producing Brecht for the Contemporary American Theatre Audience." *Gestus: The Electronic Journal of Brechtian Studies* 2, no.3 (1986): 207-213.

Weber, Bruce. "Uptown Boys." *New York Times,* 3 February 2004, AR6+.

Weber, Carl. "Is There a Use Value? Brecht on the American Stage at the Turn of the Century." *Bertolt Brecht: Centenary Essays.* Ed. Steve Giles and Rodney Livingstone. Amsterdam: Rodopi, 1998. 227-239.

Broadway & The Depoliticization of Epic Theatre: The Case of Erwin Piscator

Ilka Saal

In the fall of 1935 Bertolt Brecht warned his friend Erwin Piscator "to stay away from the so-called leftist theaters" in the United States, which were "dominated by scribblers and [had] the worst producer manners of Broadway, albeit without the latter's know-how."[1] Brecht was referring to his own experience with the New York Theatre Union, whose production of his epic drama *The Mother* in November 1935 had ended in a heated argument between theater and author. Ignoring Brecht's adamant insistence on principles of epic theater, the theater company had adapted the play in the naturalist Broadway fashion, thereby producing an incongruity between script and performance that could only but fail.[2] Yet, his friend's warning notwithstanding, Piscator agreed a few months later to a production of his own epic drama *Case of Clyde Griffiths* by the renowned Group Theatre. The play even though directed by Lee Strasberg and performed by the Group's most talented actors flopped as well, prompting Group member Clifford Odets to conclude: "America is not going in Piscator's direction."[3]

Three years later, Piscator emigrated from the Soviet Union to America. Forced into exile by the National Socialists, he found a new artistic home at Alvin Johnson's New School for Social Research in New York in 1939. For the next twelve years he was to remain there as director of the Dramatic Workshop. The Dramatic Workshop produced some of America's finest actors, playwrights, and directors—among them Tennessee Williams, Marlon Brando, Walter Matthau, Harry Belafonte, Tony Curtis, and Judith Malina. Piscator himself, however, was unable to

---

[1] Trans. mine. Brecht, *Werke*, 535.
[2] See my essay "How Brecht Failed Broadway: The Political Theater of the New Deal" (2007).
[3] Strasberg in Ley-Piscator. *The Piscator Experiment*, 40.

leave a distinctive mark on the American theater. Although he tried to carry on his work in epic theater, he quickly realized that its militant aesthetics could not be realized in the political climate of the American forties. America continued to refuse to go in the epic direction. In contrast to 1936, though, Piscator now began to adjust his agenda to this refusal. His productions and publications of the 1940s reveal a deliberate effort to deradicalize epic theater, to dissociate it from the militant modernism of the Weimar Republic, and to widen its aesthetics and politics for a broad liberal audience. Epic theater, however, did not survive this dissociation of theory and praxis. In this essay, I shall show how Piscator's productions of the forties, such as *All the King's Men* (1948), forfeited their claim to epic drama by replacing the demand for social change with a broad appeal to truth and action. Gone was the moral and political imperative for theater to be a weapon of class struggle; a general appeal to humanism was now taking its place. While a few technical vestiges of the old epic theater still remained, politically Piscator's productions of the forties were but stylized versions of the Schillerian *Schaubühne*.

Moreover, I shall argue that this transformation or reduction of epic theater from a radical form of cultural intervention to the basic bourgeois conception of theater as a tool of enlightenment reflects not only Piscator's accommodation as an immigrant with American capitalism, but also the rapprochement of political theater in the US with the bourgeois Broadway stage and its concomitant loss of radicalism. Piscator's work in New York thus illustrates that in political theater form cannot be divorced from content and that both are ultimately contingent on concrete cultural and political vectors. A second question is to what extent epic theater is a concrete historical form of cultural intervention and to what extent it is capable of surviving as a ubiquitous form of cultural critique. Although critics have frequently applied the term "Epic Theater" to the work of contemporary artists like Anna Deavere Smith and Tony Kushner, it remains to be seen how useful the concept is for a description of cultural praxis beyond that of Brecht and Piscator.

I. *Case of Clyde Griffiths*
Weimar Militancy on Broadway

Case of Clyde Griffiths (1936), Piscator's first American production, still reflects the radical spirit of his work in the Weimar Republic. In the late 1920s, his radical interpretations of history and contemporary politics at the Berliner *Piscatorbühne* had drawn much public and critical attention, frequently causing the fur-coated and jewelried patrons in the front seats to frown in consternation as students and workers in the galleries rose spontaneously to sing the "Internationale." In the end, however, all of his audience—patrons of orchestra and gallery seats alike—enthusiastically applauded Piscator's bold and ingenious multimedia spectacles. For Piscator they were nothing less than "demolition acts" ("*Zertrümmerungsaktionen*"), aimed at the all-out destruction of the illusionist bourgeois stage and its replacement with a theater that could serve as a weapon in the class struggle of the workers.[4] Like Brecht, he insisted that the call for a new theater was synonymous with the call for a new social formation. And he, too, believed that it was the epic, i.e. the open narrative form that was most suited to accomplishing this revolutionary goal. While Weimar's two leading political theater artists had somewhat different ideas about the concrete aesthetics of epic theater (Brecht insisting on *Verfremdung*, Piscator also seeking the visceral affect), they agreed on its general task and function: for both of them epic theater was a "form of political activity," which by representing the interests of the working class and by propagating a Marxist worldview sought to mobilize the workers to political action.[5] Epic theater was to provide the workers with what Brecht liked to call a "workable picture of the world" ("*ein praktikables Weltbild*").[6] Piscator likewise described its purpose as delineating the various social and political factors that

---

[4] Piscator, *Schriften*, 50.
[5] See Erwin Piscator. *The Political Theatre* (1978). Brecht and Piscator had an ongoing quarrel as to who "invented" epic theater. Brecht claimed his expressionist drama *Baal* (1918-26) as the first epic play, whereas Piscator referred to his production of Alfred Paquet's *Flags* (1924). Ironically, both undermine their quarrel over authorship by acknowledging that epic theater was not a unique invention but the result of various convergences in Western drama, particularly of the emergence of a new social group, the proletariat, alongside a new aesthetic trend, naturalism. Its roots, however, go as far back as Shakespeare and medieval market square entertainment as well as to Asian performance traditions. The question of who was first to develop the concept of epic theater has also caused much debate among scholars. George Bühler settles the argument in a minute comparative study of the works of the two theater men, concluding that Piscator was first to politicize theater and introduce epic elements, while Brecht worked out the concept of the epic theater in theory and practice (*Bertolt Brecht—Erwin Piscator*, 1978). John Willett confirms this conclusion in his comprehensive study of Piscator's work (*Theatre of Erwin Piscator*, 1978).
[6] Brecht, *Brecht on Theatre*, 133; and Brecht, *Werke*, 550.

determined modern life. Like the novel it was to offer "not only dramatic action but also a commentary on it."[7]

At his theater on *Nollendorfplatz* in Berlin (the so-called *Piscatorbühne*), Piscator created some of the most ambitious and provocative examples of epic theater, among them adaptations of Ernst Toller's *Hoppla, We are Alive!* (1927), Alexey Tolstoy's and Pyotr Shchegolev's *Rasputin, the Romanovs, the War, and the People who Rose Against Them* (1927), and Jaroslav Hašek's *The Adventures of the Good Soldier Schwejk* (1928). The trademark of these productions was the integration of what Piscator called a "sociological dramaturgy" with an epic *mis-en-scène*.[8] This meant that Piscator was primarily interested in the characters' social function, the extent to which they represented a particular social group. In order to highlight this function he often changed the original text—much to the chagrin of the authors—eliminating psychological and moral motivations and focusing instead on the social and economic forces that determine a character's actions. This sociological approach was further enhanced by the overall *mis-en-scène* of the production. In collaboration with his set designers Traugott Müller and George Grosz, Piscator created some of the most innovative stage designs of the period: a multi-functional scaffolding for *Hoppla*, a revolving half-dome for *Rasputin*, and a treadmill for *Schwejk*. Often the stage machinery was so heavy, noisy, and complicated that it put a genuine strain on the architecture of the old theater on *Nollendorfplatz* and sometimes even interfered with the acting. These sets were, however, never merely illustrative; they asserted an additional, visual commentary on the dramatic action: the fundamental isolation of the liberal forces of the Weimar Republic (*Hoppla*), the self-contained universe of Tsarist Russia (*Rasputin*), Schwejk's epic march through space and time. The most effective commentary, however, was provided by the integration of documentary footage through slide projections and film. After Eisenstein, Piscator was one of the first to turn film into an integral element of stage production and to use it as a primary stimulant of visceral affect.[9] The opening documentary montage about war and inflation in *Hoppla*, for instance, was so powerful that one critic exclaimed: "It wears you down, you the gentleman in the orchestra seat! And now that the actors begin speaking, you suddenly understand what you otherwise wouldn't have

---

[7] Piscator, *Schriften,* 145. Trans. mine.

[8] Ibid., *Political Theatre,* 187.

[9] In 1923, Eisenstein integrated film projections into his staging of Ostrovsky's *Wise Man.* Piscator began to experiment with projections in 1924 (*Flags*) and with film in 1925 (*Nonetheless!*).

understood. Why the people in the cells are revolutionaries."[10] It was this complete immersion of the spectator in the spectacle, allowing no escape, that Piscator was after when he carefully orchestrated light, sound, projections, sets, acting and dialogue into a political *Gesamtkunstwerk,* a total theater.[11] The goal, however, of these multi-media spectacles was not simply to provide the spectator with an aesthetic experience, but, as Brecht put it quite astutely, "to squeeze from him a practical decision to intervene actively in life. Every means was justified which helped to secure this."[12] Brecht therefore saw in Piscator the great innovator of the modern political stage, the experimental genius of epic theater, who in striving "for an entirely new social function for the theater," broke "nearly all the conventions."[13]

It was very much in the spirit of Weimar iconoclasm and radicalism that Piscator, together with Felix Gasbarra, adapted Theodore Dreiser's *American Tragedy* for the stage in 1929/30. *The Case of Clyde Griffiths* was to be produced at the Berlin Lessing Theater in spring 1931. In mid-production, however, Piscator hurriedly left for film work in the Soviet Union thus escaping the onset of cultural reaction in Germany (as well as his accumulating tax debts).[14] He later revised the play together with Lena Goldsmith for production in the United States.[15] Piscator's interest in Dreiser's novel derived above all from a fascination with the ways in which it reduced "human tragedy to economic principles, to the opposition between poor and rich."[16] This equation of tragedy with economics constituted for him the "specifically American," and by extension paradigmatically modern, character of the story. Since this equation

---

[10] Diebold, *Kölner Operetten Revue* 15 February 1928.

[11] Piscator commissioned Walter Gropius with the design of the Totaltheater (See Walter Gropius. *The Theater of the Bauhaus*, 1996). "What I had in mind," Piscator commented, "was a theater machine, technically as perfectly functional as a typewriter, an apparatus that would incorporate the latest lighting, the latest sliding and revolving scenery, both vertically and horizontally, numerous projection boxes, loudspeakers everywhere, etc." (*Political Theatre* 179).

[12] Brecht, *Brecht on Theatre*, 130.

[13] Ibid., 130.

[14] See Willett 83.

[15] Broadway impresario Milton Shubert discovered the play in 1935 in a small production by Jasper Deeter at the Hedgerow Theater in Rose Valley, PA and purchased it for the Group Theatre. See X. Theodore Barber. "Drama with a Pointer" (1984), 62.

[16] Trans. mine. From unpublished notes to a production of the play for the Maxim Gorki Theater in East Berlin in 1957, at Akademie der Künste Berlin, Piscator Center (file 370).

simply offered itself up for a Marxist analysis, Piscator set out to lay bare the fundamental economic conditioning of the rise and fall of Clyde Griffiths, particularly of his murder of Roberta Alden and subsequent trial. His goal was to demonstrate that what was widely perceived to be a "tragedy" stemmed from one primary conflict only: the irreconcilable opposition of social classes. "This is not an epic picture of 'Tragedy and Love,'" a narrator explains in the prologue to the play, "but a mathematical theorem to the effect that today a Destiny of Fate leads and governs mankind as inexorably and absolutely as Fate in a Greek tragedy,—the law of business, or in other words: Money."[17]

All in all, *Case of Clyde Griffiths*—the Group Theatre dropped the definite article in Piscator's title to highlight the universal implications of the story—is a rather schematic exercise in epic theater, lacking much of the playfulness and ingenuity of Piscator's earlier work. It nevertheless holds on to two of the most characteristic elements of his sociological dramaturgy: the use of the narrator and the functionalization of the *mis-en-scène*. As in other Piscator productions, the set was designed to visualize the fundamental idea of the play—here the existence of ubiquitous and insurmountable class barriers and the impossibility of crossing them individually. For this purpose Piscator suggested a tripartite set design (realized by Watson Barrett), which the narrator introduces as follows:

> Before me on the left will be laid the scenes representing Poverty; on the right Riches; and in the center, yes, in the center, lies No Man's Land, as it was called in the war—nobody's world—the land between the fronts, between the battlefields, between the barbed wire. Woe to him who stands there defenseless, who does not enjoy the protection of either side, who stands between the classes—...[18]

The play proceeds in the rough schematic manner prescribed by the set. The main characters are introduced in their respective play areas: the working girl Roberta Alden stage left and the socialite Sondra Finchley stage right. The social background is likewise set up in a contrastive fashion: the farming Alden family together with the factory employees on the left, and the few rich families of Lycurgus, notably the Griffiths, on the right. Factory scenes are staged on the left and high society scenes on the right, etc. Sometimes two scenes are acted out simultaneously and crosscut with each other in cinematic fashion in order to heighten their

---

[17] Unpublished English manuscript of the text, Akademie der Künste Berlin, Piscator Center (file 73, p. 1).

[18] Picator, *The Case of Clyde Griffiths*, 1.

contrast. For example, while Clyde is working in the factory stage left, Sondra is playing tennis stage right. The middle ground, "the No Man's Land," however, is reserved for Clyde. Here his forlorn social climb takes place. This is where he obtains top hat and tuxedo for his social engagements with the Finchleys and Griffiths, and where he is rejected by his factory co-workers after breaking up their strike: "Yes, it's Clyde Griffiths, who spoiled our strike. He doesn't belong to the others yet, but he certainly doesn't belong with us anymore."[19]

The second distinctive epic feature of the play is the narrator, or Speaker, a figure familiar to us from numerous other Piscator productions, who is supposed to represent the "objective" voice of the play. In the manner of a Greek chorus, the Speaker guides the audience through Clyde's tragic rise and fall. Leaning against the apron of the stage, pacing up and down in front of the audience, he introduces sets and protagonists and provides extensive commentaries, documentary facts and statistic, all meant to illuminate the economic background of the story. Aside from that, the Speaker acts as Clyde's confidant, often giving voice to his erratic class consciousness. "Marry Roberta," he admonishes Clyde. "She is good and she loves you. [...] Throw away your crutches. Stand on your own feet and carry on your life, the life of the majority of us."[20] Clearly, Piscator's Speaker is not a neutral observer of the unfolding drama but a fervent advocate of the working class viewpoint. As such he frequently intervenes in the stage action. He agitates the workers to go on strike for higher wages. He reproaches characters (and by implication audiences) about their ignorance as to the economic premises of their actions: "You know that at the same time you are playing tennis, work is being done," he informs Sondra. "And that you can play only because work is being done."[21] And he takes up the role of the defense attorney in the courtroom scene. Turning directly to the audience and asking them for their verdict, he argues that the murder of Roberta Alden was but a consequence of Clyde's futile strife for social recognition and as such, the tragic but logical product of rigid class structures. Hence, Clyde is guilty of killing Roberta only in a second instance, his actual crime consisting in the renunciation of his class. Seen from this angle, the turning point of the play is then no longer the accident on the lake (as in Dreiser's novel) but the strike in the factory. As the Speaker insists, in betraying the strike, Clyde also gave up the one form of social agency available to him: collective action.

---

[19] Ibid., 75.
[20] Ibid., 84.
[21] Ibid., 30.

With the reduction of Dreiser's *American Tragedy* to class conflict, Piscator radically preempts the popular sentimental reading of the story as the tragedy of an individual failing to achieve the American Dream—a reading that had been successfully rehearsed in a previous adaptation of the novel by Patrick Kearney as well as the film version by Josef von Sternberg.[22]   To ensure that any lingering assertions of this national mythology are completely demolished, Piscator concludes with the following exchange: When Clyde's mother passionately exclaims after the verdict, "he dies as a sacrifice to his rebellious, yearning heart, and he will be forgiven!," the Speaker instantly ripostes, "he dies as a sacrifice to society, and it will not be forgiven!"[23]

Case of Clyde Griffiths opened on 13 March 1936 at the Ethel Barrymore Theatre in New York and closed after only 19 performances— a definite flop by Broadway standards. Notably however, it was not so much the debunking of one of the founding myths of American national identity (a feat fervently applauded by the left and booed by the right) which caused the play to fail, but its epic form. Bourgeois critics strongly resented the play's overt didacticism and particularly the frequent interruptions by the Speaker, which for them pre-empted "the stimulation of emotional reactions" that they had previously enjoyed in the Kearney adaptation.[24] Piscator's play struck them as "contemptible intellectual" and not "sufficiently vital or gutsy" for an American audience of the 30s.[25] Labor critics concurred that due to its lack of emotional appeal, the play

---

[22] Dreiser endorsed Piscator's adaptation of his novel over an earlier one by Patrick Kearney (1926), which he rejected precisely for its rehearsal of "the from-rags-to-riches-and-back formula, really dear to the American heart, and [...] much more agreeable to the American taste for tragedy" (qtd. in program notes "The Playbill" at New York Public Library, Lincoln Center for the Performing Arts, Theater Collection). Kearney's "rags-to-riches formula," however, became the basis of Josef von Sternberg's film adaptation (1931) as well as of George Stevens's *A Place in the Sun* (1951). Before giving the job to Sternberg, Paramount had apparently approached Eisenstein about the filming of the novel, but had eventually rejected his final script for its overt leftist slant. See Josef von Sternberg. *Ich, Josef von Sternberg* (1967), 54.
[23] Piscator, *The Case of Clyde Griffiths*, 126. For more details on the production see Barber. "Drama with a Pointer."
[24] Mantle, "Theater Group Does a Beautiful Job of Restaging a Faded Tragedy," (1936).
[25] Anderson, "Case of Clyde Griffiths" (1936).

was ineffective in convincing a mass audience of a leftist agenda.[26] Faced with such predominantly negative reactions, the Group Theatre, even though it had received much praise for excellent acting and ensemble work, felt compelled to publicly disclaim accountability for the play's militant content and iconoclastic form in a letter to the major newspapers.[27] Harold Clurman explained this step as representing the opinion of the majority of Group members, who found Piscator's play "schematic in a cold way" which "definitely went against the American grain."[28]

But in what ways exactly did the play go "against the American grain"? Why did the play fail to convince an American audience? One reason was certainly the vehemence of Piscator's attack of American mores, his relentless exposure of "the cynical code of success proclaimed in every tabloid, movie, pulp-tale and true-to-life-story dedicated to the get rich theme," which found few supporters outside leftist circles.[29] Although Granville Hicks had identified class strife as the moving force of American culture, this thesis never gained much popular purchase.[30] After all, the insistence on class ran counter to one of the constitutive myths of American nationhood: the American Dream of the self-made man. To deny the possibility of individual strife was to deny what many perceived to be the very essence of America.

The most decisive factor for the broad rejection of the play, however, was its highly theatrical form in conjunction with an overtly didactic tone—a style reminiscent of the agitprop of the early 1930s, which had played an important role in the emerging workers' theaters as well as in the organization of labor forces. The direct address and exhortation of the audience, the radical dismantling of the illusion of the fourth wall, the reduction of characters to basic economic/sociological functions had all been quite common in the amateur street theaters; and this style had also

---

[26] See Theodore Repard. "Most Significant Play in New York" (1936) as well as Stanley Burnshaw. "The Theatre" (1936), and John Gassner. "Drama vs. Melodrama" (1936), 8-9.

[27] *New York Post* 17 April 1936. See also Harold Clurman. *The Fervent Years* (1975), 176. The letter was written upon Lee Strasberg's advice, and signed by Cheryl Crawford—both of them, along with Clurman, directors of the Group. The cast of the play included such stellar actors as Morris Carnovsky, Alexander Kirkland, Phoebe Brand, Margaret Barker, Sanford Meisner, and Luther Adler.

[28] Clurman, *The Fervent Years*, 175.

[29] Burnshaw, "The Theatre," (1936).

[30] Hicks, *The Great Tradition: An Interpretation of American Literature Since the Civil War*.

significantly influenced professional leftist theaters during the first half of the decade—most prominently Clifford Odets's *Waiting for Lefty* (staged by the Group Theatre just a year prior to *Clyde Griffiths*, in January 1935). By the mid-thirties, however, agitprop had been replaced with realism as the dominant paradigm of leftist theater.[31] This turn was already evident in *Waiting for Lefty*; in its attempts to add psychological depth to characters, to flesh out their family backgrounds, and to include the vernacular speech of the Lower East Side. A few months later, it became the main topic at the first American Writers' Congress of spring 1935. Most delegates agreed that it was time to substitute the "drama with a pointer" with a more verisimilar and empathetic rendition of social problems, i.e. to portray workers as individual characters with complex psychological as well as socioeconomic relations and to integrate the depiction of class struggle with domestic and sentimental issues.[32] Michael Blankfort articulated this change in aesthetics most succinctly when he called for scripts that illustrate the common human experience: "For our plays to be most effective, the common experience must always include universal and immediate wishes (for a home, for a woman, for children, for security, for love, happiness, etc.)."[33] Appealing to the shared sentimental longing for home and family, leftist theaters hoped to enable the complete identification of spectators with characters on the stage, to facilitate their absorption in the dramatic action, and to trigger the empathy which they considered indispensable to the successful mobilization of a mass audience. Not surprisingly, John Howard Lawson recommended the return to "technique in the most conservative and traditional sense," that is, drama was once again to adhere to the Aristotelian principles of conflict, action, and unity and to emulate the domestic appeal and analytical precision of an Ibsen play.[34]

Needless to say, this swing to bourgeois realism had little to do with Piscator's (or Brecht's) concept of epic theater, which was formulated as the very antithesis of the bourgeois drama of empathy. It was, however, indicative of the general reorientation of the American left in the mid-thirties. In the face of fascism and war, and particularly with the official endorsement of the Popular Front doctrine by the Communist Party in August 1935, the left was forced to relinquish its former militant, sectarian stance and to reach out to a variety of liberal forces in the population,

---

[31] See Ira A. Levine. *Left-Wing Dramatic Theory in the American Theatre* (1980).

[32] "Drama with a Pointer" is the term Richard Lockridge used in his review of *Case of Clyde Griffiths* in "The Stage in Review" (1936).

[33] Blankfort, "Facing the New Audience," 25.

[34] Lawson, "Technique and Drama," 128.

regardless of class affiliation. In terms of cultural politics this meant that the proletarian theaters of the early thirties were now encouraged to appeal to the middle classes as well. The strategic shift in leftist politics became most apparent during the election campaign of 1936, when the Communist Party changed its battle cry from "Towards a Communist America!" to "Communism is 20th Century Americanism."[35]   Evidently, Piscator's adaptation fits ill with this new inclusive populism, still evincing much of the militant oppositionality that had marked the political and aesthetic praxis of leftist theaters in the Weimar Republic.

II. The Dramatic Workshop:
Theater As A Moral Institution

On 1 January 1939, three years after the failure of *Clyde Griffiths*, Piscator arrived in New York, one of many German émigrés.   Alvin Johnson, director of the New School for Social Research, offered him directorship over the new Dramatic Workshop, which Piscator was to carry out for the next twelve years.[36] The Dramatic Workshop opened in January 1940 with some twenty students attending evening classes. Seven years later its enrollment peaked with ca. 1,000 students, a third of them full-time. Piscator enlisted a number of prominent artists as instructors in acting, directing, playwriting, and stage design, among them Carl Zuckmayer, Hanns Eisler, Ferdinand Bruckner, Stella Adler, Lee Strasberg, John Gassner, Mordecai Gorelik, and Maria Ley-Piscator.[37] Aside from providing professional training in all theater branches, the workshop was conceived with an eye towards building an ensemble, which could eventually lead to the establishment of a repertory theater. Towards this end, Piscator opened a small Studio Theater in the main hall of the New School on West 12th Street. The Studio was primarily an experimental stage, aiming to produce "plays which cannot be done on Broadway, because of their uncertain appeal, or sophisticated intelligence

---

[35] See "Text of Platform." *Daily Worker* 29 June 1936.

[36] Piscator's original plan was to stage Tolstoy's *War and Peace* for Broadway impresario Gilbert Miller. Miller, however, withdrew from the contract in the fall of 1938, considering Piscator's adaptation longwinded and tiring, entirely unsuited for American audiences. Piscator attempted to find a new sponsor for his project, but neither Clurman of the Group Theatre nor any other Broadway producer was interested. Piscator finally turned to Alvin Johnson for help (see Willett 50 and 145).

[37] For more detailed information on the Dramatic Workshop see Willett 152-167 as well as Thea Kirfel-Lenk. *Erwin Piscator im Exil in den USA, 1939-1951* (1984).

level, or overlarge cast."[38] Already in its first season, it presented three professional productions: *King Lear* (December 1940, dir. Piscator), Klabund's *Chalk Circle* (March 1941, dir. James Light), and Philip Yordan's *Any Day Now* (June 1941, dir. Robert Klein). The latter two, particularly *Chalk Circle* (starring a young Dolly Haas), were quite successful.

Piscator's own ambitious *King Lear* production, which presented the revolt against Lear's oppressive paternalism as a revolt against fascism, however, was dismissed by the press as "a mannered, pretentious and heavily Teutonic pageant."[39] The critics strongly disliked his epic modernization of a beloved classic. "Shakespearean productions are at their best when they remain within the fine and flourishing ancient ways of their native land," the Communist *Daily Worker* insisted along with many bourgeois critics.[40] Piscator's subsequent production of *War and Peace* (1942) did not fare much better. Although considered a "gallant try" in arguing for US military intervention in World War II and even praised as "a good experiment" in stagecraft, it was once again the use of a Speaker, which greatly aggravated the audience.[41] Clurman had anticipated as much when he rejected the play on behalf of the Group in 1939. While he deemed the play's short, varied, and swiftly moving episodes "scenically effective," he also considered its epic structure "an emotional failure."[42] "This sense of not being able to identify oneself with the characters," he wrote, "or to connect themselves imaginatively into their lives and milieu, which I believe is largely due to the form and structure of your dramatization, is a very serious lack, particularly from the standpoint of our American audiences, who respond much less to form and even to the excitement of stage technique than to simple characterization and situation."[43] With this assessment, Clurman incidentally also summarized why epic theater, in general, regardless of political contingencies, stood so little chance on the American stage. Its failure to focus on individual suffering and success had little appeal to an audience that firmly believed in individual strife and freedom. Aesthetic distance was, moreover, considered inimical to a professional stage (including the American left's)

---

[38] Piscator, "Bericht des Direktors an die Mitglieder des Studio-Theaters" in *Theater, Film, Politik*, 150.

[39] Watts, "A Satisfactory Lear is Still in the Future."

[40] "Piscator's King Lear."

[41] *New York Herald Tribune*, qtd. in Ley-Piscator, 194. *New York Times* 22 May 1942.

[42] Clurman in Probst, *Erwin Piscator and the American Theater*, 129-130.

[43] Ibid., 129-130.

that believed in a direct correspondence between the spectators' empathy and the box office. "The greater the [emotional] craving, the greater the release, and the greater the box office returns. Q.E.D.," Mordecai Gorelik, the scenic designer, sardonically remarked. He added that it was precisely such economical thinking which prevented the New York critics from seeing "clearly the functioning and purpose of the epic form."[44]

In October 1945, the Dramatic Workshop moved to the President Theater on West 48th Street, the Broadway neighborhood. Here the "March of Drama" repertory was inaugurated—a sequence of student performances accompanying and illustrating John Gassner's lecture series on theater history. These performances, which were open to the general public, became extremely popular. They laid the foundation for a repertory theater, which by 1947 included twenty-six plays ranging from classics by Gogol and Shaw to modern plays by Pirandello and O'Neill. In order to accommodate more subscribers and productions, a second theater was opened in the spring of 1947, the Rooftop Theater on East Houston Street. For Piscator, the President and Rooftop Theaters were a first step in the direction of developing a genuine people's theater in the tradition of Rolland and the German *Volksbühnen* movement. The goal was to acquaint a working and lower middle class audience with classic and modern plays.

At the President Theater, Piscator staged another major American production: Robert Penn Warren's *All the King's Men* in January 1948. This play was to become a milestone in the evolution of his epic theater because here, for the first time, Piscator worked with two different narrators, an extrinsic one and an intrinsic one (a device he was to use again in his celebrated re-staging of *War and Peace* at the Schiller Theater in Berlin in 1955). Warren and Piscator collaborated on the adaptation of the play from the novelist's Pulitzer Prize winning novel of the same title.[45] Based on the life of Huey P. Long, the novel portrays the rise of

---

[44] Gorelik, "Epic Realism: Brecht's Notes on the Three-Penny Opera," 36 and 29. Gorelik here referred to the staging of Brecht's *Threepenny Opera* by Gifford Cochran and Jerrold Krimsky (1933), to the Theatre Production of Brecht's *Mother* (1935) and to the Group Theatre's production of *Case of Clyde Griffiths* (1936).

[45] The novel was originally an adaptation of an earlier play by Warren in blank verse, *Proud Flesh* (1937). See James Grimshaw and James Perkins (eds). *Robert Penn Warren's All the King's Men: Three Stage Versions* (2000). The 1948 Warren-Piscator adaptation was published in German in 1957, in a translation by Piscator and Helmut Schlien, under the title *Blut auf dem Mond* (*Blood on the Moon*). It remains unpublished in English. But it became the basis for a later

Willie Stark from simple Southern farmer to one of the most powerful politicians of the region. While democratically elected, Stark can secure and extend his power only by resorting to an intricate scheme of violence, corruption, and deception. Piscator's goal in staging the play was once again the illumination of the various social and economical factors that determine Stark's form of modern dictatorship; or as the program notes put it, "to search for all the elements which influence and provoke our actions and make them good or bad."[46] In classic epic fashion, Piscator's sociological analysis proceeds via a series of flashbacks, extensively commentated by two narrators. The first, Jack Burden, a young reporter, follows the story from the inside. He is one of the characters involved in Stark's schemes during the 1930s. A second narrator, a Professor, "objectively" comments upon the events from the historical distance of the 1940s. Once again it is the epic *mis-en-scène*—a multi-functional set design (by Willis Knighton) which included a revolving stage and a projection screen—that serves to enhance this sociological approach. Piscator's student, Judith Malina, describes it thus:

> Piscator creates a stage space that one can play on, under or around. A spiral staircase rises from the center of a ramp, a small platform atop of it permitting the graphic enactment of the upward striving for power. The small stage seems to expand; a revolving platform allows for cinematic effects of action in motion. Actors walking on a turntable that revolves against them, or single spot-lit faces function as the theatrical equivalent of the moving camera and the close-up.[47]

Yet, despite such deployment of the old dramaturgy and stagecraft, *All the King's Men* remains a far cry from Piscator's original concept of epic theater. Although Huey P. Long's reign in Louisiana is certainly invoked, this historical reference is never made explicit. Rather, upon Warren's insistence the play remains deliberately fictional and allegorical in its analysis of the "Stark phenomenon."[48] I wanted my story to be personal rather than political. I wanted the issues to come to crisis in personal terms," Warren writes.[49] The astute historical and sociological analysis so

---

reworking of the play, which was published by Random House in 1960 as *All the King's Men (A Play)* (see Grimshaw/Perkins 17).

[46] Collins qtd. in unpublished program notes (PC 80).

[47] Malina, *The Diaries of Judith Malina 1947-1957*, 17. See Willet 161 for photographs of set design.

[48] Ley-Piscator, *The Piscator Experiment*, 212.

[49] Grimshaw and Perkins, *Robert Penn Warren's All the King's Men: Three Stage Versions*, 9.

typical of Piscator's previous work thus gives way to the private, ethical musing about the nature of man's dreams and actions and their inherent truth-value. Notably, the play concludes with the following exchange between the main characters:

> STARK: But I can tell you this. Truth is the dream and the act. It is the father and the child. It is the knife-edge and the wound. And to you who are dead, I who am dead, can say that this is the only reconciliation.
> JACK: And I, who am listening—who has begun to live—say this to you who are living and who, living still suffer in the awful responsibility of Time—I say that Truth is the only action. For Truth (once recognized) demands—
> PROFESSOR: Action, Mr. Burden?
> JACK: Yes, yes. For action is our only Truth. That is our Fate.[50]

Little is left in this ending of Piscator's interest in precise socioeconomic analysis, in the detailed historicization of contemporary politics; let alone of his once so fervent demand that society had to be changed—a demand that he still asserted vividly at the end of *Case of Clyde Griffiths* when the Speaker indicted society as the main culprit. *All the King's Men* contains at best a rather feeble affirmation of the need for action; but the larger question as to who ought to act on whose behalf not only remains open but also unasked. Any political commentary is framed and contained by personal reflection and feeling; the demand for collective action, moreover, gives way to the inquiry into individual failure.

If Piscator's former productions angered conservative critics precisely because of their cogent assertion of a leftist agenda for social change, they now looked in vain for any such position. Even the *New York Times* remarked that the play offered a curious mixture of "overwrought melodrama and underdone philosophizing," which suffered "from a morally muddy attitude towards its protagonist, Willie Stark."[51] *All the King's Men* received little press coverage, probably because it was considered a semi-professional production. When it was revived with a professional cast in 1950 (after the release of Warren's Academy Award winning movie), it drew wider attention. The consensus, however, was once more that the play remained "irresolute and equivocal" and that an "overly-complicated staging tended to get in the way of an overly-complicated drama."[52]

---

[50] From unpublished director's book at Piscator Center (file 670).

[51] L.B. "At the Theatre."

[52] Guernsey, "The Theaters"; and Coleman, "All the King's Men Gets 'Off-Broadway' Staging."

Piscator's subsequent production of the period—Wolfgang Borchert's *Outside the Door* (March 1949), John Matthews's *The Scapegoat* (April 1950), and Jean Paul Sartre's *The Flies* (April 1947, dir. Paul Ransom) — received little public attention. But the "March of Drama" performances at the Resident and the Rooftop continued to be well attended, thanks to an innovative and diversified repertory of plays at affordable prices.[53] Despite the mediocre reception of his American productions, Piscator enjoyed work at the Dramatic Workshop. He even came to appreciate the American theater as a theater "for the common man—with the [sic] common sense."[54] This comment, however, also reveals the extent to which Piscator was abandoning his former intention of giving contemporary theater an entirely new social function. In fact, his few theoretical writings of the period evince a concerted effort to redefine epic theater from a tool of radical intervention into an artistic means for asserting a humanist critique.

In almost thirteen years of theater work in the United States, Weimar's foremost political director never once used the attribute "political" in reference to his work. When he took up the issue of epic theater at all, it was then with much caution and diplomacy. In one of his first public statements in the US, a *New York Times* article of 1940, he described epic theater as one of many interpretative methods capable of linking man's private drama to the larger world that conditions it.[55] But even this vague and guarded assertion was prefaced by extensive praise for the achievements of the American stage. Not once in this lengthy article did Piscator mention politics. Except for a brief reference to his production of Gorky's *Lower Depths*, he moreover took great care to avoid any reference to his Berlin work. In his first "Director's Report to the Members of the Studio Theater" of 1941, he likewise asked his subscribers

---

[53] The growing deficit in Piscator's budget prompted the New School to shed the Dramatic Workshop in 1949. It continued to operate under an independent board of trustees including Gassner, Warren, Weill and Johnson Yet, by 1950 the Rooftop Theatre had to be given up due to financial problems, and a year later the President Theatre had to be closed as well. Maria Ley-Piscator continued to run the Workshop until the late 50s on two floors of the Capitol Theatre but it never regained the prominent position it once held in New York's theater life (See Willett 155-161). Piscator also participated in American theater life outside the Workshop. Together with his wife he staged Shaw's *Saint Joan* in Washington D.C., starring Louise Rainer (1940). He also directed Irving Kaye's *Last Stop* at the Ethel Barrymore in New York (1944).

[54] Piscator, "Amerikanisches Theater," in *Schriften* 2, 197.

[55] Piscator, "The American Theater: A Note or Two on Playwrights, the Box Office and the Ideal."

not to be startled by his proposal to put on *War and Peace* as an "epic" play, quickly assuaging potential fears of political and aesthetic iconoclasm by explaining that "what we call epic theater is not a modern invention as you might think but a revival of timeless trends in theater art."[56] Again there is no indication that he once considered epic theater more than a "timeless trend"—namely a concrete, historically grounded political praxis. Instead he concluded his report with a vague assertion that theater ought to fulfill more functions than mere entertainment, prudently refraining from specifying the nature of these functions. In a subsequent article "Theater of the Future" (1942), containing a somewhat more detailed exegesis, Piscator carefully explained that epic theater sought to involve its spectators in the solution of the dramatic conflict and, in this manner, to provoke an active attitude that would be useful outside the theater. But once again he was quick to add, that this approach had already been practiced with great success on the American stage with the Living Newspaper.[57] Evidently the "great innovator" of political theater now took great pains to present epic theater as a "timeless" and intrinsically *American* mode of representation, thereby rendering it as politically harmless as possible.

Such caution with regard to the practice and explication of epic theater was certainly justified given the political climate of the time as well as Piscator's precarious status as an immigrant. By the time he arrived in the US, the Popular Front was about to collapse and the period of broad leftist commitment was over. A general conservative backlash in New Deal culture was setting in with the closing down of the Federal Theatre Project by act of Congress in summer 1939. Not surprisingly, Piscator worried about his FBI file, constantly wondering "how much do they know?"[58] Moreover, since he never obtained American citizenship, Piscator was officially an "enemy alien" for the first half of his stay while the US was at war with Germany. During the ensuing cold war, the hysteria of Joseph McCarthy's witch-hunt alerted him not to draw attention to his militant theater past in Berlin, nor to his three-year tenure as president of the International Association of Revolutionary Theaters in Moscow (1932-35). In fact, he left the United States shortly after receiving a summons from the House Un-American Activities Committee in 1951. (Brecht, likewise, left immediately after his first hearing in 1947.)

---

[56] Ibid., *Theater Film Politik* 190, trans. mine
[57] Ibid., *Schriften*, 144-149.
[58] See his diary notes "Amerika" in *Erwin Piscator: Eine Arbeitsbiographie* (1986), vol. 2, 44.

Yet, Piscator's New York productions as well as his essays of the period not only bear the traces of much caution but also reveal his effort to redefine epic theater from a form of "political activity," a sharp weapon of class struggle and political intervention, into an artistic means of criticizing deplorable social conditions and fostering a general humanist attitude in the audience. He now considered epic theater as "an unparalleled instrument for the expression of all human experience and thought," defining its primary responsibility as "serving humanism."[59] Abandoning his previous Marxist standpoint for a Schillerian understanding of theater as a moral force, Piscator ironically returned to the very *Volksbühnen* diplomacy he once so vehemently attacked in the Weimar Republic.[60] With this he also abandoned his former iconoclasm and radicalism; he was now less interested in provoking the revolutionary impulses of his spectators than in soliciting their assertion of humanist values, less concerned with launching a frontal attack against the ruling system by demolishing its principal dramatic forms but with proposing corrective measures that would affirm the *status quo*. In Piscator's theoretical writings and productions of the 1940s we can thus observe a distinct deradicalization and, with regard to his original concept of political theater, also depoliticization of epic theater. What remained were a general humanist position and a few technical vestiges of the old theater (turntable, treadmill, narrator, projections). The impact of the latter was, however, "blunted by the abandonment of any extreme political stance," as John Willett rightly observes.[61]

It is not entirely clear what exactly prompted Piscator to adjust his definition of epic theater to the American culture of the 1940s. Perhaps it was the lack of cooperation on the part of American producers, dramatist, and critics. Perhaps it was a desire to accommodate himself with the American mainstream theater in order to keep his Dramatic Workshop alive, which after all sustained his existence and that of many other immigrants during the war. Perhaps he also realized that the moment of radical political intervention was over and that the one form of agency and

---

[59] *Schriften* 2, 149 and *Theater Film Politik* 215—all trans. mine.

[60] Piscator used to insist that epic theater had little to do with the *Volksbühnen* movement (a derivative of Antoine's *théâtre libre*), whose political objective consisted above all in enlightening the working and petit bourgeois classes by providing them with access to the classics. For Piscator, however, political theater was "not a question of providing the proletariat with art, but of propaganda; not of a theater for the proletariat, but of proletarian theater" (*Schriften* 1, 36, trans. mine).

[61] Willett, *Theatre of Erwin Piscator: Half a Century of Politics in Theater*, 167.

change that was left was that of humanist education and of reform. The latter position certainly was to mark Piscator's work upon his return to Germany, where he redefined political theater as *Bekenntnistheater*, as a theater of confession and assertion that was to give testimony to Germany's national guilt as well as to contribute to the assertion of a new national identity—a somewhat different but nonetheless highly political endeavor.[62]

III. Is It Epic Enough?
Legacies Of Epic Theater

Lotte Lenya once asked Brecht during rehearsals for her song *Surabaya Johnny* whether he found her interpretation "epic enough." Brecht allegedly answered: "Lenya darling, whatever you do is epic enough for me."[63] It is unlikely that Brecht or Piscator would give a similar answer with regard to the many dramas and productions that have since been called "epic" by their authors and/or their critics. In fact, the past 60 years have seen such an astonishing proliferation of this attribute in reference to the work of authors and directors that it is cause for—if not alarm—at least some pause and reconsideration of our usage of the term.

The term epic theater now seems readily applied to the most diverse works, from Thornton Wilder, Tennessee Williams, and Judith Malina to August Wilson, Anna Deavere Smith, and Tony Kushner. What these playwrights have in common is their occasional use of certain techniques commonly affiliated with the epic theater, such as presentational directness, episodic structure, documentary footage, the use of narrator and songs. These techniques alone, however, are not "epic enough" to qualify a production as epic theater. On the contrary, defining epic theater merely by a catalogue of technical devices leads to such amazingly incorrect claims as that Thornton Wilder is the founder of epic theater in the United States, and that his name stands, along with that of Brecht, as synonymous with epic theater.[64] Without doubt Wilder startled his audiences when he dismantled   the   fourth   wall   with   the   persona   of   a   stage

---

[62] See Erwin Piscator. "Die Bühne als moralische Anstalt in der Prägung dieses Jahrhunderts" (1966). In *Schriften* 2, 348.

[63] Interview with H. K. Gruber in the documentary *Lenya: Ein erfundenes Leben* (1994).

[64] Winkgens, "Das 'epische' Theater in Amerika: Thornton Wilder." In *Das amerikanische Drama* (1984), 182. It also needs to be pointed out here, that Piscator's use of the epic narrator anteceded Wilder's by two years. See also Probst 69-71.

manager/narrator/commentator in *Our Town* (1938). But his deployment of a narrator is the political antithesis to that of Piscator's, serving to mythologize rather than to historicize the everyday, to assure a middlebrow audience that "ordinary life is, after all, good."[65] Neither does Tennessee Williams's use of a narrator turn his *Glass Menagerie* (1945) into an epic play. Similar to Wilder, Williams was not interested in the historical or socioeconomic dimension of his story but in poetic effect.[66] He was primarily concerned with emotions and moods, with poetics rather than politics; and while the influence of Piscator on his work cannot be denied, his artistic heritage shows greater affinity to expressionism rather than epic theater. In general, the wide-spread application of the attribute "epic" to productions of the most varied nature shows a tendency to dissociate the aesthetics of epic theater from its politics. If epic theater is reduced primarily to an aesthetic experience, i.e. to a few technical vestiges aimed "to establish the pleasure of the critical disposition," as Peter Ferran for example suggests, then it becomes depoliticized and emptied of its very substance (as seen in the case of Piscator on Broadway).[67] However, epic theater was never just an aesthetic method aimed at showing "contemporary reality as criticizable" and at changing "the way audiences conventionally enjoy the theater" but its aesthetic agenda was always tightly intertwined with a concrete political and ideological praxis. As John Fuegi aptly reminds us, "the purpose of 'epic theatre' as conceived by Piscator and Brecht in the 'twenties was to teach and to teach from a pointedly leftist position on the political spectrum."[68] Conversely, we also need to remember that epic theater is not simply synonymous with leftist political theater *per se*. In the Living Theater, for instance, which was certainly at the forefront of the political theater avant-garde in the 1960s, the influence of Antonin Artaud is clearly more prominent than that of Piscator or Brecht, regardless of co-founder Judith Malina's frequent assertions that she had trained with Piscator at the Dramatic Workshop.[69]

There are, of course, plays where the attribute "epic" might be justified. The docudramas of Anna Deavere Smith (e.g. *Fires in the Mirror, Twilight L.A.*) have often been situated in the tradition of epic

---

[65] Ibid., 183.

[66] Probst, *Erwin Piscator and the American Theater*, 80.

[67] Ferran, "New Measures for Brecht," 22-23.

[68] Fuegi, "'Epic Theatre' in North America," 185.

[69] See Malina's published memoirs *The Enormous Despair* (1972) as well as *The Diaries of Judith Malina* (1984). See also Probst 87-94.

theater.[70] Here it is not only Smith's deployment of interviews, of video and film footage in her performances but also her anti-illusory performance style (demonstrating rather than impersonating her characters) which are reminiscent of Piscator's documentary method and Brecht's epic acting style.[71] Moreover, Smith's plays qualify as "epic" because they are interested in social change. In the manner of Piscator and Brecht, she attempts to historicize contemporary social conflict (Crown Heights, Los Angeles) by revealing the various social, economic, and political determinants behind it. And just like her modernist predecessors, she compels her audience through her selection of speeches, their editing, and their montage, to take up a critical attitude towards the narratives she portrays—notably not towards the individual characters she presents but towards the various institutional practices, economic structures, and social hierarchies that determine her characters' attitudes towards the event. In this manner, she turns theater into a forum for public debates just like Brecht and Piscator. Her goal is to initiate dialogue, an open conversation about current political problems; because, so she insists, "[h]aving an open conversation involves coming out of the house, whether it is the house of identity politics in a big way or the house of you, and being willing to walk toward something else without knowing what is going to happen."[72] Notably, however, Smith's political agenda stops here. What matters to her is the process of conversing; an interest also reflected in the name that she gives to her overall project, "On the Road: In Search of American Character." The question of social change, which certainly fuels this quest as well as her astute social analyses, thus remains open. When asked about her vision of change she even suggests that it might suffice to prompt the individual to individual action.[73] For Brecht and Piscator, however, the critical attitude of the individual spectator was not the end but the prerequisite for their ultimate goal: the total social overhaul. They viewed "changing the world" in the context of *revolutionary* activity; and at the center of their theater praxis was not the individual but the collective.[74] Smith's theater lacks this bold utopian vision, and with that

---

[70] Clark, "(Ch)oral History: Documentary Theatre, the Communal Subject and Progressive Politics," 95-122; Westgate, "This Electrifying Moment," 101-110; and Lyons and Lyons, "Anna Deavere Smith: Perspectives on her Performance within the Context of Critical Theory," 43-66.

[71] See Carl Weber. "Brecht's 'Street Scene'—On Broadway, of all Places?" (1995).

[72] Smith, "Public Lives, Private Selves," 289-90.

[73] Westgate, "This Electrifying Moment," 106.

[74] See Manfred Wekwerth. "Questions concerning Brecht" (1990), 19-37.

also an essential quality of epic theater.[75]

Perhaps it is only Tony Kushner, who still dares to dream of collective change, even of revolution in his plays. Seen from this angle, *Angels in America* (1993) is perhaps the one play that might be "epic enough" to truly deserve the term epic theater. Kushner not only asserts a fundamental critique of American bourgeois individualism (particularly in its Reaganite configuration), but he also asserts his faith that the U.S. does, after all, have the "potential for radical democracy."[76] In the concluding *tableau* of *Perestroika*, Kushner paints such a utopian vision: the WASP AIDS patient Prior Walter, the black drag queen Belize, the Jewish Reaganite Louis, and the Mormon mother Hannah are all gathered under the wings of the Angel of Bethesda in Central Park engaging in a heated conversation about perestroika, the fall of the Berlin Wall, and the ongoing Israel/Palestine conflict. With this vision of multicultural polyphony Kushner seeks to nourish the feeble collective consciousness of his spectators and ideally inspire them to collective action.

Yet, as David Savran astutely points out, ultimately Kushner's vision of "radical democracy" remains but an affirmation of American liberal pluralism.[77] Liberal pluralism has always already enlisted dissent in reaffirming consensus, or more specifically, a fundamentally conservative hegemony.[78] The utopia of a radical democracy of pluralism thus turns out to be the revolution that already took place: American nationalism in its various incarnations from the founding fathers, via Andrew Jackson and Joseph Smith to Ronald Reagan. Moreover, as Savran asserts, "revolution, in the Marxist sense, is rendered virtually unthinkable, oxymoronic."[79] For in Kushner's analysis there is no place for social class; Marxist analysis has been replaced by the identity politics of race, sex, and gender. Janelle Reinelt likewise insists Kushner's engagement of identity politics, "while useful and strategic in terms of contemporary exigencies, leaves the play with no other foundation for social change than the

---

[75] When asked about the influence of epic theater on her work, Smith stresses that her approach was primarily determined by the pragmatics of how to draw the audience into her performance. While she stresses that she admires the work of Brecht, she also makes it pretty clear that she does not understand herself as part of a Brechtian tradition (Westgate 103-4).

[76] See David Savran. "Tony Kushner considers the longstanding problems of virtue and happiness" (1994), 27.

[77] Savran, "Ambivalence, Utopia, and a Queer Sort of Materialism," 13-39.

[78] Ibid., 28.

[79] Ibid., 31.

individual subject, dependent on atomized agency."[80]   In the end—and in spite of the author's iconoclastic intentions—*Angels* is, in the words of Eve Sedgwick, "kinda subversive, kinda hegemonic,"[81] and it is precisely this quality that so quickly endeared it to critics, academics, and Broadway audiences alike, earning Kushner the Tony Award as well as securing his *Angels* a place in the great tradition of the American Jeremiad.

Not surprisingly, Reinelt concludes that while Kushner might write in the tradition of epic theater, while he might have a similar aesthetic *and* political agenda in mind, the production of his play does not necessarily turn out to be epic at all: "it is the notion that a good night out in the theater dishes up politics and genuinely horrible insights in order to accommodate them to the culinary tastes of an audience for whom these things must be rendered palatable."[82]   Ultimately, so Reinelt reminds us, epic theater has to happen not just on the page but also on the stage: "[I]f the spectators and the actors and the play form a Brechtian triangle of speculation and critique, aesthetic pleasure and political engagement, *then* the 'epic' happens."[83]

Why do we continue to bother with the term "epic" at all then; we might want to ask in conclusion. Because as Reinelt articulates, many of us are "hungrily seeking a left-wing voice in the American theater" like Tony Kushner's,[84] a voice ready to tackle "die großen Gegenstände," the massive subjects, just as Brecht and Piscator once did,[85] and because many of us are still invested in the utopia of radical democracy. Precisely this is the legacy of epic theater. However, we also have to remind ourselves that Brecht's and Piscator's dream of radical cultural and political change, of the complete social overhaul, was very much defined by a concrete historical, political, cultural situation—the intense class strife of the Weimar Republic. Both Brecht and Piscator were forced to realize in the 1930s and 1940s that their dream could not be transferred to the American stage without a significant deradicalization of its inherent political aspirations. Why then would we expect it to work now when under late capitalism the premises of cultural and political agency, even of our very concept of change, have altered so much? As Fredric Jameson put it, ours is a time when "the luxury of the old-fashioned ideological critique, the

---

[80] Reinelt, "Notes on *Angels in America* as American Epic Theater," 242.

[81] Sedgwick in Savran, 32.

[82] Reinelt, 238.

[83] Reinelt, 237.

[84] Ibid., 242.

[85] Brecht, *Schriften zum Theater*, 132.

indignant moral denunciation of the other, becomes unavailable."[86] I want to suggest that while we can certainly still affirm traces of the modernist endeavor of epic theater in the work of postmodernist artists, it might be more useful to ascertain to what extent they are developing their own, new forms of cultural praxis and political intervention, forms that speak to the particular cultural moment of the *hic et nunc*. Letting the forefathers rest might enable us to repoliticize contemporary theater praxis.

Works Cited

Anderson, John. "Case of Clyde Griffiths." *New York Evening Journal,* 16 March 1936.

Barber, X. Theodore. "Drama with a Pointer: The Group Theatre's Production of Piscator's Case of Clyde Griffiths." *TDR* 28, no.4 (Winter 1984): 61-72.

Blankfort, Michael. "Facing the New Audience." *New Theatre*, November 1934, 25-27.

Boeser, Knut and Renate Vatkova (eds). *Erwin Piscator: Eine Arbeitsbiographie*, 2 vols. Berlin: Edition Hentrich, Fröhlich and Kaufmann, 1986.

Brecht, Bertolt. *Brecht on Theatre*, trans. John Willet. New York: Hill and Wang, 1964.

---. *Schriften zum Theater*, vol. 3. Berlin and Weimar: Aufbau Verlag, 1964.

---. *Werke: Große kommentierte Berliner und Frankfurter Ausgabe*, eds. Werner Hecht, Jan Knopf, Werner Mittenzwei and Klaus-Detlef Müller. Berlin, Weimar, Frankfurt/M.: Aufbau and Suhrkamp, 1989-2000.

Bühler, George. *Bertolt Brecht – Erwin Piscator: Ein Vergleich ihrertheoretischen Schriften*. Bonn, 1978.

Burnshaw, Stanley. "The Theatre." *New Masses,* 31 March 1936.

"Case of Clyde Griffiths." *Variety,* 18 March, 1936.

Clark, Ryan M. "(Ch)oral History: Documentary Theatre, the Communal Subject and Progressive Politics." *Journal of Dramatic Theory and Criticism* 17, no.2 (Spring 2003): 95-122.

Clurman, Harold. *The Fervent Years*. New York: Da Capo Press, 1975.

Coleman, Robert. "All the King's Men Gets 'Off-Broadway' Staging." *New York Daily Mirror,* 19 July 1950.

Diebold, Bernhard. *Kölner Operetten Revue,* 15 February 1928.

---

[86] Jameson, *Postmodernism, or the Cultural Logic of Late Capitalism*, 46.

Ferran, Peter W. "New Measures for Brecht." *Theater* 25, no.2 (1994): 9-24.

Fuegi, John. "'Epic Theatre' in North America." *Actes du VII Congrès de l'Association Internationale de Littérature Comparée*, eds. Milan V. Dimić and Eva Kushner. Stuttgart: Verlag Kunst und Wissen, 1979.

Gassner, John. "Drama vs. Melodrama." *New Theatre* 16 (1936): 8-9.

Gorelik, Mordecai. "Epic Realism: Brecht's Notes on the Three-Penny Opera." *Theatre Workshop*, April-July 1937, 29-41.

Grimshaw, James and James Perkins (eds). *Robert Penn Warren's All the King's Men: Three Stage Versions*. Athens: U of Georgia Press, 2000.

Gropius, Walter (ed). *The Theater of the Bauhaus*, trans. Arthur Wensinger. Baltimore: Johns Hopkins UP, 1996.

Guernsey, Otis. "The Theaters." *New York Herald Tribune,* 19 July 1950.

Hicks, Granville. *The Great Tradition: An Interpretation of American Literature Since the Civil War*. New York: Macmillan, 1933.

Jameson, Fredric. *Postmodernism, or the Cultural Logic of Late Capitalism*. Durham: Duke UP, 1991.

Kazan, Elia. *Elia Kazan: A Life*. New York: Knopf, 1988.

Kirfel-Lenk, Thea. *Erwin Piscator im Exil in den USA, 1939-1951*. Berlin: Henschel, 1984.

L.B. "At the Theatre." *New York Times,* 19 January 1948.

Lawson, John Howard. "Technique and Drama." *American Writers' Congress 1935*, ed. Henry Hart. New York: International Publishers, 1935.

Lenya: Ein erfundenes Leben. Erinnerungen und Anekdoten über Lotte Lenya, dir. Barrie Gavin. ARTE musica/Hessischer Rundfunk, 1994.

Levine, Ira A. *Left-Wing Dramatic Theory in the American Theatre*. Ann Arbor: U of Michigan Press, 1980.

Ley-Piscator, Maria. *The Piscator Experiment*. Carbondale: Southern Illinois University Press, 1967.

Lockridge, Richard. "The Stage in Review." *New York Sun,* 14 March 1936.

Lyons, Charles R. and James C. Lyons. "Anna Deavere Smith: Perspectives on her Performance within the Context of Critical Theory." *Journal of Dramatic Theory and Criticism* 9, no.1 (1994): 43-66.

Malina, Judith. *The Diaries of Judith Malina 1947-1957*. New York: Grove, 1984.

—. *The Enormous Despair*. New York: Random House, 1972.

Mantle, Burns. "Theater Group Does a Beautiful Job of Restaging a Faded Tragedy." *New York Daily News,* 15 March 1936.

Piscator, Erwin. "The American Theater: A Note or Two on Playwrights, the Box Office and the Ideal." *New York Times,* 21 January 1940.

—. *Schriften*, 2 vols., ed. Ludwig Hoffman. Berlin: Henschel Verlag, 1968.

—. *Theater, Film, Politik,* ed. Ludwig Hoffmann. Berlin: Henschel, 1980.

—. *The Political Theatre*, trans. Hugh Rorrison. New York: Avon Books, 1978.

"Piscator's King Lear." *Daily Worker,* 16 December 1940.

Probst, Gerhard F. *Erwin Piscator and the American Theater*. New York: Peter Lang, 1991.

Reinelt, Janelle. "Notes on Angels in America as American Epic Theater." *Approaching the Millennium: Essays on Angels in America*, eds. Deborah Geis and Steven Kruger. Ann Arbor: U of Michigan, 1997.

Repard, Theodore "Most Significant Play in New York." *Daily Worker,* 17 March 1936.

Saal, Ilka. "How Brecht Failed Broadway: The Political Theater of the New Deal." *Interrogating America through Theatre and Performance*, ed. William Demastes. New York and London: Palgrave Macmillan, 2007.

Savran, David. "Ambivalence, Utopia, and a Queer Sort of Materialism: How Angels in America Reconstructs the Nation." *Approaching the Millennium: Essays on Angels in America*, eds. Deborah Geis and Steven Kruger. Ann Arbor: U of Michigan, 1997. 13-39.

—. "Tony Kushner considers the longstanding problems of virtue and happiness." *American Theatre* 11, no.8 (1994): 20-27.

Smith, Anna Deavere. "Public Lives, Private Selves." *Black Genius: African American Solutions to African American Problems*, eds. Walter Mosely, Manthia Diawara, Clyde Taylor, and Regina Austin. New York: Norton, 1999. 272-290.

Sternberg, Josef von. *Ich, Josef von Sternberg*. Velber: Friedrich Verlag 1967.

"Text of Platform." *Daily Worker,* 29 June 1936.

Watts, Richard. "A Satisfactory Lear is Still in the Future." *New York Herald Tribune,* 17 December 1940.

Weber, Carl. "Brecht's 'Street Scene' – On Broadway, of all Places? AConversation with Anna Deavere Smith." *Brecht Then and Now/ Brecht damals und heute*, eds. Marc Silberman et al. *The Brecht Yearbook/Das Brecht-Jahrbuch*, vol. 20. Madison: The International Brecht Society, 1955. 51-63.

Wekwerth, Manfred. "Questions concerning Brecht." *Re-interpreting Brecht: his influence on contemporary drama and film*, eds. Pia Kleber and Colin Visser. Cambridge: Cambridge UP, 1990. 19-37.

Westgate, J. Chris. "This Electrifying Moment." *Writing on the Edge* 15, no.1 (2004): 101-110.

Willett, John. *Theatre of Erwin Piscator: Half a Century of Politics in Theater*. London: Methuen, 1978.

Winkgens, Meinhard. "Das 'epische' Theater in Amerika: Thornton Wilder." *Das amerikanische Drama* (Studienreihe English 40), ed. Gerhard Hoffman. Bern: Francke, 1984. 182-201.

PART II:

IN THE SHADOW OF SEPTEMBER 11TH: RENEWED INTEREST IN BRECHT ON BROADWAY

BETWEEN BROADWAY & GROUND ZERO: THE *ARTURO UI* CASEBOOK, NYC 2002

NORMAN ROESSLER

To be sent to hell is to be in very good company. To be excluded from Broadway—likewise. Excluded from regular production—staged in the hope of a long run—are most of the great plays of the world from those of Aeschylus on. Even the greatest playwright in our own language, Shakespeare, is now very seldom launched for an unlimited run in the regular way of show business. How then could we expect to see lesser Shakespeare or foreign ones on Broadway?[...] So Bertolt Brecht is not exactly being discriminated against. Not one German playwright has ever had even the semisuccess on Broadway of a Shaw, a Pirandello, a Chekov. Shouldn't we really be asking why a Broadway success was ever expected for Brecht?[1]

real use of dialectics: to permit you to work with contradictory units. ie not just to be relativistic. dialectics more or less force you to seek out the conflict in all processes, institutions, ideas (russo-british alliance, british-american alliance, germano-japanese alliance, soviet democracy, tory strategy etc etc) and to use it. on the other hand (at the same time) the opposing classes operating together in nazi germany etc.[2]

The question of Brecht and Broadway (for the purposes of this article, Broadway is a synonym for commercial American Theater) leads generally to one of three conclusions: absence, failure, and erasure. That is: Brecht *Stücke* are rarely, if ever, produced on The Great White Way; if a Brecht production is mounted it has only a limited or abbreviated run; and if a Brecht work is produced and then reviewed, the review article will erase the details of the actual production by means of meta-critical, philosophical diatribes on Brecht's politics, aesthetic theories, or personal life. Intuitively, this state of affairs is understandable; after all, what other result would there be but absence/failure/erasure when a Teutonic (hence grim and humorless), Marxist (hence anti-capitalist and anti-democratic),

---

[1] Bentley, *Bentley on Brecht*, 136-137.
[2] Brecht, *Journals 1934 – 1955*, 194.

and avant-garde (hence non-commercial) playwright tried to make it on Broadway, the institutional embodiment of the capitalistic, aesthetic-dope industry of spectacle, escapism, and melodrama? Concretely, a quick search of the Internet Broadway Database[3] confirms these intuitions: between 1933 and 2006 fewer than twenty productions of Brecht's work have been mounted on Broadway, running on average about one month. Take away, *The Threepenny Opera*, the most produced work of Brecht on Broadway as well as the one work that has scored something approaching a "hit" (1955-1961) and a critical success (1976), and the record is even more depressing, especially for such a canonical writer.

Yet this dire state of affairs points not to dismal answers, but rather to dismal questions. As Eric Bentley makes clear in a 1965 review piece, Brecht is not alone with his "meager" record on Broadway.[4] Most of the great playwrights of the Western Canon—Shakespeare, Ibsen, Beckett—have been consigned to the purgatory of Broadway failure or indifference. Hence, the standard conceptualization of Brecht and Broadway is, at first glance, a project which is an intellectual dead end. Indeed, a project that supports both the leftwing and rightwing of the Brecht Industry producing the high-pitched shrill of dogmatic opponents, proclaiming either the failure of Brecht to capture Broadway or the failure of Broadway to embrace Brecht. Brecht and Broadway is a question—an important one at that—but it must be constructed in a dialectical manner substantiated by an actual theatrical event which resolves into a nexus of consonance and contradiction; i.e. an *Auseinandersetzung*. The result of this dialectical engagement is neither the success nor the failure of either Brecht or Broadway, but rather deeper illuminations of American performance culture and its interaction with Brecht.

Instead of asking why Brecht does not work on Broadway, or why Broadway does not embrace Brecht, we rather should ask: when, where, what, how, and why does American Theater reach for Brecht? And in the case of this article a more specific articulation of the question: when, where, what, how, and why does American Theater reach for Brecht after the terrorist attacks on the World Trade Center on September 11, 2001, the catastrophic event which supposedly "changed everything" at the dawn of the 21st century? In the immediate aftermath of 9/11, after the trauma had begun to recede, the first major commercial production of Brecht in New York City was a production by the National Actors Theatre (NAT) of *The*

---

[3] www.ibdb.com.
[4] Bentley, 136.

Resistible Rise of Arturo Ui, and it is an analysis of this production which will form the material of this article.

My goal is to produce a dialectical casebook. A casebook, first and foremost, records the theatrical event and the various contexts which animated the production. A casebook must describe the theatrical event in enough detail so that, in effect, the theatrical event becomes a type of "text" that presents a stable ground of reference. In order to achieve such a stable ground a casebook mediates the author's own experience at the theatrical event, as well as draws upon the commentary and articles of other reviewers who witnessed the event. Secondly, a casebook organizes this "text" of the theatrical event into dialectical interventions: i.e. analytic frameworks that maintain the integrity of the "text" of the theatrical event, while at the same time engaging critical-philosophical questions that further illuminate the production, without taking it over and rendering the theatrical event a mere byproduct of the scholarly text. In the case of the 2002 *Ui* production in New York City, I have organized three dialectical interventions: 1) the *mise en scene* constructed by the director Simon McBurney; 2) the celebrity aura of the principle actor, Al Pacino; and 3) the English-language adaptation of George Tabori used by the production.

I. Between Broadway Spectacularity and Brechtian Theatricality

Simon McBurney, founding member and artistic director of the London-based Complicité theater company, was charged with negotiating the various theatrical, cultural, and political contexts, mediating them through the *Ui* text, and distilling them into a coherent production.[5]

---

[5] *The Resistible Rise of Arturo Ui* was produced by Tony Randall's National Actors Theater (NAT) from October 3—November 10, 2002 at the Michael Schimmel Center at Pace University located in Lower Manhattan's Financial District (a few blocks from Ground Zero, the former site of the World Trade Centers), using an adaptation by George Tabori, directed by Simon McBurney, from London's Complicité Theater with a cast including: Al Pacino, Steve Buscemi, John Goodman, Dominic Chianese, Billy Crudup, Charles Durning, Linda Emond, Paul Giamatti, Chazz Palminteri, and Tony Randall.

Several interesting contexts are to be noted. First, the state of NAT in 2002. Artistic Director, Tony Randall, had founded the NAT in 1991 and originally secured a location for it in the heart of Broadway—the Lyceum Theater at 149 W. 45th St. Yet his attempt to form a national theater and repertory company was unable to sustain itself and by 2002 found itself exiled and fighting for survival as a guest at the Michael Schimmel Center in Lower Manhattan. The *Ui* production

Founded in 1983, Complicité has been one of Britain's leading experimental physical theater companies, which over its lifespan has mounted successful revivals *The Caucasian Chalk Circle* (1997), *The Chairs* (1997), *The Visit* (1989) as well as its own adaptations and theater pieces, *Mnemonic* (1999), *The Street of Crocodiles* (1992), and *The Three Lives of Lucie Cabriol* (1993). Influenced by Jacques Lecoq and Peter Brook, the company emphasizes a freedom from the playscript through creative physical theater, which builds collaboration between the ensemble and "complicity" with the audience. Extensive rehearsal, bare stage design, innovative and eclectic use of music and technology, and a highly physical and kinesthetic theater are the hallmarks of the company. Politically, McBurney and his Complicité group tend toward a form of cultural liberalism rather than overt political activism, a cross somewhere between Richard Foreman and Julie Taymor. The term complicity is emblematic of McBurney's political engagement: building communal awareness by engaging both actor and audience in the performance, but leaving political consciousness and praxis ambiguous.

Ui provided McBurney the opportunity to work in New York Theater with a star ensemble and to negotiate the immediate post-9/11 political context. At the same time, he understood the obstacles such a production

---

represented an attempt to reclaim a place for the NAT at the New York City Theatrical Table. The All-Star cast was part of a fundraising campaign for the NAT and hence led to the $115 ticket price (including a mandatory $50 membership fee), which surpassed the average regular ticket price of $100 on Broadway at the time. A production of Brecht at $115 next to Ground Zero in order to get back to Broadway, to say the least, stretches the most flexible of ironic dialecticians.

Second, the NAT was capitalizing on the resurgence of the American fascination with Hitler. Premiering on April 19, 2001 Mel Brooks' *The Producers,* starring Matthew Broderick and Nathan Lane in an adaptation of his 1968 film, was by October 2002 a certifiable hit and, as of 2006, still running on Broadway. A two-part television movie, *Hitler: The Rise of Evil,* based on Ian Kershaw's biography and starring Robert Carlyle, would debut in Spring 2003 and was already generating buzz. *Max,* a mainstream film starring Noah Taylor and John Cusack, which explores Hitler as a young artist, was in production and the source of newspaper articles. Finally, Chaplin's classic Hitler parody, *The Great Dictator*, had been re-released throughout the world to mark its 60th anniversary.

Finally, the premiere of *Ui* in early October 2002 intersected with several anniversaries: the disputed 2000 American presidential election, the 2001 World Trade Center attacks, the 2001 enactment of Patriot Act legislation, and the 2001 bombing of Afghanistan. Additionally, the current Iraq War was in its immediate prologue phase which would lead to the invasion of Iraq in early 2003.

would have to overcome. In terms of subject matter, *Ui* presented a simplistic parody of Hitler; i.e. an aesthetic reduction of an already reduced musealized figure of evil, which has been so overused in post-World War II American Culture as to be almost worthless as a reference point and a history lesson. In terms of theatrical presentation, *Ui* runs the risk of becoming a star vehicle, which has been supported in the production history of the play with the examples of Ekkehard Schall and Martin Wuttke in Germany, and Leonard Rossiter and Antony Sher in England. McBurney summarized these thoughts with Ed Vulliamy from the *New York Observer* during rehearsals:

> My initial reaction to the play was that it was not possible to stage. What relevance does Hitler have to today's political landscape? But as I read it, I realized that each time I had seen the play it had been cut to the central character. In other words, the resistance – or the lack of it – which is central to the idea of the play went unnoticed, because of the way it would be played purely as a star vehicle. After all the premise of the play is: a) the consequence of financial corruption on a huge scale; b) the taking advantage of catastrophe; c) the feeling among all people that the political threat is so risibly stupid that it can be contained, until it is too late; d) that the central idea of the gangster is to propose "a national security system."[6]

Hence, Mc Burney was acutely aware that if left unchecked, the production would turn itself into a cartoon of sorts, either a historical one or a Broadway one, and so the *mise en scene* he constructed sought to decentralize and deconstruct this centripetal force by bringing stage, technology, and music together in a largely dissonant fashion.

A minimalist stage, typical for Complicité, was presented to the audience—a chair, a few minor sets—and this allowed Mc Burney ample room to integrate choreography, technological effects, and music. Movement, gesture, spacing, and location (especially in the group scenes) exhibited a fluid, choreographed theatricality, evocative of the best of avant-garde theater (e.g. Robert Wilson, La MaMa) as well as Broadway Musical Theater. It was particularly impressive because McBurney was not working with his usual ensemble, used to extensive rehearsals and the demands of physical theater onstage, but rather a group of mostly Hollywood actors (only Pacino, Emonds, and Buscemi had any solid and recent theater credentials) used to the industrial production techniques of cinema and not the theatrical stage.

---

[6] McBurney in Vulliamy, "Reich Here, Right Now—Brecht's Allegory of Hitler's Rise Has a Chilling Resonance."

Texts and images were projected on the upstage screen, at times working in consonance and at times in dissonance with the musical score. The initial projections were generic 1930s-era cosmopolitan city images, which were produced through IMAX-type screen effects and induced vertigo-like feelings: apt metaphors for the chaotic rise of Hitler and perhaps also an allusion to the late grandness of the World Trade Centers. As the production progressed, these images gradually segued into more specific images and supertitles with both contemporary and historical resonance. Documentary footage of Hitler and his rise to power was slowly added to the mix accompanied by supertitles from the Tabori adaptation. On the one hand, it was a historical primer, which importantly showed Hitler as a historical figure, and not some force of nature who imposed himself on Germany and the world. More specifically, it documented the rise of Hitler from the late-1920s to mid-1930s, a history which has often been ignored in favor of the monstrous war-and-genocide Hitler of the 1940s. At the same time, it was also a part of the *Doppelverfremdung* effect: Brecht juxtaposing the Chicago Gangster World onstage with the rise of Hitler in the projections and supertitles.

The last noteworthy element of the McBurney production was the musical score. Building on the 1958 and 1995 Berliner Ensemble musical scores, McBurney drew upon avant-garde compositions (John Cage, Dmitri Shostakovich), Tin Pan Alley standards ("Ain't Misbehavin,'" "My Melancholy Baby") and songs from Tom Waits. Waits supplied old songs "Rainbirds" as well as two recent songs from his collaboration with Robert Wilson on *Woyzeck* (Waits's CD is entitled *Blood Money*), which coincidentally played a month later across the river at the Brooklyn Academy of Music. The score was both dissonant yet recognizable; the Cage and Shostakovich pieces so ubiquitous that they have been used in advertising and political campaigns.

The choreography, visual effects, and music all came together during the Warehouse Fire Trial scenes: a constellation of seven sub-scenes which use the blackout effect to quickly move the narrative from the beginning to the end of the trial. In the NAT production, each blackout led to the entire cast moving itself and the set and props to a slightly different location, thus altering the audience's perspective of events. Moreover, in the crucial scene where the doped defendant begins to regain consciousness, which in turn prompts the doctor to rush to give him another drugged drink, a new choreographic element was added: the doctor delivered the drink in slow motion. The cumulative effect of these aesthetic techniques constructed what Brecht called an "exercise in complex seeing"[7] and which he detailed in his essay "The Street Scene: A Basic Model for an Epic Theatre." In this essay, he describes how a simple traffic accident can be used to develop a distanced and critically conscious exploration of a simple, everyday, historical event and thus achieve epic theater: "The actor use(s) a somewhat complex technique to detach himself from the character portrayed: he force(s) the spectator to look at the play's situations from such an angle that they necessarily bec(o)me subject to his criticism," which in turn, "portray(s) social processes as seen in their causal relationships," and ultimately empower the spectator to "intervene socially."[8]

The scene then moved to the verdict. As the judge handed down his guilty verdict with a southern accent accompanied by the laughing of Giri (John Goodman) the Bill of Rights from the United States Constitution was projected on the entire auditorium wall, spilling off not only the supertitle screen, but the proscenium arch as well. This projection remained for a distressingly long time, enough for Steve Buscemi as Givola to come out and sing the "Song of the Whitewash," channeling his best Tom Waits impersonation. As the audience gazed upon the sacred words of American Democracy (here presented only in the selections that seemed to stand out the most at the time) …

> We the people of the United States, in order to form a more perfect Union, establish Justice, insure domestic tranquility, provide for the common defense [...] (Preamble);
>
> The right of the people to be secure in their persons, houses, papers, and effects against unreasonable searches and seizures, shall not be violated [...](4th Amendment);
> In all criminal prosecutions, the accused shall enjoy the right to a speedy and public trial […} (6th Amendment)

it heard Buscemi's voice croon,

> But all we need is whitewash, fresh new coats of whitewash,
> 'Cause the pigsty's giving in to stress.
> Give us whitewash, please! We'll do a bright wash!
> Whistling while we work, to cover up the mess!
> There's something new and nasty, peeling
> Right across the kitchen ceiling!
> And that's no goof (Not very good)

---

[7] Willett in *Journals 1934 – 1955*, 44.
[8] Brecht, *Brecht on Theatre*, 122.

Look, another crack, dear,
In the front and back, dear!
Ah, the system don't work like it should! [...]
So we need more whitewash, lots and lots of whitewash,
'Cause the pigsty's just about to quit!
Give us whitewash please! We'll do a bright wash!
Whistling while we work, to cover up the shit![9]

In this culminating moment right before the intermission, Mc Burney brought his entire *mise en scene* together—stage, choreography, technology, music—decentering Brecht's playscript, and delivering a political message like a hammer. It is hard to express the emotional shock which McBurney was able to deliver, even to the most seasoned of theatergoers. In a theater only six blocks from Ground Zero, and in the midst of remembrances of 9/11 and the fear and anxiety associated with the Patriot Act, Anthrax scares, and coming war, it seemed that most spectators were prepared for the *Ui* production as a general reminder of chaos, war, and dictators of the Osama bin Laden and Saddam Hussein kind, but not as a particular reference to George W. Bush and his domestic and foreign policies. McBurney had delivered Brechtian politics with a vengeance, and for the political left of the spectators, the analogies and references were acceptable. On the other hand, a good amount of the audience and reviewers (*Wall Street Journal, Financial Times, National Post, The Times, New York Post, New York Daily News*) were not only shocked but also disgusted by the lack of historical and moral clarity. For these reviewers, Mc Burney's production was "fundamentally dishonest"[10] and ultimately little bit more than a cartoon.

II. Bewteen Aura and Alienation

Regardless of whether one considered Mc Burney's *mise en scene*, in the end, to be productive or reductive, Political Theater or Cartoon Central, its use of alienation effects succeeded in granting the spectator a critical consciousness of the Brecht drama, the historical material, and contemporary events. At the very least, the director brought a centrifugal force, a disturbing yet accessible multiplicity, to bear on a playscript that is often highly reductive, historical material which is musealized, and contemporary events that were fraught with political and psychological

---

[9] Brecht adapted by Tabori, *The Resistible Rise of Arturo Ui: A Gangster Spectacle*, 82.
[10] Vitullo-Martin, "An Irresistible Urge to Heap Abuse on the White House," D8.

difficulties. This general alienation fulfilled one element of Brechtian Theatre praxis, i.e. making the spectator aware and allowing them to engage critical-creative perspectives; but the second element, i.e. persuading the spectator to critically intervene, and change the world, (and not just sit around and talk about changing the world) remained an open question. However, whether or not the production would deliver a true Brechtian theatrical aesthetic became a secondary concern as the production centered more and more on the lead actor, Al Pacino.

If McBurney brought a centrifugal force to bear, then the Hollywood aura of celebrity which pervaded the production ran the danger of bringing a centripetal force to bear, and turning the production into what McBurney most feared, i.e. a star vehicle which would denude the production of the aesthetic and political praxis of epic theater. After all, Pacino or "Big Al" as he is known in some circles is the legitimate heir to the Hollywood Gangster tradition of Cagney, Robinson, and Bogart, if not its quintessential paradigm. Consider his acting career: his breakthrough roles comes as Michael Corleone in *The Godfather* (1972) which he later reprised in *Godfather II* (1974) and *III* (1990); his first comeback occurred in 1983 with his updating of the 1932 Gangster classic *Scarface* as the Cuban mobster Tony Montana; his second comeback (*Sea of Love*, 1989) included a parody of his Gangster genealogy as Big Boy Caprice in *Dick*

Tracy (1990). Moreover, we could add to this cinematic genealogy of gangster - villain the role of John Milton, i.e. Satan, in *The Devil's Advocate* (1997) and his quest to find Richard III in *Looking for Richard* (1996). Additionally the play Big Al by Brian Goluboff, about an obsessed screenwriter trying to write the "quintessential" Al Pacino script for the actor himself to star in, was playing on Off Broadway during the Arturo Ui run. Despite his Hollywood pedigree, Pacino is no novice to the stage, nor *Arturo Ui* and its Shakespearean genealogy. He trained at the Actor's Studio in the 1960's, developing an intense friendship with his mentor Lee Strasberg and has a relatively strong theater resume for a Hollywood actor (Mamet's *American Buffalo* in the early 1980's, numerous theater roles from the mid-1960s to early 1970's as well as film and TV adaptations of plays—Mamet's *Glengarry Glen Ross* (1992) and Kushner's *Angels in America* (2003). He had played the Ui character in a 1975 production at David Wheeler's Theater Company in Boston; and his interest in *Richard III* dates back to productions in Boston (1973) Broadway (1979), and is captured most succinctly in the film *Looking for Richard* (1996).

At first glance, Pacino—Hollywood Celebrity / Strasbergian Method Actor / Gangster Character icon—seemed to be the ultimate Brechtian nightmare. As a student of Strasberg and as a product of the Hollywood system, Pacino has become synonymous with the roles he plays. Pacino the actor becomes the character he plays, at least on film or on stage. With the addition of celebrity, the cinematic character morphs into a cultural icon. Brecht had considered such a combination of method acting and cultural power when he reflected on Hitler and the Nazis theatrical expertise in his essay "On the Theatricality of Fascism":

He's an individual, a hero in the drama, and it's his purpose to make the people (or rather the audience) say what he says. Or more precisely, feel what he feels. So it all depends on the fact that he himself feels, intensely. And in order to feel intensely the house painter speaks as a private individual, to private individuals [...] In all this, his audience follows him emotionally, they participate in the speaker's triumph, adopt his attitudes. Without doubt, the house painter (as some call him, since he can only daub whitewash over the cracks in a building that's ripe for demolition) has taken up a theatrical method, by which he can persuade his audience to follow him almost blindly. He induces everyone to abandon their point of view, and to adopt his, the protagonist's viewpoint, to forget their own interests, and to pursue his, the protagonist's interests. He involves his audience in himself, implicates them in his movements, lets them "participate" in his troubles and his triumphs, and dissuades them from any criticism, even from a fleeting glance at their surroundings from their own viewpoint.[11]

Pacino built the character of Ui physically and linguistically from the ground up. Similar to Martin Wuttke's 1995 BE performance, the audience witnessed the evolution of Ui from proto-human street thug to a more polished, celebrity dictator. In the opening "line-up" scene set against the background of a police mug shot, Pacino's Ui appeared as a drugged-out zombie: disheveled hair, gaunt and pale face, catatonic eyes, slumped shoulders, hanging, ape-like arms, and a stumbling gait. The stooped shoulders and a lethargic left foot were, for the astute observer, reminiscent of Richard III. Vocally, Pacino spoke like a punch-drunk boxer: laboriously slow to respond, slurred speech, always running out of air, and ending each sentence with a scratchy gasp. Linguistically, Pacino emphasized incorrect syntax, mixed metaphors and malapropisms (all of which are more emphasized in the Tabori adaptation as a later section of this article will explore). As Ui ascended the political and social world of Chicago, his physical and linguistic mannerisms improved dramatically.

The key scene of this transformation is the Actor's scene at the Mamouth Hotel, usually the highlight of any *Ui* production, and certainly for the NAT production. In order to polish his image for his new role as leader, Ui has an old Shakespearean actor (Tony Randall) give him lessons on posture, gesture, walking and speaking. This "construction of Hitler scene," which incidentally seems to be a part of every Hitler parody (*The Great Dictator, The Producers, To Be or Not to Be,* The Three Stooges' *You Nazty Spy* and *I'll Never Heil Again,* and Tabori's *Mein Kampf*), is crucial to unmasking the theatrical element behind fascism. As Pacino's Ui learns classic poses through Shakespearean models, the audience was treated to the development of classic Hitler gestures: goosestep, finger-stabbing-the-air gesticulation, head thrust back with a visionary look, folded arms across the chest with a tucked-in chin. The audience responded to the evolution of Ui and the craft of the star actor with laughter and applause. At the crucial moment of breakthrough (the goosestep), Pacino came downstage toward the audience, and generated the biggest applause and laughter of the evening. Relatively unreported was a technical addition to the moment: as the audience became entranced by the Ui / Hitler / Pacino transformation, a projection of Hitler was shown for a split second, so short that it went unregistered by most spectators. One wonders whether it should have been projected for a longer period of time (such as the later Warehouse Fire Trial scene) in order to really

---

[11] Brecht in *Brecht on Art and Politics*, 198-199.

engage the possibility of dialectical alienation? Because this moment was intentionally or unintentionally "missed," the construction and celebration of postmodern-fascist celebrity went unexplored.

Instead, we were left with a meditation upon the actor Pacino. As Brendan Lemon of the *Financial Times* stated: "Just as *Arturo Ui* furnishes a short course in the playwright, so does this staging produce a kind of Portable Pacino, In his performance there's the sleazy volatility of *Scarface*, the ruthlessness of Michael Corleone, the obligatory references to the crookback king of Searching for Richard (sic); nearly everything, that is, except the "Hoo-ah" of *Scent of a Woman.*"[12] Ben Brantley of the *New York Times* considered the production a review of the actor's career as well as well, but a critical one, which made the spectator conscious of the various levels of evil Pacino has portrayed throughout his career: "What this production offers as compensation is a lively deconstruction of the Pacino persona. You start to think about how Richard III really is a template for so many characters Mr. Pacino has played, of how he has specialized in incarnating either Faust or Mephistopheles and sometimes both at the same time. To see this embodied with such scary energy and focus on a stage goes a long way in offsetting the evening's ennui. Hard-core Pacino fans might even consider $115 a bargain."[13] Brantley seems to suggest that the best we should hope for in the 21st century is alienation from the tabloid identification we have with our celebrity actors. In a production in which we are meant to become aware of the Hitler phenomenon, to de-mystify it, and at the same learn how to fight it, we are instead asked to become aware of the phenomenon of Pacino and the cult of celebrity. McBurney's dissonant *mise en scene* appeared fundamentally undermined by the celebrity aura of Pacino, especially in the Actor's Scene.

III. Between Alienation and Tragedy

The production used George Tabori's translation, which was originally commissioned for the 1963 Broadway premiere of *The Resistible Rise of Arturo Ui* starring Christopher Plummer and directed by Tony Richardson. Closing after thirteen performances, the 1963 production has been largely (and perhaps unfairly) consigned to the ash heap of theater history; however, the Tabori translation has lived on and in the intervening years

---

[12] Lemon, "Intelligent Artificiality: Review of *Arturo Ui.*"
[13] Brantley, "Scarface? Richard Crookback? The Godfather? Nope, It's a Hitlerian Thug," E1.

has been used in the 1967-69 Leonard Rossiter-led production in England, and most recently in a production by the San Francisco Theater Company in 1990. Since Stefan Brecht had both commissioned and praised Tabori's translation,[14] it seemed a foregone conclusion that it would be used for the 2002 production; however, other translations of the play were theoretically available for the NAT production. These included: H.R. Hays, 1941 (used to shop the play around New York Theaters in 1941, but apparently never used in production); Ralph Manheim, 1981 (first used onstage in New York City 1991 in a production with John Turturro); and Rangit Bolt, 1991 (commissioned for the Antony Sher-*Ui* in London of the same year).

Tabori's translation grew out of his long experience in America from 1947-1969 and his intense translation work with Brecht's work in the 1960s. After performing a scene from *Die jüdische Frau* during his time at the Actor's Studio in New York in the late 1950's, he and his then wife, Viveca Lindfors, came upon the idea of translating a collage of Brecht's texts for the American Stage. This resulted in the 1961 performances of *Brecht on Brecht* which was a surprising critical success. After translating *Ui* for the 1963 production and *Mother Courage* for a 1967 production in Vermont, he was invited to the 1968 Brecht-Dialog in East Berlin, where after seeing Helene Weigel in a production of *The Mother*, he seemed to come to a crossroads in his engagement with Brecht, proclaiming, "I learned a lot and I learned one thing: that this wonderful theater of yours is not my way."[15]   Shortly thereafter he published his first play *The Cannibals* in 1968 and moved to West Berlin in 1969. In the ensuing thirty years he became a popular playwright and director, writing such plays as *Mein Kampf* and *Jubiläum* and directing for long stints in Vienna, Bremen, and currently Berlin, where he now works at the Berliner Ensemble. It is perhaps too much of a stretch to claim that *Ui* is some kind of *Ur*-text for Tabori, but when compared with Brecht's original text, and the standard translation of Manheim, as well as Taborori's own Hitler-drama *Mein Kampf*, it does illuminate crucial intersections where Tabori diverges from Brechtian aesthetic practices. Tabori admits that that he constructed a "free" translation, one which he very much liked. In fact, when one reads Tabori's translation, one feels that Tabori enjoyed the translation of Ui as much as Brecht enjoyed the writing of it.[16]   Crucially, what sets it apart from other translations is its singular use of American idiomatic language,

---

[14] Tabori, "Brecht Files: In Conversation with Martin Kagel (and Nikolaus Merck)," 71.

[15] Ibid., 72.

[16] Brecht, *Journals 1934 – 1955*, 140.

its sneeringly low-brow version of Shakespeare, and its tragic pathos which at times seems to undermine the Brechtian alienation effect.

With the exception of Julia Vitullo-Martin of the *Wall Street Journal* relatively little attention was paid to either Tabori's playscript (even though it was provided to critics in the press kit) or its rhetorical highlights. Linda Winer referred to the adaptation as "playfully disciplined," Elysa Gardner anointed it "stringent,"[17] and Ben Brantley termed it "bold," while C. Bernd Sucher of the *Süddeutsche Zeitung* reflected that it was "schlanker als das Original."[18] Vitullo-Martin on the other hand, thought that Tabori's translation "takes immense liberties with Brecht,"[19] but mitigated Tabori's guilt by suggesting that Tabori was just channeling the "dishonesty" of Brecht and the "fundamental dishonesty" of McBurney's *mise en scene*. Yet, probably the most significant reason why Tabori's translation was underappreciated was due to the fact that most productions have tended to emphasize the visual and physical elements at the expense of linguistic ones. Martin Wuttke's performance of Ui at the Berliner Ensemble is emblematic, both in terms of production and reception, of this emphasis. When the Berliner Ensemble briefly toured with *Ui* in 1999, Arthur Horowitz writing for *Theatre Journal*, remarked upon Wuttke's "great technical achievements," which were "informed by film clowns": "The production included performative references to Chaplin's Great Dictator (so admired by Brecht) and Jerry Lewis's stuttering, squeaky-voiced little big man. Interwoven were physical skills rivaling those of John Cleese, particularly evident in a goose-step parody which culminated in Arturo Ui shaping himself into a horrifying human swastika."[20] Wuttke's vocal delivery was mentioned but once again emphasizing the physical over what is actually said: "Depending on the moment, Wuttke's delivery of lines goes from pinched or choked to rapidly spat out, from machine-gun patter to a croak. At one point, the words are strangled in his own spit."[21] Similarly, Pacino's performance was noted for its physicality: a "hunched cockroach" and "animated sewage, a greasy, buck-toothed savage"[22]; "Here is a purely animal presence, a brute whose hands hang at his sides like deadweights and whose eye sockets register as hungry black holes"[23]; a "simian-like

---

[17] Gardner, "Do Not Resist Rise of *Arturo Ui*."

[18] Sucher, "Wer nicht für mich ist, ist gegen mich!"

[19] Vitullo-Martin.

[20] Horowitz, "Review: *The Resistible Rise of Arturo Ui*," 22.

[21] Graham, "An Irresistible Night of Theater," B1.

[22] Marks, "Arturo Ui: Hail, Hail, the Gang's All Here."

[23] Brantley, E1.

thug, clownishly dressed in a long brown leather coat (with a fur collar), plaid pants and a white undershirt"[24]; and "a sniveling weakling, curled into himself like a tightly coiled bud that will blossom into some ghastly weed. His voice has a rasping quality, as if his nasal passages coated every utterance with noxious vapors."[25]

But what Tabori's translation does differently than the Brecht original or the Manheim translation is to show how Ui linguistically evolves over the course of the production. Brecht does draw attention to Ui's evolution in his playscript. In scene 6 before he meets the actor, Ui states: "*Man hat mir zu verstehen gegeben, daß meine Aussprache zu wünschen übrig läßt*"[26]; and then later in scene 12, right before he is to meet the Dullfeets for the first time, Betty Dullfeet remarks: "*Ui hat gezeigt, daß er den rauhen Ton jetzt lassen will.*"[27]   In this second quotation, it is a more general reference that Ui has reformed or improved his general behavior, not specifically his grammar; however, Tabori's translation does add this aspect: "His manner and grammar have much improved."[28]   Brecht indicates a gruffness of Ui but only presents this through mediocre metrics and rhythms; whereas Tabori brings this language issue front and center.

He achieves this effect through heavy use of hip-Gangster slang, vulgarisms, American idiomatic expressions, malapropisms, bad syntax, repetitive use of vocabulary, and doggerel Shakespearean verse. For example, upon meeting Dogsborough for the first time, Ui assesses his life and what he will do for Dogsborough. For the sake of comparison I include three sources—Brecht, Manheim, Tabori:

Brecht

> Herr Dogsborough. Ich weiß, Sie kennen mich nicht.
> Oder nur vom Hörensagen, was schlimmer ist.
> Herr Dogsborough, Sie sehen vor sich einen
> Verkannten Mann. Sein Bild geschwärzt von Neid
> Sein Wollen entstellt von Niedertracht [...]
> Nicht ganz efolglos war, hatt ich um mich nur
> Sieben brave Jungens, mittellos [...]
> Sie werden fragen: Was will Ui von mir?
> Ich will nicht viel. Ich will nur eines: nicht
> Verkannt sein! [...]
>   Ich bin entschlossen, ihn

---

[24] Kuchwara, "Pacino Mesmerizing in *Arturo Ui*."
[25] Kissel, "Meaty Performances, But Jokes Wear Thin."
[26] Brecht, *Große kommentierte Berliner und Frankfurter Ausgabe*, 49.
[27] Ibid., 91.
[28] Brecht adapted by Tabori, 103.

Zu schützen. Gegen jeden Übergriff.
Wenn's sein muß, mit Gewalt.[29]

Manheim

Mr. Dogsborough. I am well aware that you
Don't know me, or even worse, you know me but
Only from hearsay. Mr. Dogsborough
I have been very much maligned, my image
Blackened by envy, my intentions disfigured
By baseness [...]
Inglorious, my only followers
Were seven youngsters, penniless like myself [...]
　　But now your wondering: What
Does Arturo Ui want of me? Not much. Just this
What irks me is to be misunderstood
To be regarded as a fly-by-night
Adventurer and heaven knows what else [...]
　　The vegetable
Trade needs protection. By force if necessary.
And I'm determined to supply it.[30]

Tabori

　　Sir, Mr. Dogsborough!
I am well aware you don't know me from nothing,
Or maybe just from hearsay which is worse.
You see before you, sir, a man misunderstood,
And almost done to death by sland'rous tongues,
His name besmirched by envy, and his dreams
Misrepresented by a world replete
With Jews and bicyclists [...]
I did it all alone but for the help
Of seven solid buddies standing by
Without a pot to piss in, like myself [...]
You ask yourself, I guess: "What's Ui want?"
Not much. One thing, that's all I want from you.
I don't want to be misconstrued no more,
And treated like some greaseball racketeer,
Or whate'er else they may call me in this town.
I want respect [...]
I sucked pimento with my mother's milk!
And I'm determined to protect the Grocers.
From force and violence. With force and violence

---

[29] Brecht, *Große kommentierte Berliner und Frankfurter Ausgabe*, 33-34.
[30] Brecht translated by Manheim, 30-31.

If necessary.[31]

Tabori uses a great deal of non-standard formulations, "don't know me from nothing," "without a pot to piss in" which are colorful and wordy. The sheer wordiness of these formulations combined with the fast pace of the production forced Pacino to speak the way he did. The use of the word "misunderstood" for *verkannt* is also noteworthy. *Verkannt* in this sense means to be misjudged, unrecognized, underestimated, i.e. not to be seen in the way one wants to be seen, or seen as valued. The Manheim translation provides an elegant solution with the word "maligned," while the Tabori translation is a bit lowbrow. But "misunderstood" is far closer to the lower strata language speaker that Ui comes from. Instead of using a different word, Tabori's Ui uses a simple word and then adds a prefix to it. As we shall see in a moment this construction by addition doesn't always work, but it is a rhetorical strategy that Ui uses again and again, and one could say is a basic rhetorical strategy for a largely oral community. Tabori parses the "misunderstood" comment with the word "respect" at the end which again goes with the lower strata language speaker. The last part of the citations show how Ui continues this rhetorical strategy—he does not invent new words, but simply repeats them in a different order—e.g. with the use of "force and violence."

Ui continues these rhetorical strategies during the city hall scene as he begins to take over from Dogsborough, and relates what his initial investigations into the dock scandal have uncovered, Tabori has Ui say: "When Mr. D. persuaded me to serve the city by inquiring into what the cat brought in [...] I discovered to my greatest shock: those funds were misabused."[32] Note that Dogsborough is now rendered with a nickname, the inquiry is gilded with an unnecessary and nonsensical proverbial saying, and resolved with the terms "misabused" when "embezzled" (*veruntreut*) would have been the more appropriate expression. In the same scene, he asks rhetorically whether Dogsborough looks like someone who could be guilty of embezzlement: "Is this the face that could have maybe launched a thousand tricks?"[33] In the original Brecht had himself used "*der krumme Weg*"; however, Tabori creates a malapropism out of the saying confusing "ships" with "tricks." The effect is comical (Ui / Hitler speaking like an American mobster) and alienating (Ui / Hitler speaking like an American mobster) and repeated throughout the play. Ui

---

[31] Brecht adapted by Tabori, 38-39.
[32] Ibid., 51.
[33] Ibid., 54.

resolves the city hall scene with dialogue that Tabori takes from later in the play and augments with an Americanized twist:

> But truth is marching on! Nothing will stop it!
> Not all the scaly bums who got the nerve
> To sling their mud upon the snowy locks
> Where all suspicion crumbles into dandruff!
> Dogsborough is the father of Chicago!
> Sage of the Waterfront! Not just a name,
> Not just a man! No, he's an institution!
> Whoever is attacking him—or me—
> Attacks the town, the state, the Constitution![34]

As Ui gains power and takes acting lessons his linguistic evolution matches his physical and political evolution. Although he speaks better, it is merely a higher form of the same rhetorical strategies he showed early in the play. Ui gives his last two speeches upon a podium as stop-cut images of the speech-in-process are projected behind him. At the end of the first part of the speech, Ui/Pacino ends with the refrain:

> Who is for me? And let me incidentally add:
> Whoever is not for me is against me,
> And let him face the consequences.
> Now you're free to vote.[35]

The rhetorical strategies have not changed, they just fit the mock-heroic rhetorical mode better. Everything sounds better, but the illogic and irrationality are still there, and we hear and perceive this disconnect. Seen in this light, Tabori brought an Eichmann-like linguistic banality to the production which seemed perfectly balanced for the American stage, achieving the desired alienation effects. Yet, as previously stated, Tabori's translation was largely overlooked, or if noticed at all, its most noticeable lines were attributed to either Brecht or McBurney. And the reason, is that spectator and reviewer alike could not escape the inescapable similarities of Ui's rhetoric with that of the American President, George W. Bush. Malapropisms, tortured syntax, incorrect neologisms, and repetition of words are hallmarks of Bush's rhetorical presentation.

And these similarities did not just occur in the small scenes, but were also striking in the major political speeches of Ui at the end of the play. With the anniversary of 9/11 and the case for war against Iraq, Bush's

---

[34] Ibid., 56.
[35] Ibid., 125.

political speeches and their rhetorical dimensions were very much in the air. Tabori's Ui as acted by Pacino seemed to parody not only the everyday rhetoric of Bush, but also Bush at his most dignified and statesmanlike. For example, in his September 20, 2001 speech, one of his greatest and most effective speeches, to a Joint Session of Congress and the American People, Bush used the following phrases:

> "Whether we bring our enemies to justice, or bring justice to our enemies, justice will be done."
> "And we will pursue nations that provide aid or safe haven to terrorism. Every nation, in every region, now has a decision to make: Either you are with us, or you are with the terrorists."
> "Al Qaeda is to terror what the mafia is to crime. But its goal is not making money; its goal is remaking the world."

> "This is not, however, just America's fight. And what is at stake is not just America's freedom. This is the world's fight. This is civilization's fight. This is the fight of all who believe in progress and pluralism, tolerance and freedom."

> "I will not forget this wound to our country or those who inflicted it. I will not yield; I will not rest; I will not relent in waging this struggle for freedom and security for the American people."[36]

Likewise, the projected titles and commentaries tended to linguistically and rhetorically merge with contemporary events. In Tabori's translation he often appended words or phrases which sensationalized the descriptions, acting in some ways as tabloid headlines. For example the placard after the title scene includes "Mockery of Justice,"[37] the murder of Roma and his associates is appended with the phrase "Massacre at Tavern,"[38] after Dullfeet is murdered, the placard states "Rape of Austria,"[39] and the last placard highlights the "Terrorized Electorate."[40] However, it was the placard at the end of Scene 7, which caused the most consternation. In the Brecht original it reads: "*Im Februar 1933 ging das Reichstagsgebäude in Flammen auf. Hitler beschuldigt seine Feinde der Brandstiftung und gab das Signal zur Nacht der langen Messer*"[41]; the

---

[36] Bush, "Address to a Joint Session of Congress and the American People."
[37] Brecht adapted by Tabori, 81.
[38] Ibid., 103.
[39] Ibid., 119.
[40] Ibid., 127.
[41] Brecht, *Große kommentierte Berliner und Frankfurter Ausgabe*, 128.

Tabori adaptation: "February 1933: Reichstag building in flames. Frame up to crush opposition. Hitler starts reign of terror. 'The Night of the Long Knives.'"[42]   The production's supertitle used the Tabori adaptation with one change: "Hitler's starts reign of terror" with "Hitler's uses fear of terrorism to crush opposition." This had a jarring linguistic effect. The word "terrorism" had been in the air ever since September 11; but it is a post-1968 word which is not often associated with Hitler (although Hitler was, of course, a terrorist).

---

[42] Brecht adapted by Tabori, 71.

The reviewers who negatively reviewed the play operated under the misconception that this was Brecht and McBurney providing distorted historical analogies, but in truth it was Tabori's free translation which uncannily resonated. I say uncannily because he wrote the translation in 1963 with overt allusions to the popular culture and language of the time—the language and tabloids of heroic platitudes between Hitler and Cold War—and for the audience there was not a distinction. It seemed like the production was a *roman á clef* of post-9/11 American Culture.

If Tabori's translation brought a tabloid contemporaneity to the production through language and images, at the same time it also injected a tragic pathos to the production as well. As the production drew the audience nearer to the post-9/11 world, it drew the spectator into the emotional vortex of it all. Brecht, of course, emphasized the idea of distanciation so that dialectical-critical thinking and socio-political praxis could be accessed. Moreover, he admitted to himself that *Ui* particularly ran this danger:

> In Ui the problem was on the one hand to let the historical events show through, and on the other to give the "masking" (which is an unmasking) some life of its own, ie it must—theoretically speaking—also work independently of its topical references. Among other things, too close a coupling of the two plots (gangster plot and nazi plot)—that is, a form in which the gangster plot is a symbolic version of the other plot—would be unbearable, not least because people would constantly be looking for the "meaning" of the this or that move, and would always be looking for the real-life model for every figure. This was particularly difficult.[43]

Additionally, to engage the audience on the level of emotion and to tug on the heart strings of fate and tragedy—the mystification of life, which led to not doing anything, but just accepting one's plight—this was absolutely anathema to Brecht's aesthetic. Yet, along with the tabloid contemporaneity, Tabori's translation also brought this element. And as Martin Kagel has speculated, this space between tragedy and alienation, seems to be the inheritance of Tabori from Brecht:

> Tabori's own work in theater is certainly indebted to Brecht, yet it seems that he uses the concept of Verfremdung dialectically, in order to create a new immediacy: distance creating proximity. Exemplary in this respect is his programmatic introduction to the fourth draft of the play *The Cannibals* (1968) itself an excellent application of Brechtian techniques of distancing. In the context of numerous statements about the "epic structure" of the

---

[43] Brecht, *Journals 1934 – 1955*, 137.

play Tabori writes that its goal is to achieve "a catharsis through reconciliation and relief." The latter seems true for most of his productions in theater.[44]

This idea of tragic closeness was brought home in the epilogue. After making his final political speeches, Pacino as Ui descended the podium, walked downstage toward the audience, took off his Hitler mustache, and addressed the audience directly. Here are the three versions:

Brecht
Ihr aber lernet, wie man sieht statt stiert
Und handelt, statt zu reden noch und noch.
So was hätt einmal fast die Welt regiert!
Die Völker wurden seiner Herr, jedoch
Dass keiner uns zu früh da triumphiert—
Der Schoß ist fruchtbar noch, aus dem das Kroch.[45]

Manheim
Therefore we learn how to see and not to gape.
To act instead of talking all day long.
The world was almost won by such an ape!
The nations put him where his kind belong.
But don't rejoice too soon at your escape—
The womb he crawled from still is going strong.[46]

Tabori
If we could learn to look instead of gawking,
We'd see the horror in the heart of farce,
If only we could act instead of talking,
We wouldn't end on our arse.
This was the thing that nearly had us mastered;
Don't yet rejoice in his defeat, you men!
Although the world stood up and stopped the bastard,
The bitch that bore him is in heat again.[47]

In Tabori's translation, he replaces the conclusive phrasing of "therefore" with the subjunctive phrasing of "if" in the first and third lines, and concomitantly changes the didactic tone to a tragic one. Brecht's epic

---

[44] Kagel in Sucher, "Brecht Files: In Conversation with Martin Kagel (and Nikolaus Merck)," 70.
[45] Brecht, *Große kommentierte Berliner und Frankfurter Ausgabe*, 7, 112.
[46] Brecht translated by Manheim, 99.
[47] Brecht adapted by Tabori, 128.

theater insists on praxis, not mourning the mysteries and terrors of the world, yet this is exactly what Tabori delivers in his translation. The phrasing seems more appropriate to a chorus from the *Oresteia* by Aeschylus than an Ansager's speech from a Brechtian parable-play. Likewise, a tragic element is exposed in the second and eighth line of Tabori's translation as Tabori introduces ideas of terror, suffering, and monstrous forces of nature. Brecht's play had insisted on de-mystifying Ui/Hitler to the point of making him a common criminal, if not a cartoon gangster. It is true that the last line of Brecht's script, *"Der Schoß ist fruchtbar noch, aus dem das kroch,"* itself bears residues of the tragic, mystery realm, but Tabori moves it further into such a realm, by making it an active monstrosity that will produce another Ui/Hitler, "The bitch that bore him is in heat again." Moreover, it is the impossibility of penetrating this force of nature, which seems to hang over us like a form of tragic fate. To "see the horror in the heart of farce" sounds dangerously close to tragic aesthetics, and its phrase, "To learn through suffering." Most importantly, however, these lines were delivered in the political context of 9/11 America, within shouting distance of Ground Zero. Whatever, one felt about the production up until the epilogue was countered by this ritualized appeal to tragic mourning. Tabori's translation, similar to Pacino's aura, countered the centrifugal force of McBurney's *mise en scene*, grounding the performance in a very Americanized, very 9/11 context.

Conclusion

Returning to the original question—When, where, what, how, and why does American theater turn to Brecht after 9/11?—we can easily answer three out of the five questions: American theater reached for Brecht almost exactly one year after the World Trade Center attacks, in a theater less than half a mile away from Ground Zero, with one of Brecht's least critically yet most popularly successful works, *The Resistible Rise of Arturo Ui*. It was not performed in the 2001-2002 performance season, but rather inaugurated the 2002-2003 performance season; it was not on Broadway, not even really off-Broadway, but in a temporary, rented space; it was not *Mother Courage* or *The Threepenny Opera*. Why American Theater turned to *Ui* in these contexts seems evident: *Ui* presented the quickest, most entertaining, and most historically-relevant (Hitler and American Culture) method to present Brechtian political theater. Brecht is still the artist with the aesthetic toolbox that provides the forum and roadmap for political expression and engagement; and this is what American theater reached for after 9/11. It is the last question, how

American theater turns to Brecht in this moment, which is most interesting and problematic. As this analysis has shown, the theater event was almost three separate productions, or at least three separate interpretations, at once. McBurney's *mise en scene* delivered Brechtian epic theater, aesthetically and politically, exploding static conceptions of the play, the historical Hitler, and the contemporary 9/11 American political scene: critical awareness, intellectual engagement, and perhaps a dawning sociopolitical engagement that the world can and should be changed. Yet, Pacino and the Hollywood Cast supporting him, appeared to work against this *mise en scene* and return the production to the all-too-familiar realm of American performance culture: the familiarity and comfort of the celebrity actor, who polarizes the performance, denuding multiplicity, and draws all theatrical energy upon himself and his aura. The contemporary celebrity actor as the modern hero—the person who can tame the gangsters and monsters of history—and make them a commodifiable and digestible element for American culture. Finally, Tabori's translation brought tragic catharsis, something so decried by Brecht, but so desperately needed by American culture in 2002. To stare into the abyss, the monstrous mystery of tragedy, mystery, fate? Not answering the questions like Brecht would have us do, or forgetting the questions like most of American performance culture would have us, but forcing ourselves to gaze at the evil and destruction around us, and in ourselves, be conscious of it, but have no critical means to act upon it, to change the world.

It is the answer to this last question, which should serve as a cautionary tale for the exploration of Brecht in American theater. The production was not standard Brecht, perhaps it was not even successful Brecht. Rather, it was schizophrenic Brecht, but a version of Brecht that somehow worked on the American stage and which only a dialectical casebook could truly illuminate.

Works Cited

Bentley, Eric. *Bentley on Brecht*. New York: Applause, 1998.

Brantley, Ben. "Scarface? Richard Crookback? The Godfather? Nope, It's a Hitlerian Thug." *New York Times*, 22 October 2002, sec. E1.

Brecht, Bertolt. *Große kommentierte Berliner und Frankfurter Ausgabe* (GBA), 7. Berlin / Frankfurt a/M: Aufbau / Suhrkamp Verlag, 1991.

—. "On the Theatricality of Fascism." *Brecht on Art and Politics*. Eds. Tom Kuhn and Steve Giles. London: Methuen, 2003. 193-201.

—. *Journals 1934 – 1955*. Trans. Hugh Rorrison. Ed. John Willett. New York: Routledge, 1993.

—. *The Resistible Rise of Arturo Ui: A Gangster Spectacle*. Adapted by George Tabori. New York: Samuel French, 1963.

—. *The Resistible Rise of Arturo Ui*. Trans. Ralph Manheim. New York: Arcade Publishing, 1981.

Bush, George W. "Address to a Joint Session of Congress and the American People." 20 September 2001. <http://www.whitehouse.gov/news/releases/2001/09/20010920-8.html> (25 October 2002).

—. "Speech to the United Nations." 10 November 2001. <http://www.september11news.com/PresdentBushUN.htm> (25 October 2002).

—. "President's Remarks at the United Nations General Assembly." 12 September 2002. <http://www.whitehouse.gov/news/releases/2002/09/20020912-1.html> (25 October 2002).

Foot, Paul. "With Friends Like These." *The Guardian*, 5 February 2003, 17.

Gardner, Elysa. "Do Not Resist Rise of *Arturo Ui*." *USA Today*, 22 October 2002, 4D.

Graham, Bob. "An Irresistible Night of Theater." *San Francisco Chronicle*, 3 July 1999, B1.

Horowitz, Arthur. "Review: *The Resistible Rise of Arturo Ui*." *Theatre Journal* 52 (2000): 121-123.

Holden, Joe. "The Great Dictator." *The Guardian*, 24 October 2002. <http://arts.guardian.co.uk/culturalexchange/story0,,818205,00.html> (25 October 2002).

Isherwood, Charles. "Scent of a Madman." *The Times*, 25 October 2002.

Kissel, Howard. "Meaty Performances, But Jokes Wear Thin." *New York Daily News*, 21 October 2002, 39.

Kuchwara, Michael. "Pacino Mesmerizing in *Arturo Ui*." *Drama Critic*, 23 October 2002.

Kushner, Tony. "Notes About Political Theater." *Kenyon Review* 19 (1997): 19-34.

Lemon, Brendan. "Intelligent Artificiality: Review of *Arturo Ui*." *Financial Times*, 22 October 2002. <http://search.ft.com/ftArticle?queryText=arturo+ui &ae+true&x=9&id=021025000717> (25 October 2002).

Lyons, Donald. "Pacino Takes on Hitler." *New York Post*, 21 October 2002, 41.

Marks, Peter. "Arturo Ui: Hail, Hail, the Gang's All Here. *Washington Post*, 22 October 2002, C1.

McBurney, Simon. "Waiting for the End of the Copyright Laws: Inteviewed by Holgar Teschke." *drive b: Brecht Yearbook* 23 / *Theater der Zeit* Arbeitsbuch. ed. Marc Silberman. Berlin: Theater der Zeit / International Brecht Society / Berliner Ensemble, 1998: 30-32.

Randall, Tony. "National Actors Theatre: America's Classical Repertory Company." Arts4All Newsletter 1.1 (1999). <http://www.arts4all.com/newsletter/issue1/text/randall.htm> (25 October 2002).

Schumacher, Ernst. *Gruppenbild mit Hakenkreuz: Konstanze Lauterbach und Heiner Mller inszenieren Brechts Arturo Ui. Theater der Zeit*, Juli/August, 1995: 4-6.

Stadelmaier, Gerhard. "Die Chose ist fruchtbar noch. Große Oper für Hitler: Heiner Müller inszeniert Brechts "Arturo Ui am Berliner Ensemble." *FAZ*, 6 Juni 1995: 33.

Sucher, C. Bernd. "Wer nicht für mich ist, ist gegen mich!" *Süddeutsche Zeitung*, 15 October 2002.

—. "Brecht Files: In Conversation with Martin Kagel (and Nikolaus Merck)."*drive b:* Brecht Yearbook 23 / Theater der Zeit Arbeitsbuch ed. Marc Silberman. Berlin: Theater der Zeit / International Brecht Society / Berliner Ensemble, 1998: 70-75.

Vitullo-Martin, Julia. "An Irresistible Urge to Heap Abuse on the White House." *Wall Street Journal*, 30 October 2002, D8.

Vulliamy, Ed. "Reich Here, right Now – Brecht's Allegory of Hitler's Rise Has a Chilling Resonance." *The Observer*, 13 October 2002.

Wells, Paul. "Great Art Wrapped in Political Allegory." *National Post*, 15 October 2002.

Winer, Linda. "*Arturo Ui* Proves Hard to Resist." *Newsday*, 23 October 2002.

A NEW BRECHTIAN MUSICAL?:
AN ANALYSIS OF URINETOWN (2001)

KATHRYN A. EDNEY

There has been a recent upswing of references to Bertolt Brecht and Kurt Weill in American popular culture. A 2006 television commercial campaign for the Applebee's chain restaurant featured a cabaret performance where men sang of their love for a new sirloin menu to the tune of "Mack the Knife."[1] In March 2006, the Roundabout Theater Company at Studio 54 in New York produced a new translation of *The Threepenny Opera* by Wallace Shawn.   Staring Alan Cumming as MacHeath and pop singer Cyndi Lauper as Jenny, the production, although nominated for a Tony as best revival, was not well received critically. Lauper's presence, however, guaranteed attention from media outlets not typically interested in Broadway. In February 2006, not too long after Vice President Dick Cheney accidentally shot his friend Harry Whittington, late night shows were full of jibes. It then transpired that the shooting had triggered a mild heart attack in Whittington, prompting *The Daily Show*'s fake news host Jon Stewart to downgrade the incident on his amusement scale, commenting that, "unfortunately, if he does die, the whole thing goes Brechtian."[2]

Although the current popular awareness of Brecht is perhaps unusual, it follows an established pattern. Most obviously, Brecht is nearly always paired with Weill, a function of the popularity of *Threepenny Opera* and particularly of the song "Mack the Knife," which has long been a staple of American popular song.[3] Performed in Germany in 1928, *Threepenny Opera* had its premiere in New York in 1933. However the show did not achieve true popularity in the United States until composer and playwright Marc Blitzstein's adaptation and translation of it was staged in 1954 at the

---

[1] Cebrzynski, "The Applebee's Guys Have Gone Too Far This Time."

[2] The scale ran as follows: Pant Wetting; Incredibly Hilarious; Still Funny, But, MMM Now a Little Sad, 'Funny-Strange,' Not 'Funny Ha-Ha'; Brechtian.

[3] Gilbert, *Bertolt Brecht's Striving for Reason, Even in Music: A Critical Assessment*, 137.

Theatre de Lys in New York. This incarnation of *Threepenny Opera* ran for five years, a record at the time.[4] "Mack the Knife" became a hit song twice within four years, first in a recording by Louis Armstrong in 1954 and second by Bobby Darin in 1959, with Darin's version hitting number one on the American "Top 100" chart. Other versions of the song followed over the years by artists ranging from Ella Fitzgerald to Lyle Lovett, who sings it on the soundtrack to the 1994 film *Quiz Show*.[5] Brecht's collaboration with Charles Laughton in *Galileo* is famous among scholars. *Mother Courage* makes periodical re-appearances on the American stage, most recently in New York with Meryl Streep in the title role. But Americans know Brecht best, if they know him at all, through *Threepenny Opera* and "Mack the Knife."[6]

This abbreviated popular knowledge of Brecht manifested itself in the parodic musical *Urinetown! The Musical* as well as in reviews of both the original Broadway production of 2001 and subsequent touring productions. The musical was held up by its creators and many reviewers as an inherently "Brechtian" work. Reviews of *Urinetown*, whether positive or negative, typically contained at least one of the following tropes in their attempts to educate and reassure their audiences: likening the characters of *Urinetown* to other musical comedy characters or listing the musicals to which *Urinetown* referred; explaining that the musical was not "dirty" in spite of the title; and comparing it to Brechtian theater.[7] To be sure, not all theater critics referred to Brecht in their reviews, and those that aligned *Urinetown* with Brechtian theater did so with varying degrees of specificity. However, by reading *Urinetown* as a descendent of Brecht, however distant, reviewers were remarkably consistent with how they used the term. The *Threepenny Opera* was typically the only precise referent, and provided a quick and easy interpretive tool for reviewers trying to educate potential audiences about *Urinetown*. *Urinetown*, and reactions to it, provides a means of analyzing the place of Brecht's theatrical legacy in present-day popular culture. Is Brecht now nothing more than a good

---

[4] Shout, "The Musical Theater of Marc Blitzstein," 423-424.

[5] Friedwald, *Stardust Memories: The Biography of Twelve of America's Most Popular Songs*, 76-103.

[6] Weber, "Brecht on the American Stage at the Turn of the Century," 228-234.

[7] For a review of *Urinetown* that does address its apolitical stance, see Catherine Foster, "Fight the Power in *Urinetown* and an Updated *Threepenny Opera*," *The Boston Globe* 4 January 2004. This is the only review that I could find that analyzed the differences between the two works, most likely because revivals of both shows had opened within days of each other, a rare occurrence.

punch line for a savvy Jon Stewart viewer, empty of his original political content?[8]

Brecht in Brief

Brecht advocated for an "epic theater" that made audiences aware of the fictional nature of theater by deliberately breaking down the fourth wall between actor and spectator, thus distancing, or alienating, audiences emotionally from the characters portrayed on the stage.[9] For Brecht the destruction of the fourth wall was not just a protest against the bourgeois conventions of the theater; it was an attempt to foster political self-awareness in the audiences who saw his plays. This self-awareness could only be achieved when the audience stopped being an unthinking, emotionally reactive mass, and became a group of critical thinkers and assessing individuals. He used theater to confront audience complacency and to reveal particular social inequities rather than the interior psychology of his characters.[10]

While Brecht theorized about the need for his audiences to have an emotional distance from the characters, he also saw as a fundamental requirement intellectual distance as well. How could audiences truly think about the capitalist system if they perceived that system to be perfectly normal and never gave it a second thought? For example, a play such as *Mother Courage and her Children* was in part an attempt make strange to his audiences the normalcy of capitalism by following the requirements of the system to its logical conclusions, where war is "the sum of everybody's business operations."[11] To maintain her tenuous place within the capitalist economy of war, Courage allows her children to be sacrificed, and the audience is forced to consider why this is so.

Brecht conceived of his audience as actively participating in the creation of meaning for the text as it played out in front of them; the audience should be a passionate critic of the social issues laid out by the play. To help the audience achieve the necessary intellectual and emotional distance from illusions of theater, Brecht advocated a set of

---

[8] This is not an entirely new question. The same issues were at play during the 1960s. See Manfred Wekweth, Martin Nicolaus and Erica Munk, "From Brecht Today," *TDR: The Drama Review* 12.1 (1967).

[9] There are debates about how to precisely and properly translate Brecht's German theoretical terms into English such that their sense is effectively rendered. Alienation, while clunky, is the generally accepted term.

[10] Christy, "Brecht and the American Avant-Garde," 180-183.

[11] Brecht, *Brecht on Theatre: The Development of an Aesthetic*, 221.

techniques: set the play in the past, rather than in the present; reveal the mechanics behind the staging of a production; purge the stage of sentiment; and juxtapose, rather than integrate, words, music, and action. Further, he advocated for a system of acting and stage production—*gestus*—that would prompt audiences to recognize that the actors were acting and were moreover making conscious choices about how to act in relation to the social world.[12]

However, as is perhaps most famously the case with *Mother Courage*, his audiences often chose to ignore the explicitly political and intellectual messages he was trying to convey, focusing instead on the emotional and psychological relationships between his characters. This often led Brecht to revisit and rewrite his texts in attempts to sharpen the political and social commentary which audiences insisted were not there or which they refused to see.[13]

Brecht worked out his concepts of epic theater in a disjointed manner over several decades. As many scholars have pointed out, Brecht's own theatrical works did not always successfully mirror his theoretical writings, nor did he necessarily make any attempt to impart his theories to his actors. It is also critical to remember that Brecht came to Marxism only very gradually, and that as his political views evolved, so too did his theatrical works and his theoretical writings. In addition, Brecht habitually wrote about his earlier plays in retrospect, often re-interpreting them in light of his newly acquired political ideology.[14] Simply put, Brecht is not neat and tidy, nor can his theoretical goals be understood using only one of his theatrical works as a lens, especially when that lens is *Threepenny Opera*.

Threepenny Opera has generally been understood in terms of Brecht's fundamental disagreement with Wagnerian opera, where the audience is required to be swept along unthinkingly by the force of the music. The Wagnerian model, according to Brecht, prevents the audience from thinking by using music to re-enforce that bad habit of feeling for, rather than thinking about, the characters on the stage. The music of *Threepenny Opera* is therefore deployed differently.[15] Rather than attempting to

---

[12] See Kowalke, "Singing Brecht Vs. Brecht Singing: Performance in Theory and Practice," 57-58; Brecht, 53-56 and 104-105; Ferran, "The Threepenny Songs: Cabaret and the Lyrical Gestus," 5-7.

[13] See Kowalke, 57-58; Willett, *The Theatre of Bertolt Brecht: A Study from Eight Aspects*, 175-176; and Brecht, 220-221.

[14] Lyon, "Brecht's *Mann Ist Mann* and the Death of Tragedy in the 20th Century," 513.

[15] Brecht, 43-46 and 136.

naturalize the idea of characters breaking out into song, Brecht and Weill highlight this unnatural act through staging—placing actors in front of the curtain or announcing that a song is about to be sung—and through the use of what was then considered to be vulgar musical styles, such as cabaret. And although Brecht's political and social concerns were still developing this early in his career, *Threepenny Opera* proposes that it is primarily fiscal considerations, rather than love, that structure human relationships. Placing finance and not love at the heart of a musical theater piece thus throws into question the purpose and potential of musical theater, but in a constructive, rather than destructive, manner.[16] Done correctly, Brecht argued, musicals could impart social lessons by interrupting the emotional connections audiences felt with the characters on the stage, thus reminding audiences of the theatricality of what they were watching. Further, by using music in his productions to distance audiences from the events occurring on stage, he forced them to look twice at real issues and situations they would typically perceive to be normal. For example, a typical prostitute does not sing about her place within the larger economic system; the strangeness of such an occurrence on the stage provides an intellectual jolt to complacent spectators, requiring them to look at the world again with new eyes.[17]

Urinetown was understood precisely in terms of Brecht through the medium of *Threepenny Opera*, but in very superficial ways. It is therefore important to isolate what is "Brechtian" about *Urinetown*. Doing so will demonstrate that although *Urinetown* superficially resembles a Brechtian text, the label of Brechtian that critics applied to the production had more to do with larger concerns about the relevance of musical comedies in a post 9/11 world than to *Urinetown* itself. Moreover, the importance of musicals was not perceived of in Brechtian terms, but in ways contrary to the political and social potential Brecht envisioned for theater.

A Story of Adversity: *Urinetown* Is Born

The story of how Greg Kotis and his creative partner Mark Hollmann worked to fulfill their dream of "a freak show of a musical, a Frankenstein's Monster best kept in the basement," can be described as a tale made for Hollywood.[18] Well-rehearsed in interviews and publicity materials, it is a true tale of perseverance and friendship where two regular

---

[16] Willett, 172.
[17] Brecht, 84-90.
[18] Kotis, "Introduction," xiii.

guys somehow survived both Broadway's fear of risk and a horrible title to stage a musical that would go on to win three Tony awards for best book, score, and director. The story is this: while in Paris, playwright and performer Greg Kotis ran out of money and was forced to live on the street for a few weeks; as a result, he had to strictly monitor his budget, a budget that included pennies for the public lavatories. In the middle of this experience, Kotis had the idea that control over public urination would make a great musical because the idea *for* the musical was as absurd as the idea *of* musical theater in general.[19]

Kotis approached his long-time friend Mark Hollmann, the composer of several failed musicals and a location scout for *Law and Order*, to collaborate on this "bad, bad, idea, but . . . it has to be a musical because it's so absurd."[20] The idea of *Urinetown* struck Hollmann as a good one, although to begin with very few people agreed. After many rejections, the work finally premiered at the New York Fringe Festival in 1999 and made the move to Off-Broadway semi-respectability in May 2001. It was scheduled to open in Broadway's Henry Miller Theater for press nights on September 10 and 11, 2001. But, of course, the September 11, 2001, performance never took place. The official opening was finally held on September 20, after which the show ran for thirty-one months.[21]

Urinetown opened on Broadway during a season that saw the opening of two musicals based on films—*Sweet Smell of Success* and *Thoroughly Modern Millie*—both of which received bad to mediocre reviews, as well as revivals of *Into the Woods* and *Oklahoma!*. *Urinetown* was therefore the only completely original book musical comedy by an American composer that opened during that season. This assessment excludes the "scrapbook" musical, *Mamma Mia*, a story set to 22 songs by the Swedish rock group ABBA, and the jazz musical revue *One Mo' Time* which ran for a paltry 21 performances.[22] This lackluster season seemed to cap a fifteen-year period during which the imminent or actual death of the classic American integrated musical, where song and dance numbers flow naturally from the plot, as established by *Oklahoma!* (1943), was

---

[19] Ibid., ix-xv.

[20] Kotis in McKinley, "Fitting a Little Show into a Big House," AR3.

[21] Ibid., ix-xxvii.

[22] Andrew Lloyd Webber's very British *By Jeeves* also opened that season and had a brief run of 73 performances. This list does not include musicals that opened the previous season, such as *The Full Monty*, that had not yet closed. For a complete accounting of the Broadway season (June 2001-May 2002), see: John Willis and Ben Hodges, *Theatre World, 2001-2002*, vol. 58 (New York: Applause Theatre and Cinema Books, 2004).

constantly lamented.   A central concern haunted the idea of popular entertainment as represented by musical theater: what did it matter to American society? *Urinetown's* dark and apparently Brechtian approach appeared to provide some sort of an answer.   The initial disdain that greeted *Urinetown* before it was produced on the stage, followed by its tremendous critical and popular success after 9/11, seemed to demonstrate anew what Americans could bring to the musical stage when it involved an originality that did not rely on overwhelming visual spectacle and musical bombast as represented by the British musical theater invasion.

What Kind of Musical Is This?: Rules and Reflexivity

Kotis deliberately constructed *Urinetown* to be "as good as we could make it while having this kernel of rottenness at its center."[23]   For Kotis, that kernel was the very premise of the show: because of a water shortage, the Urine Good Company (UGC) forces the denizens of an unnamed city to pay to urinate.   Given this off-beat foundation for a plot, Kotis and Hollmann needed to quickly lay out ground rules so that the central premise, and all that flowed from it, would be understandable to audiences, thus allowing audiences to get the joke.   The ground rules are immediately established visually. The main set is comprised of a series of metal ladders and catwalks that constrains the actors without overshadowing them. Signs and the strategic placement of furniture, instead of elaborate sets, designate many of the locations, including Public Amenity #9 and the main offices of the Urine Good Company. Overall, the effect is dark, gloomy, and institutional, embodying the idea that *Urinetown* is set in a time and place beset by poverty and problems. But the production is not just sparse in terms of its set design, which taken by itself could be read simply as a reflection of the uncertain timeframe and setting for *Urinetown*. The occasional special effects are done in a deliberately low-tech and visible manner that pokes fun directly at other, more massively staged musicals such as *Les Miserables*. For example, when a deceased character returns in a ghostly character, he is accompanied by a mist that is frantically and obviously sprayed from aerosol cans held by other members of the cast. Taken together, these and other visual clues (such as the utilitarian costumes) inform the audience that *Urinetown* is not a spectacular megamusical.

Having established itself visually as to what it is not, *Urinetown* continues this process textually and works to define what in fact it is. The

---

[23] Kotis in Bornstein, "The Best Bad Play Around," 10D.

first character to walk onto the stage and speak any dialogue is Officer Lockstock: "Well, hello there. And welcome—to *Urinetown*! Not the place, of course. The musical."[24] Lockstock is soon joined onstage by Little Sally who flat out asks: what kind of musical is this? Even the opening number "Too Much Exposition" reminds the audience that "your tickets should say *Urinetown*."[25] A lot of effort is expended to keep the audience from taking *Urinetown* seriously because it is "just" a musical. At the same time the multiple direct addresses to the audience remind them that they are indeed watching a musical comedy following certain conventions, no matter how silly it seems to find them.

Sally's and Lockstock's comments are often cynical. The action of the musical takes place "in a town like any town . . . that you might find in a musical."[26] But even as *Urinetown* struggles to break away from the implicit rulebook of musical theater, the show still operates within that particular framework. As Officer Lockstock makes a point of saying, "in a musical [. . .] it's better to focus on one big thing rather than a lot of little things. The audience tends to be much happier that way."[27] Apart from reminding the audience that they are an audience to a show, and not witnesses to real events, the avuncular Officer Lockstock and precocious Little Sally freely acknowledge problems within the show's structure that audiences themselves might identify. By acknowledging the various clichés and holes in the plot, Lockstock and Sally ironically provide audiences with the opportunity to put these clichés and holes aside and to simply enjoy what occurs on stage. While Kotis may find it ridiculous that anyone would suspend belief long enough to enjoy people who break out into song at moments of great emotion, the direct addresses to the audience in essence says "but that silly singing is all okay because we're following the rules."

Refusing to fix the logistical and plot flaws of *Urinetown* was an integral part of Kotis and Hollmann's deliberate strategy to destabilize the very musical conventions they needed to employ. However by using these conventions in a self-reflexive manner, internal textual tensions resulted. Two examples should suffice to demonstrate these tensions. The first example is from the finale to act one. The masses, incited by the hero Bobby Strong, refuse to pay the required fee for urination. Mr. Caldwell B. Cladwell, CEO of the Urine Good Company, and his minions descend on Public Amenity #9 to quell the popular uprising. Bobby sings

---

[24] Kotis and Hollmann, *Urinetown: The Musical*, 9.
[25] Ibid., 13.
[26] Ibid., 10. Ellipses in the original.
[27] Ibid., 28.

triumphantly of freedom, proclaiming "Don't give us tomorrow / Just give us today!"[28] The song is in march time, perfectly fitted to this militant uprising, but these last lines underline a crucial problem with the mass rebellion. Bobby and the crowd are only thinking of the moment, and not of the future. While Cladwell confidently declares "a little brutality is exactly what these people need," he also sings in a syncopated rhythm that the crowd must "think of tomorrow."[29] The conventions of musical theater have trained everyone to believe that Bobby's desire to "pee for free" is right and just. Little Sally gives voice to this implicit assumption: "This may not be a happy musical, Officer Lockstock, but it's still a musical. And when a little girl has been given as many lines as I have, there's still hope for dreams!"[30] But Bobby's desire is utterly shortsighted, and indeed his desire contradicts the typical heroic ideal of fighting for the future. Cladwell's counter-song thus reverses the role of hero and villain, with the corrupt businessman advocating for the survival of the people he is supposedly oppressing.

The second example of the tensions within *Urinetown* occurs at the show's climax. Cladwell's corrupt policemen have executed Bobby Strong. This act thrusts his lover Hope, Cladwell's daughter, to the forefront of the initially successful revolutionary movement. Hope in her turn sentences her father to death, takes control of his company, and institutes a series of reforms to allow the public to "pee for free whenever they liked, as much as they liked, for as long as they liked."[31] But her good intentions result in a worsening of the drought. In a brief, expository scene at the musical's close, Officer Lockstock explains that Hope, once loved by the people, was subsequently executed by them. Her love for the idea of the people blinded her to the realities of what her so-called reforms actually accomplished. As Little Sally complains to Officer Lockstock, "The good guys finally take over and then everything starts falling apart?!"[32] As in the beginning, Officer Lockstock and Little Sally explicitly address the audience and the codes of musical comedies, with Sally sadly commenting "can't we do a happy musical next time?"[33] There then follows an abbreviated reprise of the song "Urinetown," and a group hail to the eighteenth century philosopher Thomas Malthus, which are the last words the audience hears.

---

[28] Ibid., 51.
[29] Ibid., 52.
[30] Ibid., 49.
[31] Ibid., 98.
[32] Ibid., 99.
[33] Ibid., 100.

But not quite. This extremely dark ending is itself undercut in performance by an exuberant dance number deliberately added to the curtain call for the Broadway and touring productions of *Urinetown* by director John Rando and musical director John Carrafa. This seemingly impromptu number is not acknowledged in either the libretto or the original cast recording. According to Hollmann, "The ending [of *Urinetown*] is really about the end of the world, and the producers thought maybe we should send the audience out on a little less of a down note."[34] The dance number gives the audience a happy and very conventional send-off into the evening, if not a happy or conventional ending. The production number, in celebrating musical comedy, could be viewed as questioning all of the effort Kotis and Hollmann have put into destabilizing the entire art form. However, this second ending also serves to further distance the audience from any sense that a musical can have any sort of social message. The world of *Urinetown* comes to crashing end, but the cast is able not only able to survive, but dance. Indeed, Little Sally's ability to posit the possibility of a cheerier musical next time around provides the space for the Rando and Carrafa's happy ending. However, this "unscripted" curtain call still falls squarely outside the narrative diegesis of *Urinetown*, and thus is not analogous to the forced happy ending of *Threepenny Opera*, when the Queen's messenger arrives in the nick of time to revoke MacHeath's death sentence for no reason other than the fact that everyone is in an opera.

The double-ending of *Urinetown* uses of one of the standards of musical theater: having the entire cast together on stage as a singing/dancing community. Classic stage musicals, such as *Oklahoma!*, are formed around the idea of community and overcoming difference. Romantic love and the coming together of the boy and the girl function as a synecdoche for the larger community. In *Oklahoma!*, Laurie is a rancher, Curley a cowboy. As they come together romantically, with Laurie choosing the cowboy over the sexually deviant Jud, the feuding ranchers and cowboys also put aside their differences and learn to get along. The finale, with everyone on the stage singing together, the now-deceased Jud excepted, drives home these fundamental points: community and the negotiation of differences to preserve the community are central.[35]

---

[34] Hollmann in Brown, "*Urinetown*: Broadway's Musical-Comedy Send up of Bad Taste Hits Cleveland," J1.

[35] It must be noted that only one character in *Oklahoma!* is excluded from the community: Jud. He is constructed as Curley's antithesis. Jud is so far outside societal norms in terms of his sexual desires (he reads dirty magazines), low class status (he is a ranch hand) and questionable racial heritage (he is described as

The importance of community and its preservation are in full view for both endings of *Urinetown*. In the first ending, the murdered members of the community—including Bobby and Cladwell—rejoin their living counterparts to sing the closing cynical homage to their hometown. None of the characters of *Urinetown* so violate the social norms that they are not allowed to rejoin the community, hence Bobby's and Cladwell's ghostly inclusion with the rest of cast for the finale. The second, unofficial ending, celebrates the cast as a community who triumphed over the shortcomings of a bad title and premise to win over the audience. As a musical, therefore, *Urinetown* falls squarely within musical theater's traditionally conservative discourse.[36]

From the perspective of co-creator Kotis, "musicals are all about good intentions, doing the right thing and being rewarded for doing it. They're morality plays. We wanted to write a musical with no moral, because it's too late for morals."[37] It is clear from this that Kotis's main agenda was not, as one critic put it, to "adoringly satirize" musical comedy.[38] Instead, *Urinetown* was Kotis's attempt to prove that musicals served no real political purpose in the world. *Urinetown* is absurd because for Kotis all musicals are absurd.[39] This idea of the absurdity of the musical helps to account for the surfeit of knowing references to other musicals often considered to have an element of social conscience or political agenda, including: *Oliver!*, *West Side Story*, *Evita*, *Les Miserables*, *Annie*, *Sweeny Todd*, *Big River*, and *Fiddler on the Roof.*

Through parody, such as the central love story between Hope and Bobby that is doomed to fail rather than succeed, Kotis and Hollmann attempted to stretch the form of musical comedy past its breaking point. Doing so would illuminate their position as to why musicals no longer have a political place within modern American society, if they ever truly had such a place to begin with. *Urinetown* wants to argue that this

---

"dark"), that he cannot be incorporated within the community and is therefore killed. Multiple scholars have examined *Oklahoma!* in light of the idea of American identity and community, one of the most recent is Andrea Most, *Making Americans: Jews and the Broadway Musical* (Cambridge: Harvard University Press, 2004). See especially chapter four.

[36] It is important to note that not all musicals, even those from the "golden age," function in this conservative and community-oriented manner, although a preponderance of them do.

[37] Kotis in Foster, "Fight the Power in *Urinetown* and an Updated *Threepenny Opera*," 1-2.

[38] Moore, "*Urinetown* Smart, Sassy, and Sensational," 4.

[39] Greg Kotis, "Introduction," *Urinetown: The Musical* (New York: Faber and Faber, Inc., 2003): xv.

particular form of popular culture, with its entrenched genre rules and expectations, is too ridden with fantasy and too wedded to "boy-meets-girl" idealism to have any potential as an advocate for meaningful social or political change.

However, parody must always remain wedded to the form it mocks, and the creators of *Urinetown* had indeed created a real musical comedy. As a result, theater critics and audiences could place *Urinetown* within the history of musical theater, and experience the parody as part of that larger American cultural tradition. Because Kotis and Hollmann relied heavily on particular musical comedy conventions, most reviewers and audiences did not read *Urinetown* as destructive, but as affectionate. Romantic love, after all, forms the center of *Urinetown* because without Hope and Bobby, there would be no real narrative.

What Kind of Musical Is This? II: A Brechtian Pallette

In *Urinetown*, Kotis and Hollmann struggle with the musical comedy conventions they set out to mock. To reconcile the resultant tensions, they attempted to operate within a framework provided by Brecht's and Weill's *Threepenny Opera*. The subject matter of *Urinetown* immediately made Hollmann think of *Threepenny Opera*, and he initially used a Brecht/Weill "palette" to frame the entire score.[40] It is important to note that Hollmann never precisely defines what he means by invoking Brecht and *Threepenny Opera*. Indeed, it is difficult to say why the subject of urination would strike him as being particularly Brechtian, especially since *Urinetown*'s take on capitalism is confused at best. Is it simply that the material is "dark" or "rotten"? Or, in the words of the song, "Too Much Exposition," was it simply that a story superficially about oppressed masses is about "nothing you don't know"?[41] Oppressed masses are, as the song suggests, very old news indeed.

First and most obviously, the title of the musical proclaims itself to be about an unpleasant subject: urine. As the musical progresses, this bodily fluid is paired with an even more unpleasant subject for American audiences: class. In the first act, it is made clear that one of the central issues of the musical should be the class tensions between the poor masses who are forced to frequent public urinals such as the disgusting Public Amenity #9, various middlemen such as the police and the people who run the amenities, and the multi-national corporation Urine Good Company

---

[40] Hollmann, "Introduction," xxxi.
[41] Kotis and Hollmann, 13.

which owns the urination stations, sets the fees, and uses the profits to keep the government under control.

But the various battle lines that are drawn within *Urinetown* actually have much less to do with class divisions than with different visions of the future. Once incited by the hero Bobby Strong, the poor fall prey to his vision of "don't think of tomorrow, just give us today." They seek to overthrow the price structure of the urination system so that they may pee for free, not because they desire class equity, but because they desire instant gratification for their bodily needs.

It soon becomes clear that the villainous owner of the Urine Good Company, Mr. Cladwell, is not really the villain after all. While he makes an obscene amount of money—often paired with filth and feces in popular culture—it was his foresight that saved the city from the drought years. By instituting draconian urination laws, water was preserved and the city and its people survived. Mr. Cladwell thinks only of the future, not of his current needs or the current needs of his daughter and the poor, and it is this orientation toward the future that is at the root of his antagonism toward Bobby Strong. The two do not clash over capitalist ideology or class distinctions, but over whose attitude toward the future is the more correct.

While Hollmann abandoned the attempt to remain completely faithful to *Threepenny Opera* as a single musical influence, and instead used musical styles from a range of familiar Broadway referents, theater critics generally followed his explanation regarding the musical tone for *Urinetown* in its entirety. Two songs in particular were singled out as closely following in Brecht's and Weill's musical footsteps: "It's a Privilege to Pee," and "Don't Be the Bunny."

Toward the beginning of the end of act one, the proprietor of Public Amenity #9, Miss Penny Pennywise, sings "it's a privilege to pee / water's worth its weight in gold these days" to forcibly inform the hero Bobby Strong that no one gets a free pass at her establishment.[42]   Where Lockstock and Sally maintain and explicate the rules of musical theater for the external audience, Pennywise lays out the laws for the characters within *Urinetown*. As Pennywise sings it, because everyone must pay to urinate no one can lay claim to being better than anyone else. They are all suffering. For Kotis, Pennywise is "an absurdist Brechtian anti-heroine,"[43] and Hollmann views her as similar to Peachum in *Threepenny Opera* as he sings his morning hymn, because "it is the singers' righteous duty to tell

---

[42] Ibid., 16.
[43] Kotis, xiii.

the truth as they see it."[44] As Pennywise sees it, bodily functions act as the ultimate equalizers.

There is some basic resemblance in "It's a Privilege to Pee" to Peachum's morning hymn. Peachum's song is a wake-up call to the beggars littering the front steps of his shop where these same beggars can buy just the right gear to touch the hearts of those who might toss them a few coins. The song ironically laments the fact that the world has become so callous, forcing Peachum to constantly invent new ways of arousing sympathy and thus maintain his cut of the beggars' profits. Miss Pennywise is similarly aware of the hard-heartedness of mankind and of her own place in the economic system when she ensures that the poor always pay to use Public Amenity #9. But where Peachum maintains his cynical view of the world and his place in it—even in the face of *Threepenny Opera's* deliberately false happy ending—Miss Pennywise transforms into a urinal proprietor with a heart of gold. Ultimately, she embraces the revolution against Urine Good Company because of Hope, and not because of any real change in her political consciousness. It transpires that Miss Pennywise was once Cladwell's lover and that the ingénue Hope Cladwell is the result of this union. Pennywise cannot maintain her place in the economic system in the face of her daughter's blind optimism. Pennywise ultimately makes her choice to join in the fight against UGC based on family ties and her maternal instincts which appear to fall outside of any economic forces. The love-bound trajectory of the American musical comedy thus overrides Pennywise's Brechtian righteousness initially in evidence during the first act.

In the penultimate song of act one, Cladwell, the apparent villain, dispenses sage advice to lovelorn daughter Hope: "Don't be the bunny." Completely confused, Hope replies, "But Daddy, we're talking about people, not animals," to which her father knowingly responds, "People are animals, Hope dear."[45] The song's setting is Cladwell's gleaming corporate office, and it is sung in the patronizing style of the upper-class patrician father imparting sage advice to his sheltered daughter and, by extension, to the audience as well. The advice is harsh and cynical: the only way to survive in the world is to step on others before they step on you; always be prepared, or you will be a helpless bunny in the face of what the world can do to you.

In the end, "Don't be the Bunny" is closer to a Brechtian philosophy than "Privilege to Pee" in large part because Cladwell never abandons a

---

[44] Hollmann, xxxi.
[45] Kotis and Hollmann, 46.

sense of the larger system of which he and everyone else in the musical is a part. When Hope betrays him to the mob and takes over his company, he takes an honest look at himself and realizes that he's "the bunny this time around."[46]   Hope followed his advice to the letter. However, in spite of his newly acquired bunny status and imminent death, he remains committed to his past acts and refuses to apologize for them. Yes, he made piles and piles of cash while saving the town from oblivion, but that was just good sense.   In this regard, Cladwell is more the Brechtian anti-hero than Pennywise because he rejects the standard conventions of musical theater.   He is not allowed a change of heart and a shot at musical redemption by giving into Hope's demands. But *Urinetown* also leaves open the question as to whether Cladwell deserved to be expelled from the community; clearly it was his actions—the regimentation of urination—that kept the community from disintegrating and slipping back into the horrors of "the Stink Years." His foresight and long tenure at the head of the UGC is placed in sharp contrast with Hope's blindness and quick demise.   For the most part, however, reviewers of *Urinetown* disregarded Cladwell as a character touched by Brecht and focused on less complex characters and less uncomfortable songs.

Follow That Trope!: The Reception of *Urinetown* and Educating Audiences

In the published script to *Urinetown* and in numerous interviews about their musical, Kotis and Hollmann framed their musical either in terms of the old fashioned nature of musical theater itself or by referencing *Threepenny Opera*. Most reviewers either took these comments at face value or fell back on Brecht as a shorthanded means to classify *Urinetown* and to place it within the canon of musical comedies. Many reviewers were also quite explicit about their intentions to educate potential audiences, linking the intended target of Kotis's and Hollmann's parody to the internal logic of musicals, for example: "in Act II, for example, there's a big gospel number ['Run, Freedom, Run!'], because musicals generally have a stirring set piece in the second act."[47]

"Run, Freedom, Run" as a song was often recognized by reviewers as an exemplar of parody and as a synecdoche for *Urinetown* for several reasons. Because the song is about cowardice and not heroism, even a spectator not well-versed in musical theater conventions could understand

---

[46] Ibid., 96.
[47] Henry, "Don't Let the Title Turn You Away," 1-2.

the humor of the situation. Bobby Strong and the mob attempt to justify their escape from Cladwell and his police by linking their cowardice to their revolutionary idea to pee freely. Spectators who had seen shows such as *Big River*, *Oh! Kay*, or *Guys and Dolls*—all musicals featuring a prominent second-act gospel number—would especially appreciate the humor of the song because they could explicitly recognize the parody of a particular musical theater convention at work. As a song, "Run, Freedom, Run" is an exciting showstopper that demonstrates the credentials of *Urinetown* as a musical through its "proper" placement in act two. Those spectators less familiar with musical comedy would still get the joke because the song is an ode to cowardice sung in an incongruous manner. Although a relatively simple song lyrically, it serves the purpose for reviewers by representing the non-threatening humorous aspects of *Urinetown* and is a staple of musical comedies.

When not attempting to persuade potential audiences that *Urinetown*, in spite of its title, was in fact a proper musical comedy, theater critics turned to Brecht. This was the case regardless of whether *Urinetown* received a positive or negative review. It was the rare reviewer who spent any time actually explaining what Brechtian theater is or what it means, although there are a few notable exceptions that will be addressed. Overall, however, reviewers seemed to equate Brecht and the *Threepenny Opera* with the popular idea of "dark" or "political" theater, without any nuance. For this reason, reviewers tended to emphasize "It's a Privilege to Pee" as being a descendent of Brecht and Weill, thus replicating comments by Kotis and Hollmann in interviews. Like "Run, Freedom, Run" which often stood in for the conventions of musical theater, "It's a Privilege to Pee" stood in for Brechtian conventions without the harshness embedded in the song "Don't be the Bunny."

Reviewers often referenced Brecht and Weill simply to explain what *Urinetown* is a parody of: "Hollmann's inventive score [...] is reminiscent of those by Kurt Weill in his collaborations with Bertolt Brecht, such as The Threepenny Opera, only funnier."[48] When reviewers have deemed the parody to be a success, they then typically characterize Brecht and Weill as unfunny or as taking themselves and/or musical theater too seriously: "Unlike Brecht, authors Mark Hollmann and Greg Kotis allow themselves to have fun with their project, even when it doesn't serve the socio-political conversation they're having."[49] Kotis and Hollmann, these reviewers argue, are having the type of fun Brecht and Weill never

---

[48] Fleming, "A Royal Flush for Musicals," 1D.
[49] Heckman, Review Roundup: Bertolt Brecht Is Alive and Well and Living in Urinetown.

dreamed of. In addition, as one reviewer made plain, "the old social commentary musicals of Kurt Weill, Bertolt Brecht and later Marc Blitzstein" are ripe for mockery because the "old social commentary" no longer has any relevance.[50] This of course echoes comments made by Kotis regarding musical theater more generally.

Those few reviewers who explicitly took it as their role to educate audiences about *Urinetown* did briefly reflect on the meaning of Brechtian, or "neo-Brechtian," theater, usually along the lines of a play "defined as one that contradicts expectations, using burlesque styles in tragic situations, and breaking the fourth wall."[51] Kotis and Hollmann were seen in generally positive reviews of the educational kind as not parodying Brecht and Weill in particular, but musical theater more broadly, and as therefore applying Brechtian techniques in a fresh manner.[52]

Significantly, negative reviews referenced Brecht and Weill in a similar manner to that of positive reviews: "this new, cheekily titled musical—a Brechtian parody about a drought-plagued city [. . .] manages to succeed on every level but the most basic."[53] In these types of reviews, the parody of Brecht and Weill might be understood as a success, but that very success is ultimately a negative one because it undermines musical theater by being too self-referential and too ironic to have any real meaning. Implicitly, such negative reviews seem to take *Urinetown* to task for pushing *Threepenny Opera's* critique of stage conventions beyond the breaking point.[54] If in "Run, Freedom, Run" the "emotional sincerity of gospel music is used merely to represent sincerity" and Brecht and Weill no longer have any relevance, these reviews worried, where does musical theater in general fit within popular culture?[55] Supposedly straightforward musicals such as *Oklahoma!* are viewed in these reviews as embodying the best type of a past American idealism, while the Brecht-

---

[50] Barnes, "'Urinetown' Pure Gold," 65.

[51] Mehlman, "'Urinetown' Leg-Crossing Fun," 19.

[52] Some recent regional productions of *Urinetown*, in line with their educational outreach programs, also make positive links between the show and Brecht. For example, see: Rena Murman, *Performance Guide: Urinetown* (Weston, VT: Weston Playhouse Company, July 2006).

[53] Scheck, "'Urinetown,'" 15.

[54] This type of critique is often leveled against Stephen Sondheim in terms of his "deconstructed" musicals, although Sondheim himself is no fan of Brecht. Scott McMillin, "Brecht and Sondheim: An Unholy Alliance," *Who Was Ruth Berlau?: The Brecht Yearbook* 30 (2005).

[55] Arnest, "*Urinetown* Flush with in-Jokes," 20.

infused *Urinetown* was seen as reflecting only cynicism of the worst kind. It is important to note, however, that many of these less favorable type of reviews occur well after *Urinetown*'s original Broadway run, and thus after the initial shock of September 11, 2001 and the apparent resurgence of the Broadway musical.

Conclusion

So why did critics habitually place *Urinetown* within the context of Brecht? In part, this can be explained by the timing of musical's premiere; initially slated to open to Broadway preview audiences on September 11, 2001, *Urinetown* instead opened shortly thereafter on September 20 and was swept up in the rhetoric of "normalcy" that understandably permeated New York city following the trauma of the attack on the Twin Towers. As one New York critic put it on September 21:

> Can we laugh and thrill to a musical at a time like this? . . . When every individual spirit as well as the national one can use all the bolstering it can get, *Urinetown* is not just a recommended tonic. Its reopening under the glare of lights on Broadway places it beside *The Producers*, another great musical that makes us laugh at tyranny, as a stanchion—no, a twin tower— of pure American vibrancy.[56]

Clearly, musical theater is being positioned as distinctly American, implicitly joyous, and anti-authoritarian. Musical theater, and musical comedy in particular, is constructed here as a vibrant, living art form that constitutes an important part of America's cultural life.

The idea of the American musical as an intrinsic part of American culture is perhaps as important as the wider historical and political context in which *Urinetown* found itself. The imminent death of the American musical was variously ascribed to the post-modern style of Stephen Sondheim, the megamusical stylings of Andrew Lloyd Webber, or MTV. Using a declension model of history, and thus also reinforcing the exceptional nature of American musical theatre, critics and scholars noted the decline in popularity of this once popular form of entertainment that to all appearances had nothing new or important to say to modern audiences.[57] *Urinetown*, simply through its originality, offered a glimmer of hope to those fearing the musical's demise. But *Urinetown* also seemed

---

[56] Weber, "Theater Review," E1.
[57] An example of this "declension model" of scholarship is Mark Grant, *The Rise and Fall of the Broadway Musical* (Boston: Northeastern University Press, 2004).

to offer up something more than simple originality. Its textual nods to the dangers of corporate greed, environmental concerns, and eighteenth century philosophers, the musical echoes of Weill, and the strategic surface use of Brechtian techniques, gave the impression that Kotis and Hollmann were attempting to speak to an audience politically. However, these nods were just that: nods, and expedient ones at that, used to show the political ineffectiveness of musical theater, and its disconnect from the real world.

The methods harnessed by critics to educate their audiences can be understood using Richard Dyer's theory of the use value of film musicals as entertainment. He theorizes that audiences do not automatically or spontaneously react to a given performance in the emotionally appropriate manner. The audience must first learn, and then understand, what emotions are expected from them regarding a particular form of entertainment. Different forms signify different systems of historical and social relationships, systems that the audience may only be vaguely aware of, although it is to these systems of relationships that the audience responds. Dyer's framework helps to reveal the reasons behind the effort of the majority of critics to educate audiences about what *Urinetown* was and was not like. Reviewers needed to explain the systems *Urinetown* both referred to and challenged in order to ensure that audiences would know not to react hostilely to the ways in which *Urinetown* utilized musical theater conventions. As Dyer posits, entertainment in general, and musicals in particular, present audiences with an embodied utopianism. Musicals normally function on an emotional level, providing audiences with pleasant or reassuring alternatives to the world in which they live.[58]

Although Kotis and Hollmann employed a variety of strategies within *Urinetown* to elicit from audiences the appropriate responses to characters and the musical comedy form itself, the reactions from theater reviewers demonstrates an awareness of the dangers inherent to parodying a form while operating within it. In its heart, *Urinetown* does not aspire to the goals set by Brecht. Instead, the musical, while allowing for knowing winks toward the audience, is more concerned with critiquing the very possibility that a musical might be socially relevant. Although part of the purpose of *Threepenny Opera* was to reform opera, to disrupt the conventions of an all-encompassing sound that carried away the audience's emotions, it was also intended to demonstrate the use*ful*ness of the art form if properly constructed. *Urinetown* is about the use*less*ness of the musical theater form at a particular historical moment.

---

[58] Dyer, "Entertainment and Utopia," 271-283.

Finally, it is important to remember that as slippery as Brecht can sometimes be, both in terms of the intent of his theories and in light of how he lived his life, he did have fundamental problems with the system of capitalism and he did mean for his theatrical texts to react politically against this system. On 10 May 2002, Paul Solman, from PBS's *Online Newshour* interviewed Kotis, Hollmann, members of the production team, and various actors from *Urinetown* about the meaning of the show. During the course of the interview, Hollmann and Kotis reveal that *Urinetown* is not so much an affectionate parody of Brecht and Weill, but an outright repudiation of what they stood for. According to Hollmann, "I really don't think capitalism is bad, and I actually take some pleasure in [...] the neo-con ending of this show, which is that, you know, the liberal do-gooders out there, they actually, when you put them in power [...] mess things up."[59] Kotis follows up on this thought, noting "Bolshevik" revolutions "lead to disaster," although he tempers his claim by saying that older systems of power may or may not know what they are doing.[60] These comments suggest that perhaps in the wake of 9/11, critics and audiences were not just looking for a comedic release from horror, an affirmation of American musical comedy, or "Brecht lite." Instead, the comments by Kotis and Hollmann illuminate why reviewers were so circumspect in their definitions of who Brecht was and the type of theater he advocated beyond "breaking the fourth wall." Brecht, through *Urinetown*, becomes a promoter for capitalism and thus for the American way of life.

Works Cited

Arnest, Mark. "Urinetown Flush with in-Jokes." *The Denver Gazette,* 12 September 2003, Final ed., sec. Go, 20.

Barnes, Clive. "'Urinetown' Pure Gold." *New York Post,* 21 September 2001, sec. Pulse, 65.

Bornstein, Lisa. "The Best Bad Play Around." *Rocky Mountain News,* 9 September 2003, Final ed., sec. Entertainment/Weekend/Spotlight, 10D.

Brecht, Bertolt. *Brecht on Theatre: The Development of an Aesthetic.* Trans. John Willett. New York: Hill and Wang, 1964.

---

[59] Hollmann in Solman, *In Tune with the Times.*
[60] Kotis, ibid.

Brown, Tony. "Urinetown: Broadway's Musical-Comedy Send up of Bad Taste Hits Cleveland." *The Plain Dealer,* 18 January 2004, Final ed., sec. Sunday Arts, J1.

Cebrzynski, Gregg. "The Applebee's Guys Have Gone Too Far This Time." 5 May 2006. <http://nrnadwatcher.blogspot.com/2006_05_01 nrnadwatcher_archive.html> (1 August 2006.)

Christy, James. "Brecht and the American Avant-Garde." *Brecht Unbound.* Eds. James K. Lyon and Hans-Peter Breuer. Newark: University of Delaware Press, 1995. 179-188.

Dyer, Richard. "Entertainment and Utopia." *The Cultural Studies Reader.* Ed. Simon During. New York: Routledge, 1993. 271-283.

Errico, Marcus. *The Songs of the Century.* 28 December 1999. <http://www.eonline.com/News/Items/0,1,5801,00.html> (1 August 2006.)

Ferran, Peter Wigglesworth. "The Threepenny Songs: Cabaret and the Lyrical Gestus." *Theater* 30, no.3 (2000): 5-21.

Fleming, John. "A Royal Flush for Musicals." *St. Petersburg Times,* 16 November 2001, South Pinellas ed., sec. Floridian, 1D.

Foster, Catherine. "Fight the Power in Urinetown and an Updated Threepenny Opera." *The Boston Globe,* 4 January 2004, Third ed., sec. Arts/Entertainment, 1-2.

Friedwald, Will. *Stardust Memories: The Biography of Twelve of America's Most Popular Songs.* New York: Pantheon Books, 2002.

Gilbert, Michael John T. *Bertolt Brecht's Striving for Reason, Even in Music: A Critical Assessment.* Studies in Modern German Literature. Ed. Peter D. G. Brown. New York: Peter Lang, 1988.

Grant, Mark. *The Rise and Fall of the Broadway Musical.* Boston: Northeastern University Press, 2004.

Heckman, Kevin. Review Roundup: Bertolt Brecht Is Alive and Well and Living in Urinetown. 14 March 2006. <http://www.performink.com/ Archives/reviewroundup/2006/4-14ReviewRoundup.htm> (1 August 2006.)

Henry, Amanda. "Don't Let the Title Turn You Away." *The Capital Times & Wisconsin State Journal,* 8 February 2004, All ed., sec. Arts and Entertainment, 1-2.

Hollmann, Mark. "Introduction." *Urinetown: The Musical.* New York: Faber and Faber, Inc., 2003. xxviii-xxxv.

Kotis, Greg. "Introduction." *Urinetown: The Musical.* New York: Faber and Faber, Inc., 2003. ix-xxvii.

Kotis, Greg, and Greg Kotis Hollmann. *Urinetown: The Musical*. New York: Faber and Faber, Inc., 2003.

Kowalke, Kim H. "Singing Brecht Vs. Brecht Singing: Performance in Theory and Practice." *Cambridge Opera Journal* 5, no.1 (1993): 55-78.

Lyon, James K. "Brecht's *Mann Ist Mann* and the Death of Tragedy in the 20th Century." *German Quarterly* 67, no.4 (1994): 513-520.

Marks, Peter. "Laughing Away the Tears and Fears." *New York Times*, 28 October 2001, Final ed., sec. Arts and Leisure, AR5-6.

McKinley, Jesse. "Fitting a Little Show into a Big House." *New York Times,* 2 September 2001, AR3.

McMillin, Scott. "Brecht and Sondheim: An Unholy Alliance." *Who Was Ruth Berlau?:The Brecht Yearbook* 30 (2005): 323-32.

Mehlman, Barbara. "'Urinetown' Leg-Crossing Fun." *Times Union*, 16 September 2001, sec. Arts, 19.

Moore, John. "Urinetown Smart, Sassy, and Sensational." *Denver Post*, 12 September 2003, Final ed., sec. Weekend, 4.

Most, Andrea. *Making Americans: Jews and the Broadway Musical*. Cambridge: Harvard University Press, 2004.

Murman, Rena. *Performance Guide: Urinetown*. Weston, VT: Weston Playhouse Company, July 2006.

Phiddian, Robert. "Are Parody and Deconstruction Secretly the Same Thing?" *New Literary History* 28, no.4 (1997): 673-696.

Scheck, Frank. "'Urinetown'." *Hollywood Reporter*, 18 May 2001, 15.

Shout, John D. "The Musical Theater of Marc Blitzstein." *American Music* 3, no.4 (1985): 413-428.

Solman, Paul. In Tune with the Times. June 2002. <http://www.pbs.org/newshour/bb/entertainment/jan-june02/urinetown_5-10.html> (1 August 2006.)

Stewart, Jon and "The Daily Show." 15 February 2006.

Weber, Bruce. "Theater Review." *New York Times*, 21 September 2001, E1.

Weber, Carl. "Brecht on the American Stage at the Turn of the Century." *Bertolt Brecht: Centenary Essays*. Eds. Steve Giles and Rodney Livingstone. German Monitor. Atlanta, GA: Rodopi, 1998. 227-239.

Wekweth, Manfred, Martin Nicolaus, and Erica Munk. "From Brecht Today." *TDR: The Drama Review* 12, no.1 (1967): 118-124.

Willett, John. *The Theatre of Bertolt Brecht: A Study from Eight Aspects*. London: Methuen and Co., Ltd., 1959.

Willis, John, and Ben Hodges. *Theatre World, 2001-2002. Vol. 58*. New York: Applause Theatre and Cinema Books, 2004.

VIRTUOSIC ALIENATION: SARAH JONES, BROADWAY, & THE BRECHTIAN TRADITION

DAVID KORNHABER

The critical reception of Sarah Jones' recent one-woman show, *Bridge and Tunnel*, which premiered off-Broadway at New York City's Culture Project in 2004 and transferred to a Broadway run in 2006, hardly brings to mind the work of Bertolt Brecht. Jones' two-hour, politically charged performance, in which she personifies fourteen immigrants from the New York area assembled for a poetry reading, has been described as "virtuosic" and "dazzling," with commentators marveling at the actress's powers of imitation and transformation.[1] In short, Jones' production seems like a far cry from the distanced, presentational performances advocated by Brecht as the only means to achieve a truly political theatre. And yet, while the fervor over Jones' abilities may not conform to Brechtian expectations, I mean to argue that a close examination of Jones' performance techniques reveals something very close to the effects Brecht describes in writings like "Alienation Effects in Chinese Acting" or "The Street Scene." Moving rapidly from character to character and signaling her transformations through representative gestures or postures assigned to each persona, Jones the performer is always at the forefront of the audience's mind. We are continually conscious of the actress presenting characters to us, indicating mannerisms and patterns of speech much like the witness to the streetcar accident in Brecht's "Street Scene." Indeed, Brecht's idea of *gestus* becomes a key tool in Jones' arsenal: with only a few minutes dedicated to each character, she makes skillful use of the indicative gesture as a means of conveying character, status, and attitude, calling attention to the way in which class and history permeate individual stances and perspectives.

Brechtian acting techniques have, of course, long been anathema to Broadway audiences: witness Lewis Nichols' 1933 description of *The Threepenny Opera* in *The New York Times* as "a gently mad evening in the

---

[1] Rooney, "Bridge and Tunnel," par. 1.

theater"[2] and Mordecai Gorelick's commentary in his 1937 edition of Brecht's theoretical work that the author "showed open contempt for the audience."[3] Even today, we can turn to Ben Brantley's recent description of Brecht's alienation techniques as "self-defeating" in a 2006 *New York Times* review of *The Threepenny Opera* and director George C. Wolfe's declaration that Brecht's ideas on acting are "outmoded."[4] Naturalism in acting, particularly of the "method acting" variety developed by Lee Strasberg, Stella Adler, and others in homage to Stanislavski, has long been the coin of the realm on Broadway, even when it comes to Brecht productions. Regarding Meryl Streep's performance in a 2006 production of *Mother Courage*, Brantley lauds the actress' powers of embodiment: "Embodying a tireless entrepreneur of the Thirty Years War—determined to survive with her business and family intact, whatever the cost—Ms. Streep so blurs the lines between Meryl and Mother that for once it is hard to distinguish the dancer from the dance."[5] In the case of Sarah Jones, however, rather than being revolted by Brecht's style of acting, audiences have been, quite literally, amazed by it, declaring Jones a kind of genius. Virtuosity, in essence, has become a means of neutralizing the typical Broadway audience's response to Brecht's techniques. The work of Jones, as I intend to show, offers an effective means of making Brechtian political theatre "palatable" to Broadway tastes. Still, even Brecht might be impressed by the manner in which we are able to coolly contemplate the political issues at hand in Jones' work rather than become engrossed in any particular story, distanced as we are from the actorial embodiment that he so decried by the allure of the performer herself. The result is an intensely intellectual, rather than grossly emotional, performance that achieves its political ends in a Brechtian manner while at the same time distracting audiences from the Brechtian mechanisms at work.

To say that Jones seeks to use *Bridge and Tunnel* to achieve political ends, of course, is not the same as to say she seeks political ends that might appeal to Brecht himself. There can be little doubt that a political purpose lies behind Sarah Jones' *Bridge and Tunnel*, but it is not of a particularly Brechtian bent. Despite recent Broadway productions of plays and musicals like *A Raisin in the Sun* and *Bollywood Dreams*, minority representation on long-running Broadway shows has been scant. In this climate, Jones' cast of fourteen immigrant characters, hailing from locales

---

[2] Nichols in Brantley, *"Threepenny Opera* Brings Renewed Decadence to Studio 54," par. 8.
[3] Gorelick in Weisstein, "Brecht in America: A Preliminary Survey," 375.
[4] See Brantley; Kalb, "Still Fearsome, Mother Courage Gets a Makeover."
[5] Brantley, "Mother, Courage, Grief, and Song," par. 4.

as diverse as Pakistan, Jamaica, and Vietnam, is in itself a kind of political statement—and one not lost on New York's theatre critics. Writing in *Variety*, David Rooney describes the show as "a bracing piece of social activism, poignant and powerful, that soberly acknowledges the prevailing post-9/11 xenophobia," adding that "its liberal political agenda is apparent."[6] *New York Times* critic Charles Isherwood similarly sums up Jones' political investment: "if multiculturalism is a dirty word to you, 'Bridge & Tunnel' will probably give you hives."[7] For Jones herself, part of the purpose of the production is to give a new voice to those who are underrepresented in the mass media. "It always feels fresh because no one talks about it. These people are not on television," she told one reporter.[8] It's a purpose Jones takes seriously, having conducted extensive interviews with Border Patrol agents, illegal aliens, and recent immigrants to New York in preparation for the show. Unlike her clear predecessor Anna Deveare Smith, Jones' words and characters are fictional, but the stated intent is to communicate to a mass audience the experiences of New York's most marginalized citizens.

Still, one cannot truly call Jones' political motivations Brechtian. A description posted on her website, which can be taken as a kind of mission statement for the production as a whole, would hardly sit well with Brecht the cynic:

> Whether we are women or men; older or younger; straight-laced or queer-eyed; whether we pray Saturday, Sunday, everyday or only at football games; whether we're born here or not; barely scraping by or more comfortable than most, we are all much more connected than any of us realize. By neighborhood, by circumstance, by chance and most importantly by our basic human dignity, we are all cosmically, and of course, often comically linked.[9]

In this declaration, Jones proudly displays the kind of universalist sentimentality that one might expect of Shen Teh in *The Good Woman of Szechuan*, and this vision of the world is the cornerstone of her production.

For Brecht, of course, such sentimentality was the antithesis of a "theatre for a scientific age."[10] In the essay "Theatre for Pleasure or Theatre for Instruction," he makes a point of deprecating the kind of

---

[6] Rooney, par. 1.

[7] Isherwood, "The Voices Inside the Boarder but Outside the Margins," par. 13.

[8] Zinoman, "The Bridges and Tunnels that Bind," par. 6.

[9] "Sarah Jones Performs in NYC," par. 3.

[10] Brecht, *Brecht on Theatre: The Development of an Aesthetic*, 121.

worldview Jones unabashedly puts forth. "The dramatic theatre's spectator," he recounts, "says: Yes, I have felt like that too—Just like me—It's only natural—It'll never change—I weep when they weep, I laugh when they laugh."[11]   Theatre, according to Brecht, should not encourage the kind of empathy and universal identification Jones means to engender; rather, it should evoke skepticism and disconnection from the characters on stage, a quizzical and probing examination of the forces influencing their behavior rather than a simple acceptance of them as fellow human beings. "The sufferings of this man appall me, because they are unnecessary—I laugh when they weep, I weep when they laugh," says Brecht's ideal spectator of the epic theatre.[12]   Brecht's cynical rationalism, of course, was born of a very particular historical circumstance—Robert Brustein would describe his work and ideas as marked by a "Weimar sneer"—and Jones' bold sentimentality (part of the "Pepsodent smile" of American theatre, again according to Brustein) is not necessarily an unwelcome contribution to the Brechtian tradition in an American context.[13]   Still, it would seem that her tender portraits of New York's immigrant community, described by critics as "a sweet-spirited valentine to New York City" and a bastion of "humor, harmony, and compassion," would be an unlikely stronghold of strong Brechtian technique in the very un-Brechtian realm of Broadway theatre.[14]

The connection, however, lies not so much in the content of Jones' political message but in the means she employs to communicate it. There is nothing Brechtian in Jones' training or background. Originally a performance artist and poetry slam participant with the Nuyorican Poets, she dabbled in sketch comedy and TV acting before developing her own material. But the means by which Jones chose to pursue the realm of the solo, multi-character show, an area pioneered by artists including Anna Deveare Smith, Whoopi Goldberg, and Eric Bogosian, brought to her work certain unmistakable Brechtian elements. In eighty minutes of performance, Jones has decided to present no fewer than fourteen unique characters. And unlike Whoopi Goldberg or Anna Deveare Smith, who often presented their characters in isolation, Jones has chosen a communal venue for her ensemble; they must interact with one another physically and verbally as they jostle for attention and for the microphone at a neighborhood poetry reading.

---

[11] Ibid., 71.
[12] Ibid., 71.
[13] See Kalb.
[14] See Isherwood; Kalb.

Despite Jones' obvious talents, the resultant performances could not be called deeply informed embodiments in the Stanislavski tradition. Of course, numerous critics of Jones' performance took pains to comment on the depth of her portrayals. Isherwood describes the production as "90 minutes of acutely observed portraiture,"[15] while Rooney praises its "incisiveness, authenticity, attention to detail."[16] But the details of these reviews, not to mention the trappings of Jones' performance itself, belie these particular accolades. Isherwood marvels at Jones' ability to transform from the Pakistani host of the poetry reading, "antsy and eager in his ill-fitting jacket" to "Lorraine Levine, of Long Island, stooped with age into an S shape."[17] Likewise, Rooney remarks that "Lorraine's trembling, arthritic hands and hunched shoulders are a lifetime away from the cocky swagger of Brooklyn rapper Rashid, the fluttering, birdlike grace of Jamaican performance artist Gladys or the wired hostility of Australian poet Monique."[18] The impressiveness of Jones' ability to shift rapidly and skillfully between personas aside, what Rooney and Isherwood offer here are descriptions of quick character markers, not truly informed embodiments. One does not, for instance, note the prowess of the cast of a production of *Long Day's Journey into Night* by observing that each actor maintained a different posture and tone of voice.

No matter how sincere her purpose or how heartfelt her monologues, Jones relies on a retinue of indicators and shorthands to move rapidly between characters, presenting them to the audience rather than fully embodying them. Jones' young Vietnamese immigrant, for instance, stands firm and straight-backed, arms akimbo, the squareness of his posture invoking the forcefulness of his complaints. The old Jewish woman she embodies moves with a stereotypically crooked back, bent forward, as if hunched over a cane. The Pakistani host of the poetry reading, eternally fond of his flat sense of humor, steps nervously back and forth and wears a perpetual grin, as if always laughing at his own joke. The loquacious Latina school teacher who introduces her shy student is all hand movements, her palms and fingers making dizzying circles as she speeds through a stream-of-consciousness monologue. The Chinese mother trying to come to terms with her daughter's homosexuality stands quietly and moves her arms in slow, arcing lines. Jones' performances are a medley of fast, simple—and precise—indicators. Moving briskly between personas, she invokes not only accent and tone of voice as most

---

[15] Isherwood, par, 5.
[16] Rooney, par. 2.
[17] Isherwood, par 6.
[18] Rooney, par. 13.

reviewers were sure to note (Isherwood praises Jones' "uncanny ability to alter the texture, color and volume of her voice") but also stance and gesture: the whirling hands of the Latina teacher give way to the square stance of the Vietnamese "homeboy," which gives way to the arched back of the Jewish grandmother, which gives way to the graceful arms of the Chinese mother.[19] "Jones' astonishing range with accents and speech patterns is matched by her skill at redefining her body language," Rooney is sure to mention.[20] Watching the performance on a television with the sound muted, one would have no greater difficulty differentiating one character from another than a spectator in the audience.

In short, Jones firmly relies on what Brecht famously, and enigmatically, called "gestus" to move her performance forward. First introduced into the German language by Gotthold Lessing in the *Hamburg Dramaturgy*, *gestus* was meant as a fusion of "gist" and "gesture," an expressible attitude distinct from gesture in the formal sense. The precise meaning of Brecht's usage of the term is regularly debated, though Brecht offers a clarifying explanation in the essay "On Gestic Music." "Gest is not supposed to mean gesticulation: it is not a matter of explanatory or emphatic movements of the hands, but of overall attitudes."[21] He goes on: "Not all gests are social gests. The attitude of chasing away a fly is not yet a social gest, though the attitude of chasing away a dog may be one, for instance if it comes to represent a badly dressed man's continual battle against watchdogs."[22] *Gestus*, in short, is the revelatory action or stance, the trademark movement or "tick" of a character that uncovers his social status and class affiliation. Far more than a stereotype or archetype (one cannot truly include the stances and demeanors of the typical hero-villain-damsel personas common to the traditional Broadway musical in the realm of Brecht's term), *gestus* is the physical manifestation of the social and historical forces that Brecht believed determined one's character. Brecht's sometimes enigmatic examples of the concept *gestus* are uniformly more tied to society and history than to individual character: chasing away a dog, working, falling down and "losing face" in front of one's peers, maintaining "the look of a hunted animal."[23] Each description exemplifies a means of translating the forces of Marxist history into an actor's performance, an attempt on Brecht's part to undo "the common tendency

---

[19] Isherwood, par. 7.
[20] Rooney, par. 13.
[21] Brecht, 104.
[22] Ibid., 104.
[23] Ibid., 104.

of art to remove the social element."[24] Through *gestus*, Brecht sought to enable his actors to transcend the narrow-minded individualism of what he termed "dramatic theatre" and convey a more "scientific" (one might today say sociological) vision of human interactions. "The social gest is the gest relevant to society," Brecht explains, "the gest that allows conclusions to be drawn about the social circumstances."[25]

Though there is no indication that Jones shares Brecht's Marxist motivations, the seriousness with which she takes the political purpose behind her production seems to have led her down a similar course to Brecht's own. Jones' unique working methodology, by which she conducts extensive interviews with actual immigrants in order to construct fictional accounts of the immigrant experience, by its very nature forces each character in her ensemble to stand for far more than himself or herself. Despite the obvious connections in performance style and political goals, then, Jones becomes in a sense the precise opposite of a performer like Anna Deveare Smith. Smith's monologues, taken verbatim from her interviews, are meant to convey the particularity of a certain character and to capture the individuality of his or her unique perspective on the world. Likewise, her performance strives to emulate the physical appearance and habits of each character. Hers is a world of distinct individuality.

Jones, in contrast, forces each character to stand for something far beyond himself or herself. The act of distilling numerous interviews into one fictional character forces that persona to become an amalgamation, a kind of theatrical summary of all the immigrants of that nationality or class with whom Jones interacted. The characters that Jones presents are not then, strictly speaking, individuals. Her decision not to include any repetition of nationality within her ensemble—to show, for instance, the individual differences between two different Jamaican immigrants or two different Pakistani nationals—speaks to her drive towards representationalism. Each persona thus becomes, quite literally, a sociological survey: a representation of Jones' perception of the general status and attitude of each immigrant group. From a certain perspective, one might say Jones' characterizations are not too far removed from stereotype, perhaps even perpetuating the kind of demeaning presentations she means to combat. It is a tension Jones was not unaware of in preparing the piece: "I really thought there was no way I could do this, because everyone will think they're stereotypes," she told one

---

[24] Ibid., 104.
[25] Ibid., 104-105.

interviewer.[26]   And for many commentators, even those who had no shortage of praise for Jones' work, her negotiations on this issue were not entirely successful.   Writes Isherwood, "Inevitably, some portraits are more freshly conceived than others, and delivered with more conviction."[27] Others were more direct: "At times [the characters] traffic in self-deprecating stereotypes."[28] To classify Jones' performances in the realm of stereotype, however, is to in a sense "buy into" the naturalist assumption that studied individuation is the only true means of conveying the human experience. For a Marxist like Brecht, personality and even personal history held a far less deterministic place in the world, and it was theatre's place to help overcome these blinders to a proper understanding of history and society. Writing on what he termed "the parable type of non-Aristotelian drama" in "Notes to *Die Rundköpfe und Die Spitzköpfe*," Brecht explains that "the playing had to enable and encourage the audience to draw abstract conclusions... The representation of human behavior from a social point of view is meant indeed to have a decisive influence on the spectator's own social behavior."[29]

More than a regression to stereotype, it is this emphasis on the social over the individual that seems to be the motivation behind Jones' decision to combine her perceptions of multiple individuals into one representative persona. The common traits condensed into each persona are not, at bottom, determined by individual perspectives or personalities but by the overarching social, class, and cultural influences impacting that demographic. Despite their similarly high levels of education, the hard, square stance of the young Vietnamese man is distinct from the nervous lilt of the Pakistani host not so much because of individual differences in their personalities but because of the different statuses of their affinity groups within the United States: in common perception at least, the Vietnamese immigrant experience is traditionally closer to the physically demanding world of blue-collar labor and grueling service industry jobs than that of the Pakistani immigrant, who is often perceived to be of a higher class than his Vietnamese counterpart and traditionally embedded in the white collar technology and financial industries. (Jones' character is an accountant.)   The slow, deliberate movements of Jones' Jewish character are distinct from the frenetic movements of the Latina schoolteacher not simply because of their differences in age. The teacher, though her career represents a degree of educational and financial success,

---

[26] Jones in Chaddha, "I Am a Poet Too," par. 9.
[27] Isherwood, par. 10.
[28] Gutman, "Sarah Jones Brings Her Downtown Hit to Broadway," par. 3.
[29] Brecht, 100-101.

is enmeshed in the frenetic world of work: she must teach to support herself and presumably her family, and the work of teaching in a New York public school does not allow one the luxury of methodical deliberation. The Jewish grandmother, in contrast, is slow and deliberate in part because she can be: the implication is that she no longer needs to work; she is not financially dependent on others and she can force them to wait on her. Her deliberation is, in part, a mark of social class. The same can be said of Jones' Chinese mother, whose delicate and unhurried gesticulations indicate some degree of financial success: hers are arms not accustomed to physical labor. Contrast this posture with the Jamaican performance artist, who, despite her artistic career path, stands upright and moves with deliberation, well trained in the grueling art of carrying and looking after white children.

Surely Jones' performances do not capture the entirety of the immigrant experience for each nationality: her characters do not summarize the experience of the Pakistani laborer or Jamaican professor, the Chinese businesswoman or the elderly, working poor. What they do capture is the general economic and social status of each national group (or at least Jones' perception of these factors, based presumably on her interviews). And like Brecht, Jones has found that one of the easiest and most effective ways of communicating this information is through distinct physical mannerism. Following her quick moves from one persona to another, we are not only able to identify the different characters quickly (this could be done just as easily through non-revelatory, i.e. more individualized and individualistic, ticks and habits); we are, more importantly, able to see the economic and social differences between the characters. What we see is *gestus*.

Within this framework, Jones' work can quickly begin to take on a certain degree of what one might be tempted to call amateurishness. That is not to criticize her tremendous talents as an actress. (Indeed, more will be said on this later.) Rather, the rapid shifts from character to character and the frequent employment of gestus as a kind of semaphore and indicator begins to raise one's awareness of the distance between Jones' presentational style and that of the traditional, Stanislavski-inspired "embodiment" expected of dramatic performance in the Broadway tradition. For all her talents, Jones seems to be indicating her characters more than embodying them—and this, in general, is often seen as negative—indeed, it is something an acting coach might instruct a student to change. There is perhaps no greater indication of the pervasiveness of this perception than Isherwood's attempt to implore viewers not to cast this judgment on Jones:

Just don't downgrade Ms. Jones's talent to a mere gift for impressions, an actor's stunt. A natural affinity for precise impersonation can only be developed into a tool of artistic expression through hard work enriched with empathy for the complicated souls behind the colorful sounds. Proof that Ms. Jones has put her actorly gifts in service to something larger than self-display is found in her writing for these fully imagined characters, which is lively, compassionate, mildly sardonic and smart.[30]

Tellingly, Isherwood invokes Jones' power as a writer as a means of counteracting any claims that she falls short as a performer. But what some might see as a shortcoming of Jones' performance, Brecht describes as the very building blocks of a politically engaged theatre. In his famous essay "The Street Scene," Brecht invokes a thought-experiment as a means of describing the ideal aims of an actor in the epic theatre:

It is comparatively easy to set up a basic model for epic theatre. For practical experiments I usually picked as my example of completely simple, 'natural' epic theatre an incident such as can be seen at any street corner: an eyewitness demonstrating to a collection of people how a traffic accident took place. The bystanders may not have observed what happened, or they may simply not agree with him, may 'see things a different way'; the point is that the demonstrator acts the behavior of driver or victim or both in such a way that the bystanders are able to form an opinion about the accident.[31]

The characteristics of the man describing the accident, Brecht contends, are the same as those of an actor in the epic theatre. Like Brecht's ideal actor, the man in the street scene doesn't wish to engross the other bystanders in an enthralling story; he means to objectively convey an event that has occurred, using elements of acting and impersonation only to assist in illustrating that event. His is what Brecht elsewhere calls a scientific approach; he is a reporter more than a storyteller. Thus, he does not aim to embody the various players in the crash he has witnessed, to penetrate their individuality and psychology; he merely wishes to indicate their role in the event as a whole. "His demonstration," Brecht explains, "would be spoilt if the bystanders' attention were drawn to his powers of transformation. He has to avoid presenting himself in such a way that someone calls out 'What a lifelike portrayal of chauffeur!'"[32] The means of embodiment Brecht's hypothetical witness has at his disposal are

---

[30] Isherwood, par. 9.

[31] Brecht, 121.

[32] Ibid., 122.

essentially a primitive form of *gestus*: "The demonstrator's purpose determines how thoroughly he has to imitate. Our demonstrator need not imitate every aspect of his characters' behavior, but only so much as gives a picture."[33]   Shifting his persona quickly from that of one player to another, he establishes each character with a distinctive gesture, motion, or tone of voice (the witness may demonstrate, says Brecht, "whether the voice was an old man's or an old woman's, or merely whether it was high or low") so that he may then jump back and forth between them to convey their interactions.[34]

In short, the scenario in "The Street Scene" is a kind of primitive, unprofessional version of Jones' highly polished production.   Jones establishes each character, most notably with an accent but also with a distinct physicality, and then proceeds to convey their interactions, much like the witness in "The Street Scene," albeit at much greater length.   It would not be unfair, then, to call hers a scientific, reportorial approach. This may sound strange given her decision to present fictional material instead of the true-to-life substance of her actual interviews (not to mention the obvious sentimentality of many of her monologues), but the reference here is more in regards to performance style than written content. The epic theatre, wrote Brecht, "must report. It must not believe that one can identify oneself with our world by empathy."[35]   Like Brecht's hypothetical witness, Jones intends to convey, single-handedly, a complex event so that the other onlookers may form a judgment about what transpired.   To do so, she must essentially extricate herself from the performance—and from the expectations of a specifically Broadway audience.   To realize the force of the expectation that a Broadway actor will become one and the same with the character he or she is presenting, we need only remember the terms of Brantley's praise for Meryl Streep in *Mother Courage*: Ms. Streep, he records, "blurs the lines between Meryl and Mother," such that it is laudably "hard to distinguish the dancer from the dance."[36] But Jones manages to sidestep any such expectation, always standing just outside her characters. There is never any thought that Jones has truly "become" any of her persona: she moves too quickly and too drastically between them. (As Isherwood says, "Now, here they are before us, those strangers who pique our interest and pass by... And all inhabit the remarkable person of Sarah Jones".)[37]   Instead, Jones is now

---

[33] Ibid., 123.
[34] Ibid., 123.
[35] Ibid., 25.
[36] Brantley, "Mother, Courage, Grief, and Song," par. 4.
[37] Isherwood, par. 3.

presenting a Vietnamese character, now presenting a Jamaican one. The thrust of the show lies in the contrasts and interactions between the figures, with Jones the performer essentially remaining outside each persona.

What Jones manages to achieve is nothing short of Brecht's famous "alienation effect"—the result that is meant to be attained when one applies the techniques outlined in "The Street Scene" to a theatrical context. As Brecht explains in his famous "Alienation Effects in Chinese Acting," actors in the epic theatre should aim to present "quite clearly somebody else's repetition of the incident: a representation, even though an artistic one."[38] Going on:

> The performer shows that this man is not in control of himself, and he points to the outward signs... Among all the possible signs certain particular ones are picked out, with careful and visible consideration... The coldness comes from the actor's holding himself remote from the character portrayed.[39]

The result, essentially, is a separation of actor and character, an unhinging of what is perhaps the most fundamental illusion at the heart of traditional theatre. For the actor in the epic theatre, writes Brecht, "at no moment must he go so far as to be wholly transformed into the character played... His feelings must not at bottom be those of the character, so that the audience's may not at bottom be those of the character either. The audience must have complete freedom here."[40] (Liberated of what Brecht considered the encumbrance of mistaking a theatrical character for a real person—and thereby associating or sympathizing with him or her on a human, or psychological level—audience members could become free to bring their unclouded, rational judgment to bear on the situation. "Feelings are private and limited," Brecht would write. "Against that the reason is fairly comprehensive and to be relied on."[41] For Brecht, the end result would be to enable audience members to better see the operations of class and economic factors at work in society by presenting them in an objective, unemotionalized arena.

For Jones, the use of the alienation effect serves other ends, but it remains an essential component of her production nonetheless. Jones the actress is clearly always present in the mind of the audience and, in this

---

[38] Brecht, 93.
[39] Ibid., 93.
[40] Ibid., 193-194.
[41] Ibid., 15.

way, kept distinct from the characters on stage. Unlike other solo performers, Jones in fact promotes this separation throughout her production. Previous performers like Whoopi Goldberg were known for donning elaborate costumes or wigs during their performances—for embedding themselves inside each new character, as in the Stanislavskian tradition. Jones utilizes costumes as well; she dons a tweed sports coat for one character, a baseball cap for another, a Muslim headscarf for another. But ultimately she does not attempt, at any point, to truly disguise herself. She relies instead on variance in voice, posture, and movement. Her face, however—the same face that creates the centerpiece of the poster for the production—remains largely unchanged from character to character. Despite radical shifts in age, gender, and nationality, Sarah Jones the performer remains visible at the center of each persona. "Effortlessly and swiftly shape-shifting across lines of gender, age, race and physical type, with only minimal (uncredited) costume assists, Jones provides the thread that stitches her diverse characters together," writes Rooney.[42] As a result, we, the audience, are always conscious of Sarah Jones, the actress, presenting us with a character.

The purpose of Jones' alienation from her own characters is, as with Brecht, highly political. Like Brecht, Jones wishes her audience to draw conclusions from her production, not simply react to it on an emotional level. As cited earlier, she has gone so far as to craft a kind of mission statement for her production—although, ironically, Jones' declaration, which includes the idea that "we are all much more connected than any of us realize," conveys precisely the sort of message Brecht meant to combat through the alienation effect.[43] Brecht speaks at length against just such a worldview in "Alienation Effects in Chinese Acting":

> The bourgeois theatre emphasized the timelessness of its objects. Its representation of people is bound by the alleged 'eternally human'... All its incidents are just one enormous cue, and this cue is followed by the 'eternal' response: the inevitable, usual, natural, purely human response. An example: a black man falls in love in the same way as a white man.[44]

The problem with such an approach, says Brecht, is that it is fundamentally "unhistorical," systematically erasing all the detail that he saw as most important in understanding how society works: history, class,

---

[42] Rooney, par. 4.
[43] "Sarah Jones Performs in NYC," par. 3.
[44] Brecht, 96-97.

power.[45] It essentially prohibits actors from any attempt at "demonstration of a custom which leads to conclusions about the entire structure of a society at a particular time."[46]

But we must be careful not to underestimate the sophistication of Jones' message or her purpose in a production like *Bridge and Tunnel*. The sentimentality of Jones' online statement must be balanced against statements of another nature, recounted in interviews: "Every once in a while, you'll have an interaction with someone and there's an urgency about what they have to say. It might not be popular; they might not be a person with the sort of face you'd see on TV... Those encounters have always resonated with me... I want to hear the other side. I want to not be made so happy and so comfortable all the time."[47] The reconciliation of these two viewpoints—on the one hand what Brecht might call a mollifying universality and on the other what might be considered an almost Brechtian drive for the disquieting and uncomfortable—lies in Jones' perception of the current state of American society, particularly with regards to its treatment of immigrant populations. "To me, this is the painful irony of this moment: Going about your daily life is no longer acceptable," she told one interviewer.[48] She later elaborated: "We realized that not only did we have the September 10 issues to contend with but also the post-September 11 issues—the really nakedly racist and ethnically focused attacks on immigrants, particularly Muslims and people of Middle Eastern descent and Arabs."[49] Jones' purpose, in other words, is not merely to advocate for a kind of unhistorical, "feel-good" universality. For her, the kind of universality that Brecht saw as a means of justifying and propagating bourgeois society is in fact a *tool* for changing that same society: by giving voice to those she feels are marginalized and disenfranchised, she means to demonstrate the illusory nature of the unspoken assumptions of "difference" that undergird American racism and xenophobia and that keep immigrants under constant suspicion. From Jones' perspective, unhistorical universality is actually a radical concept, as it challenges the historically- and culturally-specific notions of difference that can prevent immigrants from "going about their daily lives," i.e. from fully taking part in the norms of bourgeois society. This is surely not a Brechtian agenda, as it ultimately offers only what we might call an expansion of the promises of bourgeois society, not a fundamental

---

[45] Ibid., 98.
[46] Ibid., 98.
[47] Jones in Shenk, "Don't Get Too Comfortable," par. 22.
[48] Ibid., par. 6.
[49] Jones in Chaddha, par. 7.

rewriting of it. Indeed, in *Bridge and Tunnel* one of Jones' characters declares "it may not be perfect, but we live in the best country in the world," a sentiment Jones has admitted to agreeing with in interviews.[50] But neither is Jones' purpose a simple matter of unthinking propaganda.

Despite its obvious sentimentality, Jones' political intent—like Brecht's—is fundamentally based more on reason than emotion. What she calls for in her performance and in her online mission statement is essentially a matter of first identifying and evaluating differences between characters and then weighing them against similarities; hence, the constant tension in Jones' performance between her content and her technique. The stories told by Jones' personas—tales of love, family, anger, and hardship—all embody the kind of universalist mentality decried by Brecht, i.e. "a black man falls in love in the same way as a white man." But they are presented amidst a flurry of historically-determined and class-specific instances of *gestus*, the product of Jones' study of different immigrant groups. The implicit question posed by Jones to her audience is: Which is more important here, the similarities inside or the exterior differences? Like Brecht, Jones has a particular conclusion in mind for her scientific experiment: namely, that we are more alike than different, irregardless of what the surface separations and current political tensions may be. To enable this kind of rational calculation, the alienation effect becomes essential to Jones. She cannot have her audience become too caught up in any one story or any one character that they lose sight of the larger experiment; and they must not be so overwhelmed with differences (as they might be were she to truly embody any one character in all his or her unique particularity) that they are unable to recognize the similarities. Just as Brecht aimed to use the alienation effect to help his audience step outside of their emotional concerns and see the larger historical forces at work in the world, so too does Jones wish to use the alienation effect to help her audience escape their emotional attachments or aversions to certain types and see the larger similarities between individuals. "The show," writes Rooney, "has been seamlessly fine-tuned to fold a broad range of real human experience into the single theme of marginalized people looking for acceptance, dignity and the right to express themselves."[51] It is a reapropriation of the alienation effect to be sure, but a usage nonetheless.

The question that remains is how Jones was able to utilize explicitly Brechtian techniques in an environment as unfriendly to Brechtian acting

---

[50] Shenk, par. 17.
[51] Rooney, par. 16.

as Broadway. Even with the growing popularity of Brecht's dramatic works in the decades since Marc Blitzstein's famous 1954 production of *Threepenny*, which ran on Off-Broadway for seven years, the auteur's ideas on acting and performance have remained particularly hard for Americans in general and Broadway audiences in particular to swallow. As a case in point, one may take the varied reactions to two recent competing Brecht productions in New York: the Roundabout Theatre's production of *The Threepenny Opera*, which opened on Broadway in April 2006, and the Public Theatre's production of *Mother Courage* during 2006's Shakespeare in the Park season. (While not strictly Broadway, the Public Theatre's Shakespeare in the Park productions traditionally utilize Broadway directors and designers, attract Broadway-caliber talent, and often transfer directly to Broadway.) While not entirely Brechtian, the Roundabout's *Threepenny Opera* did try to emulate the feel of the Berliner Ensemble's work, with painted signs, scene-setting titles, spoken asides, and cabaret-style songs that hold little relation to the plot. Writing in *The New York Times*, Ben Brantley would disparagingly remark that "this 'Threepenny' takes Brecht's notion of the theater of alienation to new self-defeating extremes."[52] In contrast, the Public's sought to connect with audiences in a much more traditional manner. Playwright Tony Kushner, in adapting the play, specifically sought out language that would help audiences better understand and identify with Brecht's characters. "Mr. Kushner's solution," writes Jonathan Kalb, "was to sacrifice the text's antique echoes and concentrate instead on conversational flow, the thrust and clarity of situations, and the play's humor, which he said was in danger of seeming 'quaint' these days. Serious as its story is, 'Mother Courage' actually contains a lot of humor, mostly of an awkward and biting sort that Mr. Kushner has deliberately adjusted."[53] As for the alienation effect, director George C. Wolfe made clear he found it irrelevant to today's theatrical world. "One of Brecht's preoccupations," Kalb continues, "was with what he called the 'alienation effect'... Such concerns are outmoded today, Mr. Wolfe said."[54]

The resulting reviews speak volumes as to the status of Brechtian production choices, as opposed to Brechtian plays, in a Broadway environment. The Roundabout's *Threepenny Opera* was generally deemed a failure. "This is one party where the hangover begins almost as soon as the evening does," writes Brantley.[55] *Mother Courage*, in contrast,

---

[52] Brantley, "*Threepenny Opera* Brings Renewed Decadence to Studio 54," par. 5.
[53] Kalb, par. 9.
[54] Ibid., par. 22.
[55] Brantley, "*Threepenny Opera* Brings Renewed Decadence to Studio 54," par. 3.

while not the subject of overwhelming praise, was evaluated favorably, with lead actress Meryl Streep in particular receiving glowing reviews.

> If you ever wanted to watch one willowy human being lift a 12-ton play onto her shoulders and hold it there for hours, even as her muscles buckle and breath comes short, join the line of hopefuls waiting at the Delacorte Theater in Central Park for cancellations to see Meryl Streep burning energy like a supernova in the title role of Bertolt Brecht's "Mother Courage and Her Children."[56]

It is easy to see how in such an environment Brechtian acting technique, with its emphasis on gestus and alienation, would have a hard time taking hold. As discussed previously, the purpose of the alienation effect in acting is to counteract or intercept the natural (Brecht might say socially or historically created) human impulse towards identification with individuals; historical and social forces, not individuals, are at the center of Brecht's plays, just as they are at the center of society in the Marxist estimation. "The epic theatre is chiefly interested in the attitudes which people adopt towards one another, wherever they are socio-historically significant," Brecht wrote. "It works out scenes where people adopt attitudes of such a sort that the social laws under which they are acting spring into sight."[57] Combined with *gestus*, the alienation effect strives to make this clear: as the alienation effect severs any ties to individual characters, gestus points towards the larger forces at work behind each individual's actions. Brecht's theories of performance are in every way connected to a Marxist understanding of society, and not to the individual.

This is understandably a difficult paradigm for most Broadway audiences to accept. Insofar as Broadway has an ideology or philosophy, it is inimitably tied-in to that of America as a whole. In his social history of the American musical, *Our Musicals, Ourselves*, John Bush Jones notes that, historically, Broadway shows "have mirrored the concerns and lifestyles of middle Americans, their primary audience. The reality of commercial theatre dictates that, no matter how brilliant or artistic, if a show doesn't interest or entertain its audiences, it won't run long enough to make back its investment."[58] Insofar as either can be spoken of generally, Broadway, like America, is decidedly individualist. Indeed, no matter how critical they may be of capitalism, the great Broadway dramas

---

[56] Brantley, "Mother, Courage, Grief, and Song," par. 1.
[57] Brecht, 86.
[58] Jones, *Our Musicals, Ourselves: A Social History of the American Musical Theatre*, 3.

have retained an individualist focus: *Death of a Salesman* is the story of an individual overlooked and trodden down by the capitalist system; *A Raisin in the Sun* is the story of one family's attempts to overcome America's inequities through their own strength of character. Even in the heyday of artists like Elia Kazan, a one-time member of the Communist Party, and Arthur Miller, who attended Communist Party meetings (but never joined), Broadway theatre retained an emphasis on individualism; Stella Adler was the great leader in Broadway acting techniques, not Brecht. There is perhaps nothing more unBrechtian than American method acting, with its supreme emphasis on understanding individual experience and trying to identify with, if not actually merge with, one's character. Broadway's bread and butter lies in individualism.

And that is precisely how Sarah Jones managed to "sneak" Brechtian acting techniques right onto Broadway—for there is an individual at the center of *Bridge and Tunnel*: Sarah Jones. One could easily make the argument that the traditional Broadway musical, with its conventional character types and pre-patterned plot, has nothing more to do with individualism than the typical Chinese opera, where archetypal characters follow traditional storylines. But there is another kind of individualism at the heart of the Broadway musical: that of the virtuosic showman. Whether it is a mesmerizing tap dancing solo, a difficult patter song, or a resounding voice, the Broadway musical centers on the display of individual talent. (Witness the Broadway success of 1996's *Bring in Da Noise, Bring in Da Funk*, which featured little more than two hours of Savion Glover's dynamic tap-dancing.) This is the tradition into which Jones fits. Her virtuosic talents of impersonation and transformation in effect act as a cover for the alienation she achieves from her characters. Indeed, issues of skill and unique, unreplicatable ability are the driving concerns of nearly every material written about *Bridge and Tunnel*. The show's promotional webpage itself advertises Jones's "dazzling virtuosity."[59] Rooney's review in *Variety* similarly calls Jones' talents "dazzling,"[60] while Isherwood raves, "These are technical skills that invite gasps of admiration, and deserve them. Admire, please. Gasp and applaud to your heart's content."[61] Even audience members point to Jones' virtuosic talents in remarking on the show. "Extraordinary performance… We should expect more amazing stuff from this very feeling [sic] lady," writes one commentator on the audience response section of *The New York*

---

[59] "Bridge and Tunnel."
[60] Rooney, par. 1.
[61] Isherwood, par. 8.

Times website.[62]   Another recent audience member wonders, "Where can someone learn how to do this? Only on the streets of the city. Only in New York. But they'd better be good because NO ONE could pull this off by themselves. Or, can they?"[63]   Jones, it seems, is not simply a performer; she is a woman capable of accomplishing impossible feats of impersonation.

Indeed, were it not for Isherwood's claims that Jones is "an astonishing mimic with an uncanny ability to alter the texture, color and volume of her voice and even the shape of her body," one has to wonder whether his plea that audience members not "downgrade Ms. Jones's talent to a mere gift for impressions, an actor's stunt" would carry any weight.[64]   It seems reasonable to conclude that were *Bridge and Tunnel* not a one-woman show, or were Jones not such a talented performer, the piece would never have made it to Broadway. An ensemble of fourteen different performers, each merely changing the tone of their voice or the arch of their back to indicate their characters, would be a completely different production. It would be, perhaps, a true Brechtian production, but not one that would likely satisfy Broadway's patrons.   The thrill, for Broadway's individualist-minded customers, is to see the feat of Sarah Jones the individual performing (or, rather, indicating) fourteen characters herself— hence, the astonished claim that "no could pull this off by themselves." In *Bridge and Tunnel*, Brecht's Marxist techniques have essentially been harnessed into an individualist framework, wherein the performer's great ability to *present* characters (rather than *embody* them) is the attraction. So much for Brecht's declaration that "the demonstrator need not be an artist."[65]

Whether or not one views *Bridge and Tunnel* as a triumphant, if perhaps unintentional, exercise in bringing Brechtian techniques to Broadway depends on one's definition of such success. As a pure exercise in Brechtian acting, unencumbered by traditional, individualist concerns, it is perhaps a failure (though one cannot say if it was ever meant to be such an exercise). It is certainly unlikely to usher in an era of wider interest in Brechtian acting on Broadway, masked as Brecht's techniques are under the guise of Jones' individual virtuosity. Nor is it likely to prompt any reconsiderations of Brecht's own agenda as a writer and a theorist, as Jones' own intentions as an artist are rarely in line with Brecht's—and often stand in sharp opposition to his ideas. And yet, as a utilization of

---

[62] "Very Sharp," par. 1.
[63] "Bravo, Sarah!" par. 1.
[64] Isherwood, par. 9.
[65] Brecht, 122.

Brechtian elements within a Broadway framework, Jones' performance is arguably one of the more successful productions of late. More so than other solo performers, and far more so than most ensemble productions, Jones manages to successfully bring the alienation effect to a Broadway stage, presenting rather than embodying her characters, and maintaining her presence as a performer distinct from her characters throughout the entire two-hour production. What's more, she uses these techniques to political ends, albeit of an unBrechtian variety. Jones essentially asks her audience to rationally consider whether the differences between characters truly outweigh their similarities as human beings in search of such grand ideals as love, companionship, and meaning—and whether this implied universality should radically alter the exclusions and differences that Jones sees in American society, particularly in regards to our treatment of immigrants. In communicating this message, Jones specifically does *not* ask audience members to feel sympathy with her characters; rather, she asks them to think about and consider their situation and the situation of society more generally—much in the vein, if not the political spirit, of Brecht. Speaking about her own artistic process, Jones' explicitly focuses on the intellectual over the emotional. "I hate it when actors go 'Oh yes, I was channeling it. It moved right through me.' I'm not saying that I'm channeling anything, but I instantly can find their perspective," she says of her means of finding characters.[66] Perhaps it is not exactly what Brecht had in mind when he sought to conquer the Broadway stage in the mid-twentieth century. But for the theorist who wrote that a good performer "must not 'cast a spell' over anyone.' He should not transport people from normality to 'higher realms,'" perhaps it might be good enough.[67]

Works Cited

Brantley, Ben. "Threepenny Opera Brings Renewed Decadence to Studio 54." 21 April, 2006. *NYTimes.com* <http://theater2.nytimes.com/2006/04/21/ theater/reviews/21thre.html>. (9 August, 2006).
—. "Mother, Courage, Grief, and Song." 22 August, 2006. *NYTimes.com* <http://theater2.nytimes.com/2006/08/22/theater/reviews/22moth.htm> (23 August, 2006).
"Bravo, Sarah!" 31 January, 2006. *NYTimes.com*

---

[66] Jones in Kennedy, "One Woman, Many Voices" par. 2.
[67] Brecht, 122.

<http://theater2.nytimes.com/rnr/theater/rnr_read.html?_r=2&fid=.f868
d34&id=1124987588913&html_title=Bridge%20%26%20Tunnel%20
%28Play%29&tols_title=Bridge%20%26%20Tunnel%20%28Play%2
9&byline=Charles%20Isherwood&oref=slogin&oref=login>
(12 August, 2006).

Brecht, Bertolt. "Alienation Effects in Chinese Acting." *Brecht onTheatre: The Development of an Aesthetic.* Ed. and Trans. John Willett. New York: Hill and Wang, 1957. 91-99.

—. "Conversation with Bert Brecht." *Brecht on Theatre: The Development of an Aesthetic.* Ed. and Trans. John Willett. New York: Hill and Wang, 1957. 14-17.

—. "Last Stage: Oedipus." *Brecht on Theatre: The Development of an Aesthetic.* Ed. and Trans. John Willett. New York: Hill and Wang, 1957. 24-25.

—. "Notes to Die Rundköpfe und Die Spitzköpfe." *Brecht on Theatre: The Development of an Aesthetic.* Ed. and Trans. John Willett. New York: Hill and Wang, 1992. 104-106.

—. "On Gestic Music." *Brecht on Theatre: The Development of an Aesthetic.* Ed. and Trans. John Willett. New York: Hill and Wang, 1992. 104-106.

—. "A Short Organum for the Theatre." *Brecht on Theatre: The Development of an Aesthetic.* Ed. and Trans. John Willett. New York: Hill and Wang, 1957. 179-208.

—. "The Street Scene." *Brecht on Theatre: The Development of an Aesthetic.* Ed. and Trans. John Willett. New York: Hill and Wang, 1957. 121-129.

—. "On The Use of Music in an Epic Theatre." *Brecht on Theatre: The Development of an Aesthetic.* Ed. and Trans. John Willett. New York: Hill and Wang, 1992. 84-90.

—. "Theatre for Pleasure of Theatre for Instruction." *Brecht on Theatre: The Development of an Aesthetic.* Ed. and Trans. John Willett. New York: Hill and Wang, 1957. 69-76.

"Bridge   and   Tunnel."   2006.   *Broadway.com*
<http://www.broadway.com/gen/Show.aspx?si=504657> (7 August
2006).

Chaddha, Anmol. "I Am a Poet Too." Fall 2003. *Colorlines Magazine*
<http://www.findarticles.com/p/articles/mi_m0KAY/is_3_6/ai_108693
824> (2 October, 2006).

Gutman, Les. "Sarah Jones Brings Her Downtown Hit to Broadway."
2004. *Curtainup.com*
<http://www.curtainup.com/bridgeandtunnel.html>

(26 September, 2006).

Isherwood, Charles. "The Voices Inside the Boarder but Outside the Margins." 27 January, 2006. *NYTimes.com* <http://theater2.nytimes.com/2006/01/27/theater/reviews/27brid.html?adxnnl=1&adxnnlx=1157368658-3yaAHJm7OpcqoDU75q9 HDg> (6 August 2006).

Jones, John Bush. *Our Musicals, Ourselves: A Social History of the American Musical Theatre.* Hanover: Brandeis UP, 2003.

Kalb, Jonathan. "Still Fearsome, Mother Courage Gets a Makeover." 6 August 2006. *NYTimes.com* <http://www.nytimes.com/2006/08/06/theater/06kalb.html?ex=1312516800&en=77215f124584885f&ei=5088&partner=rssnyt&emc=rss> (10 August 2006).

Kennedy, Mark. "One Woman, Many Voices." 28 March, 2004. *SarahJonesOnline.com* <http://www.sarahjonesonline.com/press/AP2.htm> (12 August, 2006).

Rooney, David. "Bridge and Tunnel." 26 January, 2006. *Variety.com* <http://www.variety.com/review/VE1117929367?categoryid=33&cs=1> (6 August 2006).

"Sarah Jones Performs in NYC." 15 January, 2004. *SarahJonesOnline.com* <http://www.sarahjonesonline.com/bridge/sarah.htm> (7 August 2006).

Shenk, Joshua Wolf. "Don't Get Too Comfortable." July/August 2004. *Mother Jones* <http://www.mojones.com/arts/qa/2004/07/07_100.html> (4 October 2006).

"Very Sharp." 31 January, 2006. *NYTimes.com* <http://theater2.nytimes.com/rnr/theater/rnr_read.html?_r=2&fid=.f868d34&id=1124987588913&html_title=Bridge%20%26%20Tunnel%20%28Play%29&tols_title=Bridge%20%26%20Tunnel%20%28Play%29&byline=Charles%20Isherwood&oref=slogin&oref=login> (12 August, 2006).

Weisstein, Ulrich. "Brecht in America: A Preliminary Survey." *MLN* 78, no.4 (1963): 373-396.

Zinoman, Jason. "The Bridges and Tunnels that Bind." 8 February, 2004. *SarahJonesOnline.com* <http://www.sarahjonesonline.com/ press/ NYTIMESBandT.htm> (9 August 2006).

PART III:

A NEW CENTURY?
THE FUTURE OF BRECHT & BROADWAY?

THE RESISTIBLE RISE OF JERRY SPRINGER:
HOW AN OPERA REVIVED
THE POLEMICAL STAGE

DOMINIC SYMONDS

Should men be better? Should the world be changed?
Or just the gods? Or ought there to be none?[1]

Productions of Bertolt Brecht's plays have not been particularly
common in recent British theatre, at least since Margaret Eddershaw's
review of British Brecht productions ten years ago: the Royal National
Theatre's output has been restricted to the classics—*The Threepenny
Opera* (2003), *The Good Woman of Setzuan* (2001), *The Caucasian Chalk
Circle* (1997) and two productions of *Mother Courage* (1995, 1993). Only
its 1991 production of *The Resistible Rise of Arturo Ui* with Antony Sher
and the Donmar Warehouse's futuristic *Threepenny Opera* from 1994
really stand out.

This is a situation that seems somewhat surprising given the accepted
significance of Brecht in the UK narrative of theatre. In the drama
curricula of schools, colleges and universities, Brecht competes only with
Shakespeare as a playwright and only with Stanislavski as a practitioner,
so influential and important is his work and theory. Furthermore, recent
canonic British figures are all seen as following the Brechtian mold—
Bond and Brenton, Churchill and Godber, even Kane and Ravenhill in the
90s. Each of these, and therefore implicitly the tradition of quality British
theatre in the late 20th century, has taken on something of a neo-Brechtian
aesthetic, linking recognisable political issues to a bold theatrical style. As
a result, a certain use of "Brechtian" "devices" has become somewhat
expected in new British theatre, and a generation of theatre practitioners
has grown up using the vocabulary of this aesthetic. For a post-1956
theatre whose identity contrasted itself with conventional, middle-class,

---

[1] Brecht, *The Good Person of Setzuan*, 111.

linear, Aristotelian drama, Brechtian theatre has been the way that theatre is "done." Brecht*ian*, yes; so why not *Brecht's*?

2006 marks the 50th anniversary of Bertolt Brecht's death, and this season the situation seems rather different. A survey of London's theatre listings seems to confirm him as a major canonic figure on the mainstream British stage. Productions of *Galileo*, *Mother Courage* and *The Caucasian Chalk Circle* have all been scheduled at the Royal National Theatre, a major outdoor production of *The Caucasian Chalk Circle* is being staged by The Steam Industry at Tower Bridge, and the English Touring Theatre is taking *Mother Courage* to the regional theatres. It is not only the classic plays that are being celebrated: the newly revamped Young Vic is hosting a "Big Brecht Fest," with four new translations of lesser known plays and episodes: *A Respectable Wedding*, *Señora Carrar's Rifles*, *The Jewish Wife*, *How Much is your Iron*, and the nearby Royal Festival Hall on London's South Bank is presenting "Brecht's Poetic Legacy."

In his memorial year such an abundance of Brecht's own writing might be expected; nevertheless, we should ask if the otherwise scant representation of Brecht's work on the British stage reveals his theatre to be passé. *Should* we expect Brecht's plays to be staged nowadays, or even taught in the classroom? As the immediate presence of his theatre recedes to a historical perspective, does the new location of his work become ever more removed from the world that shaped it and with which it negotiated? "Is there not something itself profoundly unBrechtian in the attempt to reinvent and revive some 'Brecht for our times,'"[2] asks Jameson, a view that recognizes the contextual specificity of Brechtian theatre not only in sociohistorical terms but also dramaturgical.

Brecht's legacy, as at least the British system sees it, is to have made theatre valuable by giving plays a political function through a concomitant revisioning of theatrical form. Before we unproblematically accept this representation, however, the substance of both function and form requires some examination.

Ostensibly, Brecht's politics are manifest (left wing Marxist), and are very much situated within a particular sociopolitical tension (the rise to power of the fascist right in Germany). Nevertheless, they are complicated by his relatively late introduction to Marx, his somewhat nonchalant activism, and contradictions both within his plays[3] and his life.[4] These

---

[2] Jameson, *Brecht and Method*, 5.
[3] See Wright's analysis of *Puntila*'s Matti in *Postmodern Brecht: a Re-Presentation*, 57-59.
[4] For a detailed interpretation of the complex Brecht, see Fuegi's controversial biography. Perhaps the most obvious contradiction, however, is his renunciation of

contextual matters contribute a subtlety to the ways in which we must decode Brechtian theatre and its legacy. The immediate political context of Brecht's theatre has nowadays a historical rather than a contemporary significance. Furthermore, Brecht's own political agency (his evasion of military service, his exile and his 1947 flight from the US) and even the content of his writing reveals Brecht's political commitment to be philosophical rather than confrontational.

The dramaturgical aspect of Brecht's theatre, identified as epic rather than propagandistic and his strongest legacy, is perhaps less problematically able to relocate itself for the use of later generations. Brecht's aesthetic famously attempts to create in the audience a feeling of "alienation,"[5] which Wright explains as the "theatricalisation of experience."[6] This theatricalisation "does not do away with identification" (as might be assumed from Brecht's anti-Aristotelian stance), "but examines it critically."[7] A vision of the world and our place in it is revealed such that the spectator is able to conceptualise his/her habitual social self as alienated. In epic theatre

> both actors and directors are invited, even incited, to play a part in the construction of a narrative other than the one that the received version of history proposes.[8]

The enablement of such an objectifying stance has been discussed in detail elsewhere and the reader is referred to Hilda Brown's discussion of perspective[9] to expand upon the complex experiential dynamic of the spectator in epic theatre. This dramaturgy, however, demands in its understanding a synthesis with the political context, and with the political and social act of "reading" or engaging with the works. As Jameson discusses, the nature of epic theatre offers a "process of transcendence"[10] wherein "the frame and focus of the representation suddenly enlarge to include the world itself, and Being."[11] This is reminiscent of Brecht's own

---

Communism in front of the House Un-American Activities Commission in 1947, an ironic postscript to Galileo's comparable renunciation in the eponymous play.

[5] In this respect Brooker (79) quite rightly recognises Brecht's alienation to effect a "de-alienation" in Marxist terms.

[6] Wright, 99.

[7] Ibid., 19.

[8] Ibid., 2.

[9] Brown, *Leitmotiv and Drama: Wagner, Brecht and the Limits of 'Epic' Theatre*, 1-24 and 68-107.

[10] Jameson, 145.

[11] Ibid., 147.

comment locating the value of theatre in reaching beyond the confines of its own interiority: "Every artist knows that subject matter in itself is in a sense somewhat banal, featureless, empty and self-sufficient. It is only the social gest—criticism, craftiness, irony, propaganda, etc.—that breathes humanity into it."[12]

As this year's glut of London productions shows and as the curriculum idolatry implies, however, the way in which Brecht's plays *nowadays* reach beyond their subject matter may have subtly changed. Do Brechtian productions *still* reveal the social self as alienated and thereby enable us to see our true situation in the world? It seems to me that instead, contemporary perspectives on Brecht (for example, as a canonic writer, in memorial celebration of his death, or even as the progenitor of a legacy) indulge a self-referentiality that insistently fetishises his personality or the surface trappings of his theatrical style. Our understanding of the gestalt relationship of the Brechtian text with its context risks being occluded by the more immediately obvious techniques of Brecht's theatrical style and their attendant jargon (*Verfremdungseffekt*, *Gestus*, *Episch*), devices which Hilda Brown calls "comparatively ephemeral."[13]

How effectively canonized classics refracted through a cult of personality can achieve an ideological unveiling is, I think, questionable, since they themselves remain trapped by the ideology they would seek to reveal. On the one hand, audience anticipations colour reception as they "encounter the text via the framework of the prefabricated ideological categories of modern literary criticism"[14]; on the other hand, as Wright recognizes, "epic elements [are] too easily absorbed into the old theatre"[15] where they are used not as *gestic* signifiers but as mere indicators of a theatrical style. Thus a "Brechtian" aesthetic has become "the universal language of contemporary theatre, irrespective of its ideological origin."[16] In becoming institutionalised as "great" "art," which this portentous rhetoric with its assumptions of "timelessness" and "universality" effects, the contemporary and particularly practical efficacy of a Brechtian theatre risks becoming diluted.

I have taken some time to interrogate received assumptions about Brecht's theatre (its political function and its theatrical style) because I think careful analysis reveals a subtle shift in practice and rhetoric that has

---

[12] Willett in *Brecht Collected Plays: Six*, 105.

[13] Ibid., 18.

[14] Herhoffer, "Bertolt Brecht: An Aesthetics of Conviction?" 224.

[15] Wright, 30.

[16] Ibid., 113, citing Wirth, "Vom Dialog zum Diskurs: Versuch einer Synthese der nachbrechtschen Theaterkonzepte."

disempowered its dialectical potential. If we can no longer count on revivals of Brecht's plays removed from their original context to "change the social reality"[17]—an expectation of Brechtian theatre that, frankly, has always seemed rather disingenuous—it is not to say that Brecht's theoretical agenda cannot be revisited in order to reinvigorate his philosophical dialectics. In this respect we should not forget that a central tenet of his theory involved remodelling the apparatuss—"pedagogical refunctioning"[18]—a fundamental strategy for disrupting the theatre-going experience and thereby provoking critical thought. Brecht himself advocated that the apparatus of opera should be challenged in his notes accompanying *Mahagonny*,[19] though Wright wryly observes that his own epic theatre "exposes the contradictions [of society] while perpetuating the institution which produces them."[20] Recently, however, the high-profile success of *Jerry Springer: The Opera* on the London stage has done just that not only with opera but also with the West End musical and the trash TV talk show, and it is the ensuing provocation of critical thought, public debate and political exchange that reveals the still active potential of Brechtian dialectics and makes this show a powerful example of (neo-) Brechtian theatre.

Jerry Springer: The Opera is a musical, inspired by the US talk show *The Jerry Springer Show* and conceived by composer Richard Thomas in 2000.

> "I'd get back from jobs late at night and sit watching Jerry on cable," he recalls. "There were always six people screaming at each other with a crowd baying for blood; you couldn't understand what people were saying half the time. It struck me – that's opera."[21]

The piece was initially mounted in February 2001 at Battersea Arts Centre in London, a thriving venue for innovative works in development that are showcased and workshopped through "Scratch" performances. At this point in *JS:TO*'s inception, when it was entitled *How to Write an Opera about Jerry Springer*, the audience was invited to respond to an early performance draft of the show, which consisted simply of what is now the first act—an 'episode' of *The Jerry Springer Show* sung in the style of

---

[17] Ibid., 24.
[18] Giles, "Marxist Aesthetics and Cultural Modernity in *Der Dreigroschenprozeß*," 56.
[19] Willett and Mannheim, *Bertolt Brecht: Collected Plays*, Vol 2iii, 33-42.
[20] Wright, 13.
[21] Thomas in Sella, "Aria of the Lesbian Dwarf Diaper Fetishist," 50.

grand opera. Following this appearance, comedian Stewart Lee joined Thomas as co-writer of the libretto and lyrics, and two further draft versions were performed over the next two years, followed by a stint at the Edinburgh Fringe Festival. Success on the Fringe further encouraged Royal National Theatre director Nicholas Hytner's interest, and the show's full version was mounted at the (subsidised) RNT in 2003. Thereafter it transferred to the West End's (commercial) Cambridge Theatre, was scheduled to tour the regions, and was screened by the BBC in January 2005.

Crucially, however, *JS:TO* is *not* an opera, much as it carries some of the signifiers of the form: it is true to say that much of the vocal aesthetic is more characteristic of an operatic rather than a musical theatre sound; nevertheless it is not staged in an opera venue, and as such avoids the trappings of the institution and its ideological identity. On the other hand, its identity as a musical is complex: it shares few of the integrated techniques or expectations of the traditional model espoused by the likes of Rodgers and Hammerstein; nor does its provenance on the alternative stage afford it the same commercialised agenda as the megamusicals endemic to the West End stage. In this confusion of musical theatre and opera, as in the semiotics of the title, a battle between high and low art forms is announced and the very machinations of the apparatus centred as a focus of the show's content.

The Jerry Springer Show sung in the style of grand opera is, ostensibly, the full extent of act one. Jerry introduces several guests to his show, each of whom indulges in a confessional outpouring of their guilty secrets, desires or fantasies: Dwight is sleeping with both crack and dope addict Zandra and hermaphrodite Tremont, whilst his fiancée Peaches admits to urinating over strange men in public lavatories; Montel confesses to his fiancée Andrea a fetish for wearing diapers and defecating with fellow diaper fetishist Baby Jane; Shawntel's husband Chucky is disgusted by her poledancing but is exposed as being a member of the Ku Klux Klan. The format of these three scenes is presented as if the theatre audience is a part of the studio audience, and as such the episode itself is preceded by a lengthy warm up, and the individual scenes interspersed with mock commercial breaks. The show's chorus play additional members of the studio audience, who, as in the TV show, are extremely vocal. Their heckles, chants and interspersions are sung, as are the guests' and Warm-Up Man's lines; Jerry's dialogue is spoken throughout, and is written to mimic precisely the phrasing and tone of the real Jerry Springer. Indeed, a significant contribution to the humour of the musical is in its all but direct mimicry of recognisable features of *The Jerry Springer Show* and the presentation of these elements in operatic style: characters such as the head of security Steve, the audience chants "Je-rry, Je-rry" and typical idioms spoken (sung) by guests, such as "Talk to the hand loser cuz the face ain't listening!" are all familiar to viewers of the original talk show, whilst melismatic cadenzas, repetitious choral passages and reference to Jerry's "Inner Valkyrie" are all direct references to opera.[22]

Each of these referenced texts self-consciously inculcates its own specific implied audience. The consumption of source text *The Jerry Springer Show*, for example, works as (one example of) a counter-cultural object of attachment for a youth audience traditionally distanced from the mainstream. The antisocial behaviour of the depicted characters is celebrated, partly as a vicarious playing out of tensions, and partly as a carnivalesque subversion of accepted social behaviour. The characters themselves—and certainly their acts—are often seen as figures of ridicule, though they are associated with a certain constituency of American society that has a comparable representation in the UK. For the mainstream British public this constituency's affront to sociable behaviour is linked to a decline in public responsibility, educational standards, family values, and threatens to erode moral decency. Opera, on the other hand, for those who attach themselves to *The Jerry Springer Show*, is seen as unattainable, undesirable and elitist. The consumption of opera is associated with a comfortable and conservative middle class, the very constituency that sees itself as upholding moral decency etc.

So anomalous are the opposing referenced texts of *JS:TO* that (as with the term "rock opera") a negotiation of the middle ground is immediately invoked. Such a piece requires an audience to understand the sensibilities and languages of overtly popular texts (in this case *The Jerry Springer Show*) *as well as* high-brow cultural forms (opera). Needless to say, the process by which this set of anomalous signifiers can work in conjunction with each other is one that relies on its audience consuming both high and low texts. The existence of such an audience is testament to a sociocultural development in reception (which detractors may see as a degradation), together with significant preparatory texts that incorporate both high and low elements. We might mention Baz Luhrmann's *Romeo and Juliet* as a high-profile example of such a text, and should acknowledge that significant agents in this sociocultural development have been the mass

---

[22] In fact, the musical referencing of *JS:TO* does not limit itself to operatic style, including as it does musical theatre and pop references "from Herbert Howells (the theme-tune trio), to Sondheim (a swaggering paean to infantilisation), to Stevie Wonder (the glorious melismatic transvestite aria, 'I'm a Man')". (Picard, n.p.).

cultural forms (TV and film) that simultaneously promote artistic (high) and entertainment (low) imperatives.

In short, the status-aware sensibility of contemporary cultural audiences allows for a convergence of high and low aesthetics within the same text, in which convergence the paradox of a cultural hierarchy becomes the defining generator of meaning.

As both Springer and Hytner suggest in program notes for the RNT production, the stories of the show's guests resemble the dramatic tragedies of traditional opera, "universal issues, core human drama."[23] Nevertheless, in both TV show and musical this drama is side-stepped in favour of the stylistic resurfacing of its delivery. Given the episodic structure of the TV show there is also little opportunity for narrative or character to develop, and in this respect the placement of song resists the conventions of the Broadway or West End (integrated) musical, in which song is traditionally used as a developmental device within the dramaturgy. Indeed, although many of the songs are outpourings of heightened emotion, the only song in act one that resembles the sort of internalised monologue most familiar to the language of musical theatre is the Warm-Up Man's "The First Time I Saw Jerry," which is not a part of the content of the Jerry Springer episode, and which is sung directly to the audience. Though this backstage scene/song may allow us to relate to the characters of the Warm-Up Man and Jerry, we neither care nor commit our interest to the plights of the guests,[24] and if we empathise with any character, it is Jerry himself, replicating much the same relationship we have with the real Springer in the TV show, in which forum we have equally little empathy for the guests.

However, empathy is hardly the point in this text—nor is the plight of the working class characters depicted. Instead, we marvel at the wit and irony of the convergence of forms: the naughty delight of hearing obscenities sung to operatic music; the musical soundscape (which composer Richard Thomas has termed a "sonic canvas"[25]) that reflects the chaos of the studio set during *The Jerry Springer Show*; and the quite literal denigration of a high art form into an accessible commodity divested of its pretensions. As such, we neither commit ourselves to a relationship with the characters, nor does the music serve to engage us with their emotional trajectory. Instead, the musical language of *JS:TO* is

---

[23] Springer, Program notes for *Jerry Springer: The Opera*.
[24] Here I challenge Soto-Morettini.
[25] "I don't really view musical styles as styles – just as textures," Thomas says. "You've got your sonic canvas, and you've got all these amazing colors. And I like to paint bright" in Sella, 50.

functional, serving primarily as a referent to the style of the form that is pastiched, and secondarily serving to construct and consolidate a particular audience interaction with the text. Thus the surface rather than the content of the text becomes its signifying plane.

A referential use of signification has been noted as a feature of postmodern texts, incorporating the use of recognisable narrative, stylistic and thematic material and its reprocessing. In this context musical and performative styles are both particularly significant: the audience recognises idioms from both opera and trash TV and is able to translate the use of such material into an engagement with the text as commentary on the form. It is partly this idiomatic referencing that helps construct and consolidate a particular audience interaction with the text: much of the show's structural rhetoric is symptomatic of referencing assimilated speech patterns, rhyming meter etc. However, the relationship the audience has with the text is further aided by an internal rhetorical structure that uses many traditional musical theatre elements (Opening Number, "I Want" song, act one cliffhanger, etc.), but which uses them as effective epic devices.

Beyond this, the stand-up training of Lee has enabled the writers to develop the communicative strategies of comedy potential within the musical discourse of *JS:TO* by manipulating the structure of language. Interviewer Marshall Sella reveals that, for the authors, "beautiful rhythm in music is parallel to precise comic timing,"[26] and this is a sentiment expanded on by Thomas and Lee.[27]   The *JS:TO* script allows for (numerous) vulgarities, whose expletive nature renders them interchangeable as adjective, noun, verb, etc. Due to this, they can be positioned unproblematically at any point within a phrase with the effect that its rhythm can be manipulated to serve the comic timing.

This use of structural rhetoric maximises the grammar of musical theatre to divert the audience away from an engagement with the interior content of the narrative and into an engagement with the surface of the text. The ramifications of this for both audience and text are complex. The story becomes superficial: it is difficult to say that it *ceases* to exist, but its role changes to one of cipher (and with it the role of character). Accordingly, as we have implied, the audience's engagement is distanced, and directed instead towards the mechanics of referencing. The emphasis of receptive processing is located less around the *what* than the *how*: how is the material reinterpreted? The adaptation itself becomes part of the text,

---

[26] Sella, 50.
[27] Rose Bruford College Symposium (Thomas & Lee 2003, n.p.).

to the extent that it is the encounter of text B (the reinterpretation) in relation to text A (the original) that becomes a meaningful transaction in the audience's consciousness. The fact that the interior storyline becomes less significant in the communicative intent creates important shortcuts in the way in which the piece is constructed. The performance text is able to restrict itself to real-time interaction, for example, which Thomas and Lee recognise as a device that audiences have become familiarised to through TV culture, and which is again endemic of the referencing process. Here, informational or atmospheric "memory" is indexed through a real-time quotation: "When you're watching [TV], it's completely normal to be subjected to four or five different styles in a few minutes. So you can use that pacing, use short cuts, if you like, in order to build up a classic piece where you create space to expand."[28]

This expansion reminds us of the sort of epic magnification that Suvin and others claim for Brechtian theatre: Suvin talks of Auerbach's "figural interpretation," an allegorical "connection between two events or persons, the first of which signifies not only itself but also the second, while the second encompasses and fulfils the first."[29] We shall return to this use of allegory in due course, but for now it is enough to recognise the capacity to effect this within the postmodern language of referencing. Although we can see from a similar use of referencing in film that this is a trait of postmodern texts in general, the metaphorical transaction of music that we have already noted affords the musical a particular ability to exploit this, and in doing so to treat it as an epic device.

There are two claims we can make concerning such a use of referencing: the first is made by Kinkade & Katovich who suggest that postmodern pieces themselves become "stable cultural document[s]"[30] through their critique of previous texts.[31] The second claim is that the appropriation of a previous cultural text re-evaluates the perception of the original. It is tempting to say that this re-evaluation is an authentication of

---

[28] Thomas in Picard, "Jer-ry! Jer-ry! Jer-ry!"

[29] Suvin, *To Brecht and Beyond: Soundings in Modern Dramaturgy*, 173-174.

[30] Kinkade and Katovich, "Toward a sociology of Cult Films: Reading Rocky Horror," 203.

[31] The question this presents us with is, why does this not happen to *every* postmodern piece? We can justifiably claim that *The Rocky Horror Picture Show* (Kinkade & Katovich's focus) is a stable cultural document due to its ongoing appeal, and in the fervour of *JS:TO*'s recent success, we might bestow upon it a similar kudos, but perceptually at least, pieces such as *Forbidden Broadway* (which presents a similarly postmodern critique of Broadway shows) have achieved less status and stability, despite positive critical acclaim.

the original, and we can certainly see that the use of *The Jerry Springer Show* within a different cultural form (and particularly under the aegis of the Royal National Theatre) has the effect of magnifying its imprint on the contemporary cultural lexicon. In a similar way, many otherwise disposable texts have developed in cultural significance through second generation reflection (the iconographic soundtracks of the Tarantino movies, for example). However, the re-evaluation of the original text is not necessarily a step towards authentication, for instinctively we understand *JS:TO*'s particular convergence of anomalous texts as denigrating the status of opera more than it raises the status of *The Jerry Springer Show*. Instead, the former identity of both original texts becomes divested of their original signification(s) and in a way neutralised.

This discussion is particularly interesting in relation to act two of *JS:TO*, by which stage the identity of both *The Jerry Springer Show* and opera have been so neutralised. Now the piece attempts to use that neutral space to construct meaning within what has previously been the stylistic exercise of converting *The Jerry Springer Show* into grand opera. The cliffhanger of act one is that Jerry gets shot, which turns out to have been a ploy by Satan to transport Jerry first to Purgatory (act two) and then to Hell (act three), where he can resolve the chthonic battle between good and evil.

> Jerry: Ya know from time immemorial Heaven and Hell have been at war. But is there a way of reconciling the irreconcilable and give both parties a sense of closure and a chance to move on?[32]

That this happens within the narrative is really little more than a twist in the plot, a second gag to trump the stylistic convention of the first which has by now worn thin. However, the coup de grace of *JS:TO*, and the seed of not a little controversy, is the fact that the same characters from act one reappear as biblical figures in acts two and three: Satan is sacked Warm-Up Man Jonathan, Jesus is diaper fetishist Montel, Mary crack and dope addict Zandra, Adam klanman Chucky and Eve poledancer Shawntel, etc. This turn of events reverses the hollow perspective on the characters that has been constructed in act one, such that the ciphers become the ciphered.

It is in this layering of one world upon another that *JS:TO* realises Jameson's "process of transcendence,"[33] and here that we return to Auerbach's "figural interpretation" as the diegesis, internal world and social understanding of (audience) Self are brought into a relationship of

---

[32] Thomas and Lee, *Jerry Springer: The Opera.*
[33] Jameson, 145.

clarity that "inaugurate[s] the allegorical process itself."[34] The allegorical process as Jameson understands it moves beyond a simple use of allegory as clearly defined by Suvin[35] to have "symbolic as well as epistemological meaning"[36]; the very act of engaging in the allegorical transaction itself invokes and enables us to perceive our simultaneous engagement in the epic process of alienation (de-alienating ourselves).[37] The V-effect is "dialectical in its very form."[38]

In one sense it would be sufficient for *JS:TO*'s narrative allegory to expose the chthonic battle as mundane, to humanise the biblical characters and render trailer trash characters valuable human beings. This level of analysis would further enable us to recognise the show's criticism of trash TV and could easily be sited within a debate on commercial culture and exploitation. However, conflating the characters is really no more than the religious narrative already does (in Christ's hypostasis and the inheritance of the meek), and criticising popular culture for exploitation hardly shows groundbreaking insight. Crucially, however, and allowing it to serve its Brechtian epic function, the achievement of *JS:TO* is to reveal the religious narrative and its projection of our social Self as ideologically constructed. The layering of one world upon another reflects itself the process of our own allegorisation, our understanding of the piece in epic terms, which Hilda Brown refers to as a "network of perspectival devices which fan out over a drama, interacting to form dominant, authoritative or 'overarching' viewpoints."[39] In other words, due to the complex interplay of discordant references in act one that confounds institutionalised expectations of both popular TV (that it is puerile and meaningless) and opera (for instance that the subject matter is unquestionably worthy and dramatic, a term that itself is ideologically loaded with value implications),

---

[34] Ibid., 128.

[35] Suvin, 254.

[36] Jameson, 47; see also Wright, who refers to the Lacanian "Symbolic Order" (19-20).

[37] Jameson's abstraction allows us to clearly conceptualise the process and is worth noting in full: "The mediaeval four levels of meaning are both retained and complexified in the new scheme: they rose, as will be remembered, from the literal level, the historical fact (let us say, of the people of Israel coming up out of Egypt), to the allegorical level of Christ rising out of the grave and returning from Hell, and on to the twin signifying levels of the moral and the anagogical: the soul cleansing itself from sin in its conversion, and the human race facing its own collective resurrection in the Last Judgement," 128.

[38] Wright, 20.

[39] H. Brown, 3.

the introduction in act two of biblical references actually becomes more resonant.

> The show manages to drag profound metaphysical questions of humanity into the dirt – or perhaps it elevates Jerry Springer to the level of high philosophy. The distinction has been blurred beyond recognition.[40]

The invocation of divine characters is something we recognise in Brecht's own work, most obviously in the three visiting Gods of *The Good Person of Setzuan*, through which we might observe a similar perspectival space being opened up in the dramaturgy (and a similar epic dialectic being established). It is significant that by contrast to these incarnations of eastern religious figures, his perspective on Christianity is often critical, and in *The Threepenny Opera* and *Galileo* linked to corruption and ideological power. The earlier work's corrupt Peachum espouses the moralistic rhetoric of Christianity to recognisably religious intonations in the music; this, if we accept the common three-phase model of Brecht's career (Esslin, Suvin), represents a rather simplistic confrontation of institutionalised religion. *Galileo*'s confrontation of the Church is integral not only to the entire plot, but to the epic qualities of the play. The epicization clearly metaphorises Brecht's own artistic practice, but more importantly implicates the ideological ruling forces as a fundamental cause of the earth's ills. The specific target of Brecht's antagonism changed in each incarnation of the text, as for example Bentley[41] details; nevertheless, the spectator's experience is analogous in each case, in that s/he is inculcated on one or other side of a contemporary political issue, supportive of that ideological power or not. The self is perceived as social being.

Given that *Jerry Springer: The Opera* was named Best Musical at the Olivier Awards, the Evening Standard Awards, the What's On Stage Awards and the Critics' Circle Awards, we can consider it to have been accepted as a valuable new piece of art in what I have maintained is an epic model. Nevertheless, we must concede some space to the criticism of *JS:TO*, for which the show has gained its notoriety. Although the musical received little in the way of negative publicity during its initial stage runs (even at the RNT), the decision to broadcast a televised version in January 2005 provoked an enormous outcry. The musical has been lobbied insistently by Christian groups for its offensive language, derisive content and treatment of religious characters.

---

[40] Sella, 50.
[41] Bentley, *The Brecht Commentaries 1943-1980*, 183-214.

It is easy to see why the content of *JS:TO* might be found offensive. The cross-casting of characters is clearly provocative; the script has been claimed to have 8,283 swear words,[42] and all of the biblical characters talk (sing) in the vernacular of typical talk show guests; the character of Jesus admits to being "a bit gay" ("Satan and Jesus Spat," Act III); and Mary is referred to as having been "raped by an angel, raped by God" ("Adam and Eve and Mary," Act III).

The BBC received an unprecedented 55,000 complaints prior to its televising of the show and 8,000 afterwards. It was subsequently taken to court by the Christian Institute for breaching the guidelines of its Royal Charter and the human rights of Christians. TV lobby group mediawatch-uk challenged the BBC for breaching the Communications Act 2003, the terms of its Licence Agreement and its own Producers' Guidelines on language and religious sensibility. The media regulator Ofcom received a record 16,801 complaints, The British Board of Film Classification received seven requests to refuse the DVD a certificate, and high street stores Sainsbury's and Woolworths bowed to pressure to remove the product from shelves. Protestors gathered at the BBC's London headquarters in Wood Lane, where they proceeded to burn their TV licences; pressure groups published personal contact details of BBC executives, thereby exposing them to hate mail; and the controller of BBC Radio 3 resigned in protest.

In parliament the broadcast was the subject of Early Day Motions condemning it,[43] supporting it,[44] calling for the abolition of the Blasphemy Law,[45] criticising the BBC for screening it,[46] campaigning for Freedom of Expression for scriptwriters and producers[47] and finally standing for the rights of freedom of expression in the sale of the DVD.[48] Perhaps the general outcry is best expressed in the text of the first of these motions, "BBC and *Jerry Springer: The Opera*":

> That this house regards with dismay the decision by the BBC to broadcast *Jerry Springer: The Opera* on BBC2, causing widespread offence to Christians and those of other faiths by its mocking portrayal of Jesus

---

[42] Malvern, "West End Swears by Springer Success" and "Is This another Row for Springer, the Opera?"

[43] Donaldson, "BBC and Jerry Springer: The Opera."

[44] Harris, "BBC and Freedom of Expression."

[45] Harris, "BBC and the Abolition of the Blasphemy Law."

[46] Smyth, "BBC Policy on Content of Programmes."

[47] Cryer, "Freedom of Expression for Scriptwriters and Producers."

[48] Foster, "*Jerry Springer* DVD Withdrawal."

Christ, Holy Communion, and some of the central tenets of the Christian faith; condemns the show's juvenile and offensive use of repeated profanity in an attempt at humour; further notes that it is particularly serious that the show should have been transmitted by the publicly-funded national broadcaster and questions whether it places the Corporation in breach of its charter; laments the dismissal of Christian concerns by the Director General of the BBC; condemns the serious decline in general of the moral and spiritual content of programmes aired by the BBC; and calls on the Government to publicly rebuke the Corporation for its attack on the religion adhered to by over 70 per cent of the UK population and for its lowest common denominator approach to ethics in its attempts to chase ratings.[49]

The show was referred to on the floor of both parliamentary houses in several debates, including Commons discussion of the BBC Charter Renewal on 8th February, the Lords Blasphemy debate on 3rd March, the Future of the BBC in the Commons on 9th March and the Lords discussion of the Serious Organised Crime and Police Bill on the 14th March. Most significantly, it became a crucial part of policy discussion in the formulation of the Racial and Religious Hatred Act 2006. Here, a central tension was established between the institution of a Bill to outlaw religious intolerance, and the threat that such a law might contravene freedom of expression clauses in the European Bill of Human Rights. An Australian act of parliament was cited which "prohibits incitement to serious contempt, severe ridicule and so on, of a religion,"[50] under which terms a show such as *JS:TO* would be seen as unlawful; this raised the concern, expressed by opposition MP David Davis, that a similar Bill might

disproportionately curtail freedom of expression, worsen community relations as different religious and belief groups call for the prosecution of their opponents, create uncertainty as to what words or behaviour are lawful and lead to the selective application of the law in a manner likely to bring it into disrepute.[51]

In the Second Reading of the Racial and Religious Hatred Act 2006, Home Secretary Charles Clarke was clear to point out that "The Bill does not stop anybody telling jokes about religion, ridiculing religions or engaging in robust debate about religion. It will not stop people from

---

[49] Donaldson.

[50] Her Majesty's Government. "Racial and Religious Hatred Act 2006. Second Reading," Col. 670.

[51] Ibid., Col. 684.

proselytising and it will not curb artistic freedom."[52] Ultimately, the final document schedules an amendment to the Public Order Act 1986 explicitly relating to theatrical productions:

> If a public performance of a play is given which involves the use of threatening words or behaviour, any person who presents or directs the performance is guilty of an offence if he intends thereby to stir up religious hatred.[53]

In Marxist terms the contradiction Brecht has always faced is that relating to Marx's Eleventh Thesis on Feuerbach. This posits that (specifically) philosophy but by extension art and theatrical texts, no matter how didactic, are incapable of changing the world because of their impotent position in the superstructure. We see from the relationship between Brecht's own plays and social change that for all his claims, epic theatre appears to offer little in the way of direct political engagement. There are relatively few shows that have caused the controversy of *JS:TO* and provoked the explicit response of a state power. Having said this, we must be careful not to simplify our discussion by claiming that a simple cause and effect transaction operates in this case between artwork and policy. Despite its clearly offensive nature (deliberately provocative at that), the show's theatrical incarnations received nothing like the same level of attention; televising of *The Jerry Springer Show* itself (with similar levels of profanity and explicit discussion of unconventional fetishes) attracts relatively little hysteria, though it does have the reputation of being "trash" TV; and similar manifestations of counter-cultural free expression on TV have not outraged the public to anything like the same extent. Why has the TV screening of *JS:TO* been so threatening that it has earned *JS:TO* such notoriety and (for the purposes of this study) a Brechtian mantle?

The reason, it seems to me, is to do with the contemporary revisioning of the epic apparatus that *JS:TO* has effected; one which takes into its service, in a way that we sense Brecht would have applauded, the technological vehicles of mass communication and propaganda, and which coerces the engagement of those who wield real political power. This new epic apparatus works on a fundamentally dialectical model, and importantly activates the dialectical process on several different levels—textually, symbolically and (meta-)theatrically.

---

[52] Ibid., Col. 668.
[53] "Racial and Religious Hatred Act 2006."

The dialectic that works within the text of *JS:TO* is the humiliation in Marxist terms of the divine, such that the proletariat are seen to share human values with a higher order, and such that received Christian doctrine is exposed as ideological.[54] Simultaneously, devices of postmodern referencing and the revisioning of several cultural apparatuses (commercial musical theatre, opera, TV talk show) draw in various audiences whose engagement with the text is itself dialectical and symbolic (ie., in judging the validity or not of the piece the spectator announces his/her own ideological position). That the debate generated by this confrontation then radiates out through media channels increases the potency of the initial text and, effectively, enlarges the theatrical space. The debate itself, centred on the "juvenile and offensive use of repeated profanity [...]; serious decline in general of the moral and spiritual [...]; lowest common denominator approach to ethics"[55] is a further example of this symbolic metonymy, in which the detractors' (superficial) consideration of the show reveals and therefore undermines their own ideological standing. A truly active dialectic, this chain of responses increases exponentially at each level the agency of the motivating epic forces.

That *JS:TO* operated so effectively in this contemporary epic model is, as we have explained, due to a very specific cultural and ideological mood, and it is unlikely that the show will be 'read' in the same way in a different climate. Such is the particular and contextual nature of epic theatre, and if this means that productions of Brecht's own plays become historical, it is merely testament to the dramaturgical and political Gestalt of the epic theatre that defines his legacy.

---

[54] Such confrontation of the Church finds theoretical support in Althusser's writings on Ideological State Apparatuses. Although the dominance of the Church in pre-capitalist times is no longer explicit ("the School-Family couple has replaced the Church-Family couple", 146), the authority of religious (Christian) values underpins the moral and ethical codes of this country. For all the claims of increasing secularisation in Britain, Blair's candid commitment to religion (eg, *Parkinson* 04/03/06) has led to accusations of faith influencing policy on several occasions: regarding the Faith Communities Liaison Group (Jones), Faith Schools (Walker, n.p.) and a pervasive "faith culture" (Callum Brown 3), for example.

[55] Donaldson.

Works Cited

Althusser, Louis. *Lenin & Philosophy and Other Essays*. Bristol: NLB, 1971.

Bentley, Eric. *The Brecht Commentaries 1943-1980*. London: Eyre Methuen, 1981.

Brooker, Peter. *Bertolt Brecht: Dialectics, Poetry, Politics*. London: Croom Helm,1988.

Brown, Callum. '"Best Not to Take it Too Far": How the British Cut Religion Down To Size', 2006. <http://www.opendemocracy.net/xml/xhtml/articles/3335.html> (9 January, 2006).

Brown, Hilda Meldrum. *Leitmotiv and Drama: Wagner, Brecht and the Limits of 'Epic' Theatre*. Oxford: Clarendon Press, 1993.

Cryer, John. "Freedom of Expression for Scriptwriters and Producers." Parliamentary Information Management Services EDM 822, 2005.

Donaldson, Jeffrey. "BBC and *Jerry Springer: The Opera*." Parliamentary Information Management Services EDM 502, 2005.

Eddershaw, Margaret. *Performing Brecht: Forty Years of British Performances*. London and New York: Routledge, 1996.

Esslin, Martin. *Brecht: A Choice of Evils*. London: Eyre & Spottiswoode, 1963.

Foster, Don. "*Jerry Springer* DVD Withdrawal." Parliamentary Information Management Services EDM 1270, 2005.

Fuegi, John. *The Life and Lies of Bertolt Brecht*. London: Flamingo, 1995.

Giles, Steve. "Marxist Aesthetics and Cultural Modernity in *Der Dreigroschenprozeß*." *German Monitor* 41 (1998): 49-61.

Harris, Evan. "BBC and Freedom of Expression." Parliamentary Information Management Services EDM 531, 2005a.

—. "BBC and the Abolition of the Blasphemy Law." Parliamentary Information Management Services EDM 532, 2005b.

Herhoffer, Astrid. "Bertolt Brecht: an Aesthetics of Conviction?" *German Monitor* 41 (1998): 211-226.

Her Majesty's Government. "Racial and Religious Hatred Act 2006. Second Reading." *Hansard* (435:20) Col. 670, 2005.

—. "Racial and Religious Hatred Act 2006. c1. Schedule: Hatred Against Persons on Religious Grounds." London: Her Majesty's Stationery Office, 2006.

Jameson, Fredric. *Brecht and Method*. London and New York: Verso, 1998.

Jones, Lynne. "Influence of Faith Groups on Government." Parliamentary Information Management Services EDM 812, 2005.

Kinkade, Patrick T. and Katovich, Michael A. "Toward a sociology of Cult Films: Reading Rocky Horror." *The Sociological Quarterly* 33, no.2 (1992): 191-209.

Malvern, Jack. "West End Swears by Springer Success." *The Times*, 15 November 2003. <http://www.timesonline.co.uk/tol/newspapers/sunday_times/britain/article1101691.ece> (3 April 2007).

—. "Is This Another Row for Springer, the Opera?" *The Times*, 30 October 2004. <http://www.timesonline.co.uk/tol/news/uk/article500848.ece> (3 April 2007).

Picard, Anna. "Jer-ry! Jer-ry! Jer-ry!" *The Independent*, 19 August 2001.

Sella, Marshall. "Aria of the Lesbian Dwarf Diaper Fetishist." *The New York Times*, 17 March 2002, Late Edition—final, 50.

Smyth, Martin. "BBC Policy on Content of Programmes." Parliamentary Information Management Services EDM 584, 2005.

Soto-Morettini, Donna. "The Clowns of God: *Jerry Springer the Opera.*" *Contemporary Theatre Review* 14, no.1 (2004): 75-88.

Springer, Jerry *et al*. Program notes for *Jerry Springer: The Opera.* Royal National Theatre, directed by Stewart Lee, 2003.

Suvin, Darko. *To Brecht and Beyond: Soundings in Modern Dramaturgy.* Brighton: The Harvester Press, Ltd., 1984.

Thomas, Richard and Stewart Lee. *Jerry Springer: The Opera.* Libretto, 2001.

—. "In Conversation," chaired by Nesta Jones, *Soundings: Innovations in, and Reflections on Music Theatre.* Rose Bruford College Symposium, 7 July, 2003.

Thomson, Peter and Glendyr Sachs, eds. *The Cambridge Companion to Brecht.* Cambridge: CUP, 1994.

Walker, Jonathan. "Blair's Faith Under Scrutiny." *Birmingham Post*, 21 October 2005.

Willett, John. *Brecht in Context: Comparative Approaches.* London: Methuen, 1984.

—. ed. *Brecht On Theatre: The Development of an Aesthetic.* [1964] London: Methuen, 1993.

Willett, John, and Ralph Mannheim, ed. *Bertolt Brecht: Collected Plays, Vol 2iii. The Rise and Fall of the City of Mahagonny / The Seven Deadly Sins.* London: Eyre Methuen, 1979.

—. eds. *Brecht Collected Plays: Six.* London: Methuen, 1998.

Wirth, Andrzej. "Vom Dialog zum Diskurs: Versuch einer Synthese der nachbrechtschen Theaterkonzepte." *Theater Heute* 1 (1980): 16-19.

Wright, Elizabeth. *Postmodern Brecht: a Re-Presentation.* London and New York: Routledge, 1989.

BRECHT'S "U-EFFECT": THEORIZING THE HORIZONS OF REVOLUTIONARY THEATRE

WILLIAM J. BURLING

As a key component of his newly conceived theory of "epic theatre" Bertolt Brecht articulated a seminal conceptual strategy that he would apply widely and often for the rest of his life, *Umfunktionierung*. Perhaps the least understood (especially by Americans) of his many theoretical concepts pertaining to the relationship of politically committed theatre to actual social change, this term—which is variously translated as "rebuilding," "readapting," "functionally transforming" or "refunctioning"—I shall call the "U-effect." Among the many complexities of the U-effect are its implications for revolutionary theatre. Given the advantage of historical hindsight, we can now assert with some confidence that Brecht's views of the limits and possibilities of revolutionary theatre were, and continue to be, powerfully insightful. Brecht developed his theory within modernist ontological notions of art and politics, but, as we shall see, his analyses remain relevant in the era of postmodernist culture.

A term that appears most frequently in Brecht's theorizations on the strategies for revolutionary theatre is "innovation," but part of my purpose here is to suggest that Brechtian scholarship has increasingly ignored, downplayed, or misinterpreted this term. Ironically—for Brecht meant the concept to refer to radical political possibilities—innovation instead has been understood via humanist aesthetic assumptions, i.e., *the very opposite* of what Brecht meant. When properly understood, innovation is synonymous with the essence of the U-effect, i.e., the recasting of theatre into a vastly different form *for entirely dialectical and subversive purposes counter to the capitalist status quo*. The U-effect thus encapsulates the very essence of Brecht's artistic strategy and explains why Broadway and West End productions, bearing the ideological impetus of capitalist aesthetics encoded as humanism, *must* necessarily "misread" and thus misrepresent Brecht's plays. In other words, his plays are now always "un-refunctioned."

While Brecht's contemporaries, as we shall see, understood the U-effect's significance, the concept's centrality is no longer emphasized. For example, Peter Brooker's otherwise excellent essay "Key Words in Brecht's Theory and Practice of Theatre" in the *Cambridge Companion to Brecht* nowhere even mentions the term, though Roswitha Mueller rightly (but briefly) recognizes that it represents "the pivot between artistic and social production,"[1] and Christopher Baugh mentions it four times in his "Brecht and Stage Design," though without special consideration. Likewise Mary Luckhursts's excellent discussion of Brecht's theory and practice of the dramaturge is silent on refunctioning.

If the *Cambridge Brecht*, arguably one of the most important consensus introductions to Brecht's work, fails to emphasize the U-effect, then, I contend that this lack of emphasis in recent scholarship represents a major distorting absence and reinterpretation of Brecht's entire artistic project. Further this misreading parallels the hegemonic practices in other venues wherein the U-effect *must* be ignored or downplayed if Brecht is to be read and performed in present-day classrooms and theatres in a manner consistent with and congenial to the ideological impulses of capital.

The following essay seeks, therefore, to argue for renewed recognition and study of the seminal significance of the U-effect and to re-illuminate its complexities. The first section will briefly outline the salient points of the U-effect and discuss by way of example Brecht's conscious "innovations" in *Mahagonny*, now properly understood as refunctionings. The second and third sections, focusing on content and form, respectively, pertain especially to Brecht's refunctioning of so-called "classical" plays for his own purposes, particularly *Coriolanus*, which he was refunctioning as *Coriolan* in the years leading up to his death in 1956. With special attention to contemporary theatre as a cultural institution, I will discuss particularly Rickman's and Viner's recent *My Name is Rachel Corrie*. My central contention is that even the most politically charged production on Broadway (or any other commercial venue), *has no concrete political effect whatsoever and only the slightest possibility of social effect*. Quite to the contrary, as Brecht's U-effect theorizes, even the most outrageously political plays merely serve to perpetuate via their commodity form the latent interests of the very political systems they wish to critique on the manifest level of content.

---

[1] Thomson and Saks, *The Cambridge Companion to Brecht*, 81.

I will conclude, in the spirit of Brecht's U-effect, with my own intervention in an attempt to "refunction" some of the current debates concerning the relationship of theatre to social change, or rather, in Brecht's view, to revolution. Among my conclusions will be the one perhaps most relevant to the present essay collection: just as an artist cannot use the capitalist mode of production on Broadway or the West End against itself, so, ultimately and for a myriad of reasons, one cannot produce Brecht's plays in support of capitalism's values without utterly misrepresenting them and thus eviscerating them of their revolutionary spirit.

Understanding the U-effect

Despite decades of extended study by scholars, Brecht's theoretical positions are still yielding important corrections and insights that bear strong relationships to the present argument. Douglas Kellner, for example, forcefully restated Brecht's intellectual debt to Karl Korsch in order to counter the emerging liberal humanist falsification in the 1970s that Brecht was never "really" a Marxist playwright. Likewise Brecht's most famous and challenging theoretical concept, *Verfremdung*, has been understood by all scholars since John Willett as "alienation" and referred to as the "A-effect." [2] As both Peter Brooks[3] and Fredric Jameson argue[4], however, "alienation" in German is actually *Entfremdung* and is Marx's term for a different concept altogether. Thus *Verfremdung* "had better be rendered 'estrangement' in keeping with its Russian ancestor."[5] Both Brooks and Jameson thereafter refer to it as the V-effect, a nomenclature which hereafter I will follow.[6] Also Mary Luckhurst[7] has completely reinterpreted and revalued Brecht's practice of dramaturgy. These reexaminations and re-castings of such central Brechtian concepts point immediately to why the U-effect requires close attention. I wish to argue, in fact, that *the V-effect is a subset of the U-effect, and that the latter is far more important* when attempting to comprehend Brecht's theoretical agenda. As he writes in the poem "Speech to the Danish Working-Class Actors on the Art of Observation" (1934): "To change yourselves and

---

[2] For a typical but useful overview and thoughtful consideration of the "A-effect," see Juliet Koss, "Playing Politics with Estranged and Empathetic Audience."
[3] Brooks in Thomson and Saks, 193.
[4] Jameson, *Brecht and Method.*
[5] Ibid., 85-86 n13.
[6] Kellner also makes this point.
[7] Luckhurst, *Dramaturgy: A Revolution in Theatre.*

show us mankind's world / As it really is: made by men and open to alteration."[8]   Thus the U-effect's intention of altering literary and historical material for dialectical purposes is the principal artistic strategy which embodies and empowers Brecht's general political and philosophical commitment to the possibility of social change and is the very foundation of his later renaming of "epic theatre" to "dialectical theatre."

This section will outline the general logic of the U-effect and begin to suggest how it enables theatre to be "refunctioned" so as to contribute to social change. In short, the U-effect applies in three general areas, play content, play form, and the relationship of theatre to the means of production, with the latter being the preeminent dimension.

Walter Benjamin tells us in "The Author as Producer" (written by 27 April 1934) that Brecht coined and was regularly using the term *Umfunktionierung* specifically to apply to "the transformation of the forms and the instruments of production in the way desired by a progressive intelligentsia—that is, one interested in freeing the means of production and serving the class struggle."[9] The problem Brecht hoped to solve was that of crippling mystification: the progressive intelligentsia sympathetic to the proletarian cause needed to learn that tendency in content would never be sufficient for revolutionary purposes. They had to recognize "the decisive difference between the mere supplying of a productive apparatus and its transformation."[10]   Indeed, the problem of the well-intended intellectual community's subservient relationship to the dominant productive apparatus has continued down to the present day and constitutes one of its greatest blind spots.

Recognizing that the presently existing theatrical production system, termed by him variously as "culinary" and "bourgeois" theatre, was inherently complicitous with capitalism's ideological interests at many levels, Brecht attempted to turn theatre on its head but understood the difficulty of the challenge. He flat out states ca. 1940 that "the wealthy bourgeois theatre stands no chance of achieving the simplicity that comes from searching after the truth."[11]   Rather, he argues on 31 March 1929, "only a new purpose can lead to a new art. The new purpose is called paedagogics,"[12] and its purpose is "to find the best way to behave."[13]

---

[8] Brecht, *Journals 1934-1955*.
[9] Benmjamin, "The Author as Producer," 228.
[10] Ibid., 228.
[11] Brecht, *Brecht on Theatre*, 149.
[12] Ibid., 30.
[13] Brecht, *The Messingkauf Dialogues*, 17.

Paedagogics for Brecht concerns attention to a play's 1) content and 2) form, but even more urgently to 3) the play's dialectical relationship to the productive apparatus. To accomplish his goal, Brecht created some entirely new forms of drama, such as the *lehrstücke*, but I will explore Brecht's remarks on "innovation" in the sense of refunctioning.

A sub-head near the conclusion of "The Modern Theatre is the Epic Theatre" stridently proclaims "For Innovations—Against Renovation!"[14] This clear binary opposition serves quite nicely to introduce the U-effect. Whereas renovation simply means locally limited aesthetic variations designed to update the "culinary" value of the opera or any other revival, "real innovations attack the roots" of entrenched conservative social hegemony: *Mahagonny* therefore "attacks the society that needs operas of such a sort [i.e., culinary]."[15] The content of opera is refunctioned through "innovations which allow the theatre to present moral tableaux (showing the commercial character both of the entertainment and of the persons entertained) and which put the spectator in a moralizing frame of mind."[16] In short, the innovations seek "to convert institutions from places of [mere culinary] entertainment into organs of mass communication."[17] Thus "innovation" produces the "U-effect," the refunctioning of the purpose of theatre.

The content of *Mahagonny* was meant to provide pleasure and to instruct. The pleasurable aspects of theatre Brecht never ignored, and he incessantly comments on the necessity to please, as in his remark concerning *Mahagonny* that "*its content is pleasure*"[18] (emphasis in original). The didactic element of course was always close at hand, for *Mahagonny* was "to be neither moralizing nor sentimental, but to put morals and sentimentality on view."[19] The ideological content of culinary dramatic theatre was refunctioned in many ways, however, in this opera. Of the nineteen innovations Brecht outlines in a table, several particularly exemplify crucial challenges to the *content* of bourgeois ontology: 1) the human being "is alterable and able to alter;" 2) "man as process;" 3) "jumps" in social evolution; and 4) "social being determines thought." These assumptions collectively challenge and seek to dismantle the

---

[14] Brecht, *Brecht on Theatre*, 41.
[15] Ibid., 41.
[16] Ibid., 41; n2.
[17] Ibid., 42.
[18] Ibid., 36.
[19] Ibid., 38.

ideological constraints upon which capital perpetuates itself.[20] The table also presents several innovations of dramatic *form*: 1) "each scene for itself;" 2) "montage;" 3) "in curves" (rather than linear development); and not in the table but immediately following, 4) "radical *separation of the elements.*"[21] As with those of content, these strategies of form must not be interpreted in or reduced to only aesthetic terms. Together these innovations are nothing less than strategies to refunction drama to serve the purpose of a paedagogics aiming to change not just art but society itself. In this sense innovation is the mechanism of the U-effect, the machinery intent on producing the effect of radical change.

The third component of the U-effect is the most important because it is the one seldom or never considered by the present theatrical community, *the crucial significance of the apparatus.* In fact, this dimension of refunctioning is so vital that without it the other two components (i.e., form and content of individual plays) are neutralized with respect to revolutionary potential. Understanding the U-effect with respect to the commodity apparatus is the only way to explain why when presented by the capitalist theatrical community that Brecht's plays are mis-performed and otherwise ostensibly radical political theatre in general is ineffective.

The apparatus is Brecht's shorthand term for Marx's complex system of the means and relations of production, distribution, and consumption. The "form" of a play within the apparatus is therefore simply that of the commodity, a point completely ignored in most discussions of art's "form." Long before T. W. Adorno's famous pronouncements on the same point, Brecht asserts that "Art is merchandise, only to be manufactured by the means of production (apparati)."[22] At this level of analysis, the U-effect is generated only when 1) the play comments reflexively on its own status as a commodity; and 2) the apparatus is at the least overtly challenged and at the best ostensibly altered by subverting the discipline of the commodity requirement.

In the 1920s and 30s new technologies such as radio and cinema seemed to offer enormous potential for social change. Brecht's radical strategy was to harness the technologies in the cause of social change. *The Flights of the Lindberghs* (1930), for example, which he adapted for radio from the music festival version of the previous year, "is not intended to be

---

[20] Though, to be sure, simply saying such things does not mean that an audience either understands or embraces the ideas, a point to which we will return at the conclusion of the essay.

[21] Ibid., 37.

[22] Ibid., 35.

of use to the present-day radio but to alter it."[23]   This alteration of use,
essentially rendering the play ineffective for the purposes of capitalist
consumption, is the heart of the U-effect, its revolutionary impulse.
Adorno and Horkheimer, however, soon recognized that these new
technological forms had other and quite opposite possibilities. The
resulting effect, termed by them the Culture Industry, serves capital's
agenda precisely by inculcating consumption and distracting the public
from any politically subversive activities. The Culture Industry is thus
doubly conducive to capital's "cultural logic": the cultural product as
commodity also proliferates and sustains within its product the ideological
justification for its own existence. In terms of "serious theatre," the
"ideology of the aesthetic," to use Terry Eagleton's well-known
formulation,[24] takes the form of aesthetic humanism packaged as
entertainment. Such vehicles can be deadly "serious" about whatever
cause they care to present, but never threaten the political status quo
because the message is always presented in the commodity format, a point
to which I shall return in the final section of this essay. For the present, let
us return to another application of Brecht's concept of refunctioning, i.e.,
at the level of the individual play.

Coriolan: **Refunctioning** *Coriolanus*

Probably no other way of exploring Brecht's notion of the U-effect
with respect to content and originality is clearer, more controversial, or
more illustrious than his many adaptations of Shakespeare's plays. The
Great Bard's drama has long been the object of revision: notable and
enormously popular examples include Davenant's and Dryden's musical
adaptation of *The Tempest* (1674), Nahum Tate's *King Lear* (1681), and
Colley Cibber's reworking of *Richard III* (1700). Brecht's refunctioning of
Shakespeare, however, differs markedly in two ways.

The initial question is one of purpose. Why Shakespeare? The choice
automatically invites close scrutiny and the guarantee—regularly borne
out—of unsympathetic and harsh appraisals, so what might be Brecht's
reasoning? His adaptations have no interest in the usual directorial sense
of making Shakespeare "modern" but rather comprise a dialectical
conversation with both the primary scripts and with the "meanings" as
embodied in the collective historical tradition of theatrical production. In
short, Brecht chose to rework Shakespeare's plays in part precisely

---

[23] Ibid., 32.
[24] Eagleton, "A Note on Brecht."

because they are the most famous in the English language, and the results are highly suggestive concerning the meaning and importance of the U-effect. The critical debate over the meaning and value of Brecht's adaptations has been voluminous and contentious. One of the most sensitive overviews is offered by Helen M. Whall.[25] Her thoughtful and detailed analysis of some of Brecht's uses of Shakespeare argues for what she sees as Brecht's "determined ambivalence."[26] That she can arrive right on the edge but stop short of being able to see the underlying existence of the U-effect is precisely the proof of why we must recognize and understand this crucial artistic parameter if we are to assess his work more clearly.

Brecht's adaptation of Shakespeare's *Coriolanus* is central to any understanding of both the U-effect and to Brecht's general artistic vision. He first saw the play performed in 1925, and the impression remained with him for life. Indeed he remarked that the play was "decisive in the development of the epic theatre,"[27] and at the end of his life Brecht was hard at work adapting the play for performance by the Berliner Ensemble, though it was not staged until 1964, eight years after his death, and in a version not faithful to his vision. Darko Suvin has explored at length many of the contexts surrounding Brecht's fixation on this play, so while adding nothing new to that topic I wish to revisit the adaptation for the purpose of clarifying the U-effect.[28]

Brecht routinely thought of all history and all earlier cultural production in general and literature in particular as grist for his mill. He constantly sought historical events or works to refunction, and the more famous the better. This frame of mind is captured perfectly in his poem "The Playwright's Song" (1935):

> To learn how to show what I see
> I read up on the representations of other peoples and other periods.
> One or two plays I have adapted, precisely
> Checking the techniques of those times and absorbing

---

[25] Whall, "The Case is Altered: Brecht's Use of Shakespeare."

[26] Whall also provides a convenient summary of some main critics and positions with respect to the general subject of Brecht and Shakespeare.

[27] Brecht in Suvin, *To Brecht and Beyond*, 191.

[28] The following argument owes much to Löb and Lerner's excellent article and to Arrigo Subiotto's *Brecht's Adaptations for the Berliner Ensemble*. I am most deeply indebted, however, to Suvin's analysis of *Coriolan* in *To Brecht and Beyond* (1984; chapter 7), arguably one of the very best studies of Brecht to appear in English.

Whatever is of use to me.[29]

Ladislau Löb and Laurence Lerner note this pervasive characteristic in asserting that Brecht "was always prepared to tamper with his material" to fit his "program for a theater that will change the world instead of accepting it,"[30] and Brecht as "The Philosopher" in *The Messingkauf Dialogues* (hereafter *TMD*) states flatly that one should "make fresh additions and generally use plays [by other dramatists] as so much raw material."[31] This tendency extended even to original creations. As Willett comments, "to Brecht his own raw material was always expendable, to be ruthlessly rewritten and pruned."[32] In short, no literature was sacred or untouchable; anything and everything that had any value to Brecht was revised and put to service. When "The Dramaturg" in *TMD* suggests that "The Philosopher" may not be responding as "a man of taste," the latter's retort is telling: "But like a man, I hope. There are times when you have to decide between being human and having good taste."[33] Here Brecht clearly implies that "taste" itself (*vis-à-vis* Eagleton), is one of the subjectively internalized mechanisms of ideological control that requires dismantling.

A concise example of the U-effect is strikingly seen in Brecht's refunctioning of Helmet von den Steiner's translation of a poem by the Greek author Cavafy. Willett points out in the notes to "Reading a late Greek Poet" (ca. 1953-56) that "Brecht has in effect reshaped the first two lines of the last stanza and the third to fifth lines of the first stanza to make an only faintly less pessimistic version for his own time ... [that is] at once more concrete and more obscure than the original."[34] This reshaping of someone else's poem is a quintessential but simplistic example of the Brechtian U-effect. So let us turn to his adaptation of *Coriolanus* for further amplification of the concept.

As Suvin persuasively argues, Brecht's adaptation of Shakespeare was highly complex and is not reducible to simple agitprop sloganeering. The central axis and binary opposition of the Coriolanus legend (in both Livy and Shakespeare) is that of Coriolanus and Rome, the warrior hero and the plebian populace. In this dichotomy Brecht saw possibilities and refunctioned the play as a meditation and intervention on the

---

[29] Brecht, *Poems 1913-1956*, 258-259.
[30] Löb and Lerner, "Views of Roman History: *Coriolanus* and *Coriolan*," 38.
[31] Brecht, *The Messingkauf Dialogues*, 38.
[32] Brecht, *Brecht on Theatre*, 175.
[33] Brecht, *The Messingkauf Dialogues*, 38.
[34] Willett in Brecht, *Poems 1913-1956*, 603.

contemporary matter of Stalin's relationship to the workers, and on the possibilities of enlarged democracy. Whereas Shakespeare chose to emphasize the "tragedy" of the individual hero and savior of Rome and to berate the rabble populace, Brecht offered two massive revisions. First, he incorporated "a radical change in the attitude of (and thus also toward) the plebians"[35]: he refunctioned the citizenry, depicted by Shakespeare as crude, undisciplined, ignorant, and essentially anarchical in the worst sense, both expanding their presence in the play and altering their character to that of wise and carefully acting avatars of social justice. Second, he retained the positive features of Marcius (Coriolanus), a talented general, but replaced "the attitude of 'wounded pride' in the protagonist by the newly relevant attitude of 'belief in his irreplaceability.'"[36] This second change was meant to demonstrate that while talented in one sphere (war for Coriolanus; economic revitalization for Stalin) that Coriolanus had no aptitude for leadership in another (i.e., peace/politics, respectively). Brecht's overall refunctioning of Shakespeare's play can be seen, therefore, as "not only a rewriting of Shakespeare and ancient history, but also a rewriting of the Leninist theme of state and revolution and modern German-cum-Russian history."[37] As Arrigo Subiotto rightly notes of Brecht's adaptations, "the mainsprings of dialectic that were the motive force of historicizing in his own work provided the criterion by which Brecht chose plays adaptation, with a consequent and sometimes radical change in their dramatic form and function,"[38] such that "the value of an existent work does not then lie in our ability to learn from the past (though this may appear to be the case in the first place) but in creating a perspective for fresh work; it is didactic in opening the way to a correction of false ideas, and active in its attention to influence."[39] In short, Brecht attempted to refunction Shakespeare to serve the particular contemporary situation.

We can now turn to some of the implications for theatre in the current historical situation. As we shall see, productions of both Brecht's plays and those by other dramatists take on new resonances when fully considered in light of the U-effect.

---

[35] Suvin, 205-206 n3.

[36] Ibid., 205-206 n3.

[37] Ibid., 197.

[38] Subiotto, *Bertolt Brecht's Adaptations for the Berliner Ensemble*, 13.

[39] Ibid., 10.

Refunctioning the Theatrical Apparatus

An opposition has long been theorized between theatre as a disciplinary ideological institution and theatre as "performance" seeking to inspire and participate in the shaping of society. Baz Kershaw has demonstrated at length in *The Radical in Performance: Between Brecht and Baudrillard* that even productions which ostensibly attack injustices only *appear* to do so. Instead they "occupy the established edifices of the theatrical estate today [and] trade under the unavoidable sign of global commodification"; thus they "succumb to what they attack."[40] Still those members of the theatrical community affiliated with such "established edifices," despite whatever socially progressive intentions they might express, continue to be unwilling or unable to grasp the concrete material conditions of their own complicity with capitalism. Typical of the position of even the most well intended believers in the power of theatre is a remark by Del Martin, a director at one of the most socially conscious theatrical companies in the United States, Atlanta's 7 Stages: "We can't give up on the idea that theatre can be part of the process of social change. If all we're doing is creating entertainment, where people don't have to think about ideas, we are abusing the art form. I would hope that Brecht's legacy would be in reminding us that in theatre, it's possible to put the head back on the shoulders."[41] Martin's view can serve well to suggest why a complete understanding of Brecht's U-effect is vital for any theatrical production committed to social change.

That Brecht's name is connected with both Kershaw's and Martin's remarks about the possibilities of activist theatre is, of course, neither coincidental nor surprising. Brecht demonstrated by his practice that he believed in the power of theatre to contribute to change, and yet he understood well the limits of praxis inherent in what he called "culinary" (i.e., commodified) theatre. What requires attention here, therefore, is the current lack of attention to, let alone understanding of, Brecht's strategy: the absolute requirement for rethinking the material conditions (i.e., the cultural form) of the performance's production. In his view the performance *must* at least challenge if not remove itself from and go beyond the neutralizing constraints of the capitalist theatrical apparatus. Kershaw and others have gone far toward documenting some of the experiments along these lines and elaborating new possibilities, but they have not properly credited Brecht with the theoretical foundations for

---

[40] Kershaw, *Radical in Performance*, 55, 54.
[41] Martin in Henderson, "The Persistence of Brecht."

attaining genuine radical theatre nor fully expounded his position. My contention here is that an understanding of the U-effect at the level of cultural production allows one to theorize why these plays, including Brecht's own, have little if any impact on social change when presented in currently existing venues. I will conclude by exploring the potentialities and limitations offered by Brecht's U-effect for theorizing a far more potent type of radical theatre.

Critical Theatre as Specialized Commodity

Brecht remarks that the mystifying element that subverts even the best intended of politically progressive dramatists is "in thinking that they are in possession of an apparatus that in reality possesses them."[42] In short, as long as the theatrical production neglects to address the structural relationship of its own material conditions of production and consumption relative to the prevailing interests of the capitalist apparatus and the accompanying complicitous aesthetic assumptions, then its thematic message (i.e., its content), no matter how politically committed, *is ever and always negated*, being confined to the category of entertainment, albeit of a special type—*uncensored space*. Even the most shocking, fully transparent political or social productions, and especially the most successful, such as Tony Kushner's *Angels in America* or, to the point here, *My Name is Rachel Corrie*, are doubly ineffective: 1) they generate profits and thus sustain the very system that produces the injustices that they criticize; and 2) their messages are confined to the category of uncensored space, i.e., a marketing category consisting of cultural productions critical of the status quo. The U-effect does offer insights as to what is needed to counteract capital's powers of propagation and assimilation and thus to enable genuine, concrete political praxis. We will consider those factors in the final section of this essay. All members of the theatrical community who wish to employ the theatre in some larger social cause must first recognize and understand, however, that the current theatrical apparatus cannot accommodate their intentions, and, in fact, guarantees quite the opposite effect.

The first dimension to consider is that of theatre as cultural production in commodity form. The equation is quite simple: if a theatre sells tickets, it is complicitous with capital. This essential dynamic, regularly dismissed today as a faulty Marxist premise, is precisely what Brecht means by the apparatus, the formal structure that powerfully but silently controls the

---

[42] Brecht, *Brecht on Theatre*, 34.

theatrical community. He comments at length this matter in "The Literarization of the Theatre":

> The theatre apparatus's priority is a priority of means of production. This apparatus resists all conversion to other purposes, by taking any play which it encounters and immediately changing it so that it no longer represents a foreign body within the apparatus—except at those points where it neutralizes itself. The necessity to stage the new correctly—which matters more for the theatre's sake than for the drama's—is modified by the fact that theatre can stage anything: it theatres it all down. Of course this priority has its economic reasons.[43]

The essential point here concerns the meaning of "theatre it all down." By this phrase Brecht means two things: 1) to ensure ticket sales the entertainment factor is maximized; and 2) the educational component is eliminated or neutralized. These changes are systemic across the entire range of the apparatus such that audiences are trained by the hegemonic theatrical community to expect only entertainment or wishy-washy explorations of ideas. Brecht remarks elsewhere on the net effect: "people who want unobtrusive lessons want no lessons at all,"[44] and even further "for art to be 'unpolitical' means only to ally itself with the 'ruling' group."[45]

This complicity with the status quo affects even Brecht's own plays. Wolfgang Storch remarks that in the 1976 Berlin production of the little known *The Decline of the Egoist Johann Fatzer* Brecht's play was "treated as if he were his own opposite."[46] Storch understood perfectly that "the revitalization necessary for Brecht to work is not furthered by this production."[47] If Brecht suffers this fate in Germany,[48] can we really imagine that when the *Threepenny Opera* is presented in Oklahoma (or on Broadway) that the "real Brecht" can possibly hope to emerge? The conclusion is unarguable: even so powerful a thematic playwright as Brecht can be transformed (refunctioned!) into his opposite via the inherent logic of theatre as commodity apparatus.

---

[43] Ibid., 43.
[44] Brecht, *The Messingkauf Dialogues*, 89.
[45] Brecht, *Brecht on Theatre*, 196.
[46] Storch, "Political Climate and Experimental Staging: *The Decline of Johann Fazter*," 108.
[47] Ibid., 106.
[48] The theoretical implications of this Berlin production of *Fatzer* call for a full-length study in their own right.

That Brecht's observations strike to the continuing inherent commodity kernel of theatre is also made clear by Kershaw, who points out that in the U. K., a culture arguably the most committed to cutting-edge theatre, "the structures of British culture created in the past twenty years [i.e., the late 1970s to the late 90s]—and those of its theatres in particular—seem ill-designed to contribute to a weakening of the political and economic forces that act as a deterrent to democracy."[49]   We must conclude along with Brecht, therefore, that the *formal structure* of theatre itself, expressed as commercial necessity in venues such as Broadway and the West End, ties theatre completely and inescapably to the logic and demands of capital.

Still, of course, it can be objected that some commercial theatres, such as The Royal Court, routinely present plays "of ideas," including Brecht's own, so does this situation not seem to contradict Brecht's arguments concerning the crippling effect of the theatrical apparatus? This question itself points to the most difficult issue to understand in this entire essay: *social critique is a marketing category.* As Benjamin remarks in discussing Brecht's U-effect, the capitalist "apparatus of production . . . can assimilate astonishing quantities of revolutionary themes, indeed, can propagate them without callings its own existence, and the existence of the class that owns it, seriously into question."[50] The ability on the part of capital to "assimilate astonishing quantities of revolutionary themes" may be explained by the concept of uncensored space.

Capitalism, as all theorists since Marx have observed, is not a logically consistent system; implicit contradictions can and do exist. In the case of the arts, the contradiction involves a space created by the slippage between the requirements and the relations of production, distribution, and consumption resulting from capitalism's need for fresh commodities and services that generate new possibilities for profit. This explanation has been well articulated by T. W. Adorno: "the artist works as social agent, indifferent to society's own consciousness. He embodies the social forces of production without necessarily being bound by the censorship dictated by the relations of production, which he continually criticizes by following the rigor of his *métier.*"[51] In other words, one major role occupied by the artist is precisely to generate content embodying critique of the status quo "without necessarily being bound by the censorship dictated by the relations of production." The uncensored *artwork as production* may well indeed offer the most strident critiques of the status quo, but the *artwork*

---

[49] Kershaw, "Discouraging Democracy: British Theatres and Economics, 1979-1999," 283.

[50] Benjamin, 229.

[51] Adorno, *Aesthetic Theory*, 43-44.

as commodity is nevertheless contained within the means and relations of distribution. It is precisely the failure by artists to understand the crucial linkages among production, distribution, and consumption that Brecht, Benjamin, and Adorno emphasize. *In other words, the meaning of the content of a play created by artistic production is silently altered by the capitalist conditions of distribution and consumption.* As Benjamin expresses this matter, "political tendency is the necessary, never the sufficient condition of the organizing function of a work."[52] Sufficiency emerges only when tendency merges with new formal conditions of production and consumption, a point of massive importance (see below).

The playwright, again quoting Benjamin's discussion founded upon Brecht's U-effect insight, must "not supply the apparatus of production without, to the utmost extent, changing it."[53] Benjamin, of course, analyzes the situation with respect to political newspapers, but if such a tendentious and non-artistic medium as political journalism is neutralized by the capitalist apparatus—for newspapers are also commodities—then why does theatre think capital's influence does not apply to it? The goal must be, in other words, to make the playwright acutely aware "of the decisive difference between the mere supplying of the productive apparatus and its transformation."[54] So the truly political play will be one not only offering political content but also being presented under entirely new formal conditions of production, including wholly different relationships with respect to both the performers and the audience. This model is precisely what Brecht attempted to implement with the Berliner Ensemble and which took for its model the Paris Commune theatre troupe of 1871.[55]

Brecht coined the term "thaëter" to designate the radical formal structure required to carry out his agenda. He remarks on the distinction that "much of what is considered essential to the art of the theatre we may wish to abandon for the sake of our new aims,"[56] because theatre functions by "taking any play which it encounters and immediately changing it so that it no longer represents a foreign body within the apparatus."[57] Understood in this light, Broadway and the West End always are only and ever "theatre."

---

[52] Benjamin, 233.
[53] Ibid., 228.
[54] Ibid., 228.
[55] It is thus no mere coincidence that Brecht was working upon a new play entitled *The Days of the Paris Commune* near the end of his life.
[56] Brecht, *The Messingkauf Dialogues*, 94.
[57] Brecht, *Brecht on Theatre*, 43.

Contemporary Thaëter: *My Name is Rachel Corrie*

An outstanding test case is the highly controversial *My Name is Rachel Corrie*, which premiered at the Royal Court in April 2005 (and repeated twice thereafter) to widespread notoriety and sold-out audiences. Based on the diary and other writings of American peace activist Rachel Corrie who was killed in Gaza by an Israeli bulldozer, the play is arguably as politically intentional and controversial in content as one can be, probing the flashpoint intersection of the Palestinian and Israeli situation. The New York Theater Workshop announced in early 2006 that it would produce the play but soon thereafter postponed the American premiere. As Philip Weiss reports in *The Nation*, "the Workshop had posted and then removed from its website a clumsy statement aimed at explaining itself.[58]" Immediately the Workshop and James Nicola, its artistic director, became mired in controversy and resulting claims of censorship emerged, with special attention to alleged pressure on the Workshop's board of directors from the Jewish community. The situation immediately evokes the possibility of financial manipulations, and Weiss rightly remarks, "Questions about pressure from Jewish leaders morph quickly into questions about funding" and "Nicola's statement about a back channel to Jewish leaders suggests the presence of a cultural lobby that parallels the vaunted pro-Israel lobby in think tanks and Congress."[59] The Workshop production has been moved to the West End, and the play has been tentatively rescheduled for New York in October 2006 at the off-Broadway Minetta Lane Theater. Calling this situation a "charged issue" is a screaming understatement. But of what kind?

Is London a more open society and New York more closed? Brecht's U-effect offers some timely insights, the first of which being that the conditions of distribution and consumption can reveal more about the play's actual received meaning than its contents. In this case, *My Name is Rachel Corrie* ultimately serves to focus not on what the play says one way or the other, or whether it "makes a difference" in political attitudes, but rather on the scandal surrounding its very producibility. In effect the publicity resulting from the controversy will ultimately result in massive audience demand such that the play will become far more famous and successful in larger venues than it ever would have been if it had been allowed quietly to proceed at the tiny Workshop in the first place. Ironically, however, the subsequent commercial success will overwhelm

---

[58] Weiss, "Too Hot for New York."
[59] Ibid.

its message, and the play will forever be remembered as "controversial," with the only result being artistic and financial success for all involved with the show. As Brecht would have it, "the apparati do not work for the general good; the means of production do not belong to the producer [i.e., the creative community]; and as a result his work amounts to so much merchandise, and is governed by the normal laws of mercantile trade. Art is merchandise …"[60] And controversy is good for ticket sales.

Ultimately, commercial theatrical success, however much it may serve to generate criticism of social conditions, does not equate to political action, and will not change the American (or any other) political position because, as Samuel Beckett perhaps of all playwrights best understood, theatre (or any of the other arts) under capital is not a form of collective political activity but of personal expression readily co-opted by the commodity apparatus. Brecht bluntly summarizes the result: "theatre is a serious obstacle to … theater."[61]

The Implications: Refunctioning Radical Theatre

And so we may conclude this brief overview by stressing the implications gleaned from this consideration of the U-effect. Brecht was always committed to the idea that theatre might serve to educate the public and help to support social change. Had he not so believed, he scarcely would have continued his work. But he also came to realize the enormity of the challenges, for even in the GDR the conditions of production and consumption mitigated his agenda, i.e., while the country was ostensibly communistic, assumptions concerning theatre (and all of the arts) remained tied to the capitalist formal models. Seen in this light, American (and all other capitalist theatrical production,) is simply incapable of presenting serious political drama that can offer any genuine possibility of real praxis, for the simple reasons that 1) play content is never critical of the underlying mode of production of which it constitutes a part and through which the social injustices arise; and 2) the theatrical community in the main remains totally mystified concerning the formal conditions of theatrical production, distribution, and consumption, i.e., the apparatus.

"Political theatre" on Broadway and in the West End is a marketing niche where controversy is packaged as entertainment, where the right to express a point of view is tolerated (and even encouraged!) as long as no concrete action is taken by either the dramatist or the audience to

---

[60] Brecht, *Brecht on Theatre*, 35.
[61] Brecht, *The Messingkauf Dialogues*, 91.

challenge the class interests of capital via the conditions and relations of production and consumption. *My Name is Rachel Corrie* contains not a word about how the play as cultural production is beholden to the constraints of commodity capitalism within which it is produced and consumed. The current apparatus, therefore, could never internalize and incorporate Brecht's U-effect precisely because, as Terry Eagleton rightly notes, "the theatre, then [i.e., the 1950s] as now, is the very paradigm of that warped way of looking at the world which Brecht spent a lifetime trying to subvert, and which for shorthand's sake we must call liberal humanism."[62]   Hence even Brecht's own plays are now stripped in production of their edgy awareness of and resistance to the capitalist apparatus.

No question exists concerning the efforts of many theatrical companies to present *content* which challenges the capitalist status quo. From the numerous radical theatres of the 70s and 80s in the U. K., such as 7:84, Belt and Braces Roadshow, Portable Theatre, Monstrous Regiment; to the more recent forays into interventionist theatre in Belfast, Sheffield, and elsewhere; to their less numerous but equally tendentious counterparts in the U. S. (e.g., San Francisco Mime Troupe), the evidence for ongoing, passionate commitment to social change is undeniable.[63]   But here is the point: while such radical theatrical activity serves well to stimulate possible change at the individual level, what are the actual collective political effects?   The best that can found is a continuing militant resistance and an awareness that "socialist playwrights [and theatre companies] cannot themselves change the world yet might … [contribute] to the work of those who can"[64] ; and the hope that radical performances "might ripple out into other forms of social relations."[65] At the worst the radical theatre is itself co-opted by capital, such that the shows of even the venerable San Francisco Mime Troupe, while attracting large audiences, "rarely shock or astonish anymore."[66]   As Kershaw observes: "commentators on alternative and community theatre have been

---

[62] Eagleton, 90.

[63]   Some studies include Catherine Itzin, *Stages in the Revolution: Political Theatre in Britain since 1968*; Peter Billingham, ed., *Radical Initiatives in Interventionist and Community Drama*; Baz Kershaw, *The Politics of Performance: Radical Theatre as Cultural Intervention*; Susan Vaneta Mason, ed., *The San Francisco Mime Troupe Reader*; and Jill Dolan, *Utopia in Performance: Finding Hope at the Theater*.

[64] Itzin, 339.

[65] Dolan, 34.

[66] Mason, 7.

pessimistic about the future for oppositional performance."[67]   Thus only severely limited redefinitions of goals now seem realizable for radical theatre until new broader constituencies arise and the political "situation" changes (e.g., an ecological meltdown).

As Brecht and Benjamin make clear, the only way for theatre to become truly revolutionary is by *challenging and transcending capital's requirements of form*, as well as content. The theatrical artists must "rethink their own work, their own relation to the means of production.[68] Thus the most socially active companies must 1) alter or at least challenge the prevailing personnel structures of the commercial theatre (e.g., by collectivizing); 2) make clear to the audience the constraints imposed by investors and commercial necessity; and 3) reduce or eliminate the presently understood distinctions between the audience and the "technical specialists" who are the performers. This latter point relates directly to Brecht's interest in working as much as possible with amateur performers and by the enormous attention he devoted to acting techniques which serve to subvert formal expectations of commercial theatre.[69]

Brecht calls for nothing less than the *obliteration* of the very capitalist theatrical apparatus itself. Thus the full political, revolutionary potential of the theatre will be realized *only under wholly non-capitalistic terms of production and consumption*. Brecht, therefore, theorized the essential conditions for the possibility of truly political and revolutionary "thaëter." Once we appreciate the radical extent of his agenda it comes as no surprise why his U-effect is never discussed and why so much Brechtian scholarship and criticism—from the reactionary Bentley, Esslin, and Politzer mission to portray Brecht as "really" a liberal humanist—is dedicated to willfully misreading or downplaying his allegiance to the Marxist notion of the apparatus, discrediting his artistic innovations, and thus serving to mystify his message in terms congenial to the hegemonic apparatus.

Recognizing the centrality of *Umfunktionierung* to Brecht's thought is therefore the most urgent—and most difficult—challenge to understanding and reenergizing his legacy, especially in the current era of global, multi-

---

[67] Kershaw, *The Politics of Performance: Radical Theatre as Cultural Intervention*, 255.

[68] Benjamin, 226.

[69] Craig Kinzer, for example, has written regularly on the sweeping significance of Brecht's actor training methods for internal company relations that "provide a site for the confluence of theory and praxis" that "has encouraged artists to think critically and progressively about the critical ground on which their work rests" in "Brecht and Theatre Pedagogy," 206.

national capital's "cultural logic." Let us cut through that ever-enlarging ideological mist by reestablishing the U-effect as the central tenet of Brecht's entire enterprise in all of its radical intention: "The form in question can however only be achieved by a complete change of the theatre's purpose."[70] This purpose, as we have seen, is not confined to content but must be achieved by altering the formal relations of production and consumption, first in the theatre, and then in society itself: "the socialization of these means of production is vital for art."[71] We must not allow any ambiguity on this matter: by socialization, Brecht means socialist art in the service of socialism. Let us allow Brecht, then, to have the final word regarding *Umfunktionierung*: "it is not at all our job to renovate ideological institutions on the basis of the existing social order by means of innovations. Instead our innovations must force them to surrender that basis."[72]

Works Cited

Adorno, T. W. *Aesthetic Theory*. Trans. and Introd. Robert Hullot-Kentor.Minneapolis: University of Minnesota Press, 1997.

Benjamin, Walter. "The Author as Producer." *Reflections*. Ed. and intr. Peter Demetz. New York: Schocken, 1978. 220-238.

Billingham, Peter ed., *Radical Initiatives in Interventionist and Community Drama*. Portland, OR: intellect, 2005.

Brecht, Bertolt. *Brecht on Theatre*. Ed. and trans. John Willett. New York: Hill and Wang, 1964.

—. *The Messingkauf Dialogues*. Trans. John Willet. London: Methuen, 1965.

—. *Poems 1913-1956*. Ed. John Willett and Ralph Mannheim. New York: Routledge, 1996.

—. *Journals 1934-1955*. Ed. John Willett and Ralph Mannheim. London: Methuen, 2000.

Dolan, Jill. *Utopia in Performance: Finding Hope at the Theater*. Ann Arbor: University of Michigan Press, 2005.

Eagleton, Terry. "A Note on Brecht." *Pretexts: Studies in Writing and Culture* 1 (1999): 89-92.

---

[70] Brecht, *Brecht on Theatre*, 30.

[71] Ibid., 48.

[72] Ibid., 53.

Curran, Angela. "Brecht's Criticisms of Aristotle's Aesthetics of Tragedy." *Journal of Aesthetics and Art Criticism* 59.2 (2001): 167-184.

Henderson, Stephen. "The Persistence of Brecht." Special issue. *American Theatre* Vol. 15.5 (May 1998): 12, 14-16, 54-56. On-line. EPSCO 5 June 2006.

Itzin, Catherine. *Stages in the Revolution: Political Theatre in Britain since 1968*. London: Eyre Methuen, 1980.

Jameson, Fredric. *Brecht and Method*. New York: Verso, 1998.

Kellner, Douglas. "Brecht's Marxist Aesthetic: The Korsch Connection." Weber and Heinen: 29-42.

Kershaw, Baz. "Discouraging Democracy: British Theatres and Economics, 1979-1999."*Theatre Journal* 51.3 (1999): 267-283.

—. *The Politics of Performance: Radical Theatre as Cultural Intervention*. New York: Routledge, 1992.

—. *The Radical in Performance*.New York: Routledge, 1999.

Kinzer, Craig. "Brecht and Theatre Pedagogy." *Brecht Yearbook* 22 (1997): 205-213.

Koss, Juliet. "Playing Politics with Estranged and Empathetic Audience." South *Atlantic Quarterly* 96.4 (1997): 809-820.

Löb, Ladislau and Laurence Lerner. "Views of Roman History: *Coriolanus* and Coriolan. *Comparative Literature* 29 (1977): 35-53.

Luckhurst, Mary. *Dramaturgy: A Revolution in Theatre*. Cambridge: Cambridge University Press, 2006.

Mason, Susan Vaneta, ed. *The San Francisco Mime Troupe Reader*. Ann Arbor: University of Michigan Press, 2005.

Politzer, Heinz. "How Epic is Bertolt Brecht's Epic Theatre?" *Modern Language Quarterly* 23 (1962): 99-114.

Storch, Wolfgang. "Political Climate and Experimental Staging: *The Decline of Johann Fazter*. Weber and Heinen: 106-112.

Subiotto, Arrigo. *Bertolt Brecht's Adaptations for the Berliner Ensemble*. London: Modern Humanities Research Council, 1975.

Suvin, Darko. *To Brecht and Beyond*. Totowa, NJ: Barnes and Noble, 1984.

Thomson, Peter and Glendyr Saks, eds. *The Cambridge Companion to Brecht*. Cambridge: Cambridge University Press, 1994.

Weber, Betty Nance and Hubert Heiner, eds. *Bertolt Brecht: Political Theory and Literary Practice*. Athens, GA: University of Georgia Press, 1980.

Weiss, Philip. "Too Hot for New York." *The Nation* (3 April 2006). On-line edition.

Whall, Helen M. "The Case is Altered: Brecht's Use of Shakespeare." *University of Toronto Quarterly* 51, no.2 (1981-82): 127-148.

Appendix

Productions of Bertolt Brecht's Plays

April 13, 1933

The Threepenny Opera. Empire Theatre. Directed by Francesco Von Mendelssohn

November 19, 1935

The Mother. Theatre Union. Directed by Victor Wolfson

December 7, 1947

Galileo. The Experimental Theatre, Inc. Directed by Joseph Losey.

March 10, 1954

The Threepenny Opera. Theater de Lys. Directed by Carmen Capablo.

September 30, 1955

The Threepenny Opera. Theater de Lys. Directed by Carmen Capablo.

March 28, 1963

Mother Courage and Her Children. Martin Beck Theatre. Directed by Samuel Matovsky.

November 11, 1963

The Resistible Rise of Arturo Ui. Lunt-Fontanne Theatre. Directed by Tony Richardson.

March 24, 1966

The Caucasian Chalk Circle. Vivian Beaumont Theatre. Directed by Jules Irving.

October 27, 1966

The Threepenny Opera. Billy Rose Theatre. Directed by Michael Meschke.

April 13, 1967

Galileo. Vivian Beaumount Theatre. Directed by John Hirsch.

November 16, 1967

Mother Courage and Her Children. Billy Rose Theatre. Directed by Ida Kaminska.

December 22, 1968

The Resistible Rise of Arturo Ui. Billy Rose Theatre. Directed by Edward Payson Call.

November 5, 1970

The Good Woman of Setzuan. Vivian Beaumont Theatre. Directed by Robert Symonds.

May 1, 1976

The Threepenny Opera. Vivian Beaumount Theatre. Directed by Richard Foreman.

November 5, 1989

The Threepenny Opera. Lunt-Fontanne Theatre. Directed by John Dexter.

April 20, 2006

The Threepenny Opera. Studio 54. Directed by Scott Elliott.

CONTRIBUTORS

Arminda Apgar is a Master of Arts Student in the Department of English at Missouri State University. Her academic interests include issues of Marxism and gender in American popular culture, including literature, film, and theater. She recently completed her Master's thesis entitled *Gritty Girls Undone: The Unraveling of Gender Fluidity in Pat Cadigan's Synners*.

William J. Burling is Professor of English at Missouri State University . He is the author, editor, or co-author of four books, including *The Colonial American Stage, 1665-1774: A Documentary Calendar* (with Odai Johnson) and *Summer Theatre in London 1661-1820 and the Rise of the Haymarket Theatre*. He has also published more than fifty notes, articles, and reviews in *Theatre Survey, Theatre Notebook, Theatre History Studies, Essays in Theatre, Modern Philology, Music and Letters, Utopian Studies*, and numerous other journals. He is currently editing *Mapping the Unimaginable: Kim Stanley Robinson and the Critics* (McFarland, forthcoming 2008).

Kathryn Edney is a doctoral student in American Studies at Michigan State University. Her research interests focus on issues of memory, nostalgia, performativity, ethnicity, and gender manifested in musical theater and film. She is also currently the managing editor for the *Journal of Popular Culture*.

Anne Fletcher is Associate Professor in the Department of Theater at Southern Illinois University Carbondale. Her essays and reviews have appeared in *The Eugene O'Neill Review, Theatre Journal, Theatre Symposium*, and *Theatre History Studies*. Her work is included in the *Blackwell Companion to American Drama* (David Krasner), *Experimenters, Rebels, and Disparate Voices…*(Arthur Gerwitz and James Kolb), *Interrogating America Through Theatre and Performance* (William W. Demastes and Iris Smith Fischer), *The Encyclopedia of Modern Drama* (Gabrielle Cody and Evert Sprinchorn). Her book on Group Theatre scene designer and theorist Mordecai Gorelik is forthcoming from SIU Press.

David Kornhaber is a Faculty Fellow in the Doctoral Program Subcommittee on Theatre at Columbia University and the Assistant Editor of *Theatre Survey*. His work has appeared in *The New York Times*, *The Village Voice*, and *American Theatre*, and he has been a regular contributor to *Disability Studies Quarterly* and *Alt.Theatre: Cultural Diversity and the Stage*.

Norman Roessler is the Editor of *Communications,* the performance journal of the International Brecht Society, and a Lecturer in the Intellectual Heritage Program at Temple University in Philadelphia, PA / USA. He has published essays in *Communications from the International Brecht Society* and *Focus on Literatur: A Journal for German-Language Literature*.

Ilka Saal works as Assistant Professor at the University of Richmond, VA, where she teaches drama & theater as well as American Studies. Her essays and reviews have appeared in *The Drama Review*, *South Atlantic Review*, and *Amerikastudien*. She is the author of *New Deal Theater: The Vernacular Tradition in American Political Theater*, which is forthcoming with Palgrave Macmillan in 2007.

Dominic Symonds is Senior Lecturer in Drama at the University of Portsmouth, UK. He is joint editor of *Studies in Musical Theatre*, a member of the Music Theatre Working Group of the IFTR and a Writer Associate of Mercury Musical Developments. He is also a professional director, with credits as diverse as the London cult fringe hit *Dragula* and the first ever production of *The Magic Flute* in the Republic of Moldova. He holds a PhD from London University.

J. Chris Westgate is Assistant Professor of drama in the Department of English, Comparative Literature, and Linguistics at California State University, Fullerton. His essays and theater reviews have appeared in *The Eugene O'Neill Review*, *Theatre Journal*, *Modern Drama*, and *American Drama*. He is currently finishing a book entitled *Urban Drama: The Metropolis in Contemporary North American Plays*.

INDEX